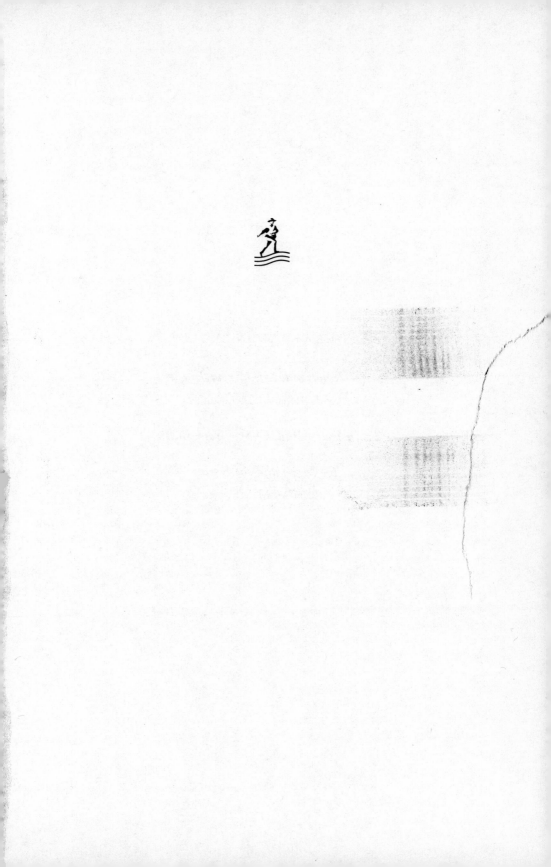

CAN'T
JUST
STOP

*An Investigation of
Compulsions*

SHARON BEGLEY

SIMON & SCHUSTER

New York London Toronto Sydney New Delhi

Simon & Schuster
1230 Avenue of the Americas
New York, NY 10020

First Simon & Schuster hardcover edition February 2017

SIMON & SCHUSTER and colophon are registered trademarks of Simon & Schuster, Inc.

For information about special discounts for bulk purchases, please contact Simon & Schuster Special Sales at 1-866-506-1949 or business@simonandschuster.com.

The Simon & Schuster Speakers Bureau can bring authors to your live event. For more information, or to book an event, contact the Simon & Schuster Speakers Bureau at 1-866-248-3049 or visit our website at www.simonspeakers.com.

Manufactured in the United States of America

1 3 5 7 9 10 8 6 4 2

Library of Congress Cataloging-in-Publication Data

Names: Begley, Sharon, 1956- author.
Title: Can't just stop : an investigation of compulsions / Sharon Begley.
Description: New York : Simon & Schuster, 2017.
Identifiers: LCCN 2016016745 (print) | LCCN 2016029889 (ebook) |
ISBN 9781476725826 (hardcover) | ISBN 9781476725840 (ebook)
Subjects: LCSH: Obsessive-compulsive disorder—Popular works.
Classification: LCC RC533 .B446 2017 (print) | LCC RC533 (ebook) |
DDC 616.85/227—dc23
LC record available at https://lccn.loc.gov/2016016745

ISBN 978-1-4767-2582-6
ISBN 978-1-4767-2584-0 (ebook)

CONTENTS

CAN'T
JUST
STOP

INTRODUCTION

JOHN MILTON, HAVING set himself the modest task in *Paradise Lost* of "justifying the ways of God" to man, was blind for most of the time he was creating his epic poem, from 1658 to 1667. So every morning, once that day's scribe—one of his three daughters or, sometimes, his nephew—arrived, he began dictating another batch of what would be the ten thousand-plus lines of verse describing the fall of humankind, lines that he crafted every night and memorized until daylight broke. (A painting hanging in the main branch of the New York Public Library, Mihály Munkácsy's 1877 oil, "The Blind Milton Dictating *Paradise Lost* to His Daughters," depicts Mary, Deborah, and Anne facing their father around an ornate table, ready to midwife the birth of one of western literature's seminal works.) If that day's designated amanuensis was late, according to an anonymous biographer, "hee would complain, Saying hee wanted to bee milkd." The bovine metaphor could not be clearer: like a cow aching to release her store, Milton had a palpable need to be unburdened of the memorized lines of verse that filled him with anxiety until he could get them out.

Hemingway's drive to write apparently had similar roots. In the characteristic monosyllabicity that inspired countless Papa-imitation contests, he put it this way: "When I don't write, I feel like shit."

Both writers' work sprang not, or not only, from a deep creative impulse and genius that could find expression nowhere except the page, but from something deeper, darker, more tortured. They were *driven* to write, compelled to get words down on paper in order to keep the psychic pain they felt at bay. Yet far from being unremittingly debilitating, even destructive, their compulsion to create brought them literary immortality. The rest of us made out pretty well, too: generations of readers have found comfort in the Fall and promised redemption of humankind, or inspiration in the self-sacrifice of Robert Jordan as the forces of the Spanish fascists approached.

There are endless motivations for human behavior, from the basic drives for food and sex to more complicated ones such as ego gratification, reputation building, altruism, compassion, envy, anger, a sense of duty, and simple pleasure, among so many others. But none of these explain behaviors that we feel irresistibly, often inexplicably, driven to engage in: compulsions. Compulsions come from a need so desperate, burning, and tortured it makes us feel like a vessel filling with steam, saturating us with a hot urgency that demands relief. They are an outlet valve, a consequence of anxiety as inevitable as burst pipes are a consequence of water freezing within a building's plumbing. But while compulsions bring relief, they bring little enjoyment, and while with one part of our brain we desperately wish to stop them, with another we are desperately afraid of stopping.

Compulsively checking your smartphone for text messages, stabbing the thing the moment you step out of a dead zone and get a signal; frantically trying to beat a level in a video game; acquiring more and more stuff, no matter how much you already have and how unfulfilled each previous hoard has left you—we feel compelled to engage in these behaviors and more because, if we don't, we feel the anxiety that drove Milton to regurgitate his memorized lines or that caused Hemingway to feel like shit.

In that sense a compulsive behavior is true to the word's etymology. We describe as "compulsive" someone who reads, tweets, steals, cleans, watches birds, lies, blogs, shops, checks Facebook, posts to Instagram, eats, or Snapchats not only frequently but with the urgency of one who is not fully in control of his behavior. Similarly, we describe as "compelling" motives, novels, reasons, evidence, television shows, arguments, scenarios, advertisements, melodramas, speeches, and candidates that create a sort of behavioral black hole: their attraction is so powerful, if we try to keep ourselves from being drawn in, if we try to look away or pull away, we feel a shiver (or more) of anxiety that can be assuaged only if we give in. Action that is *compelled* is brought about by pressure or even force, often against the will of the person executing the action; behavior that is *compulsive* arises from an irresistible, urgent drive or urge, one that loses none of its potency from the fact that it often clashes with one's conscious inclinations, wishes, and even deep desires. Our compulsions arise from a mortal ache that we will go to what seem the craziest extremes to soothe.

The "Lunatics" We Deserve

British historian Roy Porter (1946–2002) observed in a 1991 essay titled "Reason, Madness, and the French Revolution" that "every age gets the lunatics it deserves." And ever since the 1947 publication of W. H. Auden's poem *The Age of Anxiety*, ours has been an era defined by dreads both existential and trivial, societal and personal. Although Auden wrote in the immediate aftermath of Hiroshima and Nagasaki, the sources of anxiety in the twenty-first century go well beyond the specter of nuclear holocaust.

They include global warming and other forms of environmental destruction so powerful that humans have become like gods, replacing the "nature" in "natural disaster" to become the agents of floods, wildfires, hurricanes, droughts, and even the inexorable rise of the seas. They include the possibility that terrorism could again descend from an azure September sky or turn places as quotidian as an airport check-in, a subway, a concert hall, and a marathon's finish line into carmine killing fields. The sources of anxiety include, too, relentless technological advances that seem to outpace the ability of the human brain to keep up, from the banal (*Should I be on Snapchat or WhatsApp, or both, or . . . ?*) to the consequential (*What cancer treatment from which doctor at which hospital should my mother get?*). The minute-by-minute monitoring of whether one is Hot or Not and how many likes that clever post on Facebook got can ignite a smoldering anxiety that feels as if our blood has turned to lava and is seeking the weakest escape portal. Parents a couple of generations ago did not stress out over getting their children into the "right" preschool, nor did yesterday's teenagers and new graduates agonize over once-trivial choices such as what summer job to get or extracurricular activities to sign up for. And before the likes of Google Shopping and FareCompare, buying decisions did not bring the stress of wondering, *If I had just clicked through to the next page, or tried a different site, would I have found a better, less expensive version of what I wanted?* No wonder some of us must compulsively check Zappos.com's 517th pair of pumps before we can enter our credit card number.

While many of those anxieties afflict a nano-slice of American society, other forms are widespread. Experiencing, or merely witnessing, such massive economic dislocations as the financial crisis of 2008–2009 or the waves upon waves of layoffs that crashed onto America's workplaces beginning in the 1980s made us see job and financial security, not to mention career stability, as illusory, fragile, a thing of the past. A job for life, whether on an assembly line or in an office, has become as anachronistic as a pay phone. The insecurity inherent in twenty-first-century global capitalism permeates every corner of life, which seems to be cartwheeling beyond our control: play by the rules, act responsibly, and you can still wind up jobless, partnerless, and unfulfilled. How can we not feel anxious?

No wonder that by 2015 more U.S. college students suffered from anxiety than from depression, which had long been the most common mental affliction in this population. And no wonder that the malaise engulfed adults, too: according to the National Institute of Mental Health, in any twelve-month period 18.1 percent of U.S. adults suffer from anxiety intense enough to be considered a disorder, compared to 6.9 percent who suffer from major depression. And Google's Ngram Viewer, which charts the frequency of words appearing in English-language books, shows that from 1930 to the turn of the millennium use of the word *compulsive* rose eightfold.

That suggests a corollary to Porter's maxim: if every age gets the lunatics it deserves, then our age of anxiety deserves those who are in the grip of a compulsion.

For compulsions, according to a growing body of scientific evidence, are a response to anxiety. Suffused and overwhelmed by anxiety, we grab hold of any behavior that offers relief by providing even an illusion of control. We can't keep a private equity firm from saddling our company with so much debt it has to lay off half of us, or an online date from regarding us as one of countless fish in the sea. We can't keep power plants in China from burning so much coal that the resulting greenhouse effect turns a minor storm into a hurricane bearing down on our community, and we can't keep an anthrax-toting fanatic in Karachi from hopping a plane to New York. So we do what we can and control what we can, compulsively cleaning or checking, hoarding or shopping or surfing the net or wearing out our thumbs with video games. We cling to compulsions as if to a lifeline, for it is only by engaging in compulsions that we can drain enough of our anxiety to function. Against tectonic social and economic forces that feel as uncontrollable as King Canute's tides, we seize on anything that might restore a sense of agency. Compulsions are the psychological equivalent of steering into the skid: counterintuitive, initially scary, but ultimately (at least for some of us) effective.

While extreme compulsions appear odd, irrational, pitiable, and even self-destructive to outside observers, they are responses to otherwise unbearable and even paralyzing anxiety. According to a new, still-emerging understanding, even the craziest-looking compulsions are adaptive, even pragmatic, and all too human. A compulsion is at once biological balm and curse, surface madness (or at least eccentricity) and profound relief.

Consider compulsive exercise, which nearly half of those with an eating disorder are driven to engage in. After all, what feels more like it should be within our control than our own body?

Carrie Arnold* thought so. An overachieving college freshman, she began exercising regularly for fitness, but also because she was "stressed out of [her] mind" by the pressures of college and by being away from home for the first time, she told me. Whenever the anxiety got too bad she would "lace up [her] running shoes and head to the gym." Still, her exercise habits were hardly extreme—maybe thirty minutes a day, four or five days a week.

A few months into college, however, Carrie's already-intense regime exploded into something more. "I started exercising late into the night and it stopped being social," she recalled. "And it was almost all for stress relief." Every day, for hours each day, even as she carried a full load of courses, she ran and made the college gym her second home, powering herself up the stair stepper and making the stationary bike whine—all on about four hours of sleep a night.

Exercise, Carrie found, helped dampen the waves of anxiety that

---

*All of the people described in this book are real individuals, not composites or fictionalized. Where I give first and last names, those are their actual names; where I give only a first name (real or pseudonymous), it is at the request of the person interviewed.

washed over her. As a result, she felt anxious if she wasn't hitting the gym every day. By the end of her junior year her compulsion had spiraled out of control: she was exercising more in a day than is recommended for most people in a week and had lost so much weight that when her mother saw her for the first time in months, she told her she looked skeletal. "I felt I had to burn so many calories, or do so many sit-ups, and if I burned one less or if you stopped me from doing it I'd get really upset," recalled Carrie, who chronicled her compulsion to exercise in a 2004 book, *Running on Empty: A Diary of Anorexia and Recovery.* "I also had to use a specific machine, and if I didn't, I'd get frantic." Even when physicians ordered her to drastically cut back on exercise, "I couldn't just stop," she said. The compulsion to hit the Stairmaster felt like the most intense itch imaginable, one that can be relieved only by moving—intensively, energetically, even manically.

After graduating, Carrie threw herself into exercise like a dying woman reaching for a life preserver. She awoke at night and was seized by an urge to exercise; she did squats in the bathroom and ran for miles before the sun rose. "It was a horrible anxiety that got translated into, 'I have to exercise,'" she told me. "Exercise had become the way I managed my life. The worse I felt, the more miles I needed to run. I constructed my whole life around it. I had no friends or social life. The only point was seeing how many calories I'd burned, or the numbers of steps or miles I'd done." She tried to dial back, but "every time I ended up on the floor, shaking and sobbing. Exercise was the only thing that seemed to lower my sky-high levels of anxiety."

* * *

When I began this book, I viewed life-altering compulsions as foreign and almost frightening: people who scrub their hands compulsively and repeatedly; people who play video games so compulsively their thumbs seize up; people who shop so compulsively they wind up filing for bankruptcy. But in the course of my research and reporting, two things happened.

For one thing, as I got to know people who, at first blush, fit the "crazy" category, their compulsive behaviors didn't seem unreasonable at all. To the contrary, their compulsions seemed like understandable responses to angst that would otherwise eat them alive. They weren't crazy or even, necessarily, broken; they were coping, they were keeping themselves together, and they were probably functioning better than if they had allowed the anxiety to swallow them. The more I listened to the hoarder whose story most moved me, the more I found myself thinking, *Yup, if I had experienced what you had then my home, too, would be bursting from an accumulation of stuff serving as the only bulwark between me and a slough of despond.* Just because you're compulsive about something doesn't mean your brain is broken.

The second epiphany I had is that although people with the most extreme compulsions seem like outliers, the anxiety that drives them to those extremes is universal—and underlies milder compulsions, too. Actively behaving to allay anxiety is a deep and ancient impulse. That realization changed how I viewed myself and those around me: behaviors that once seemed thoughtless, selfish, controlling, or damaging now seemed like understandable responses to fear and anxiety. The mild compulsions of people who don't come close to meeting the diagnostic criteria for a mental pathology arise from the same sort of dread that drives severe ones. The compulsions serve the same function, too. It's just that deeper, more acute anxiety demands more extreme, and often self-destructive, compulsions to alleviate it, while milder anxiety has only enough power to compel us to never let go of our phones, to do the laundry according to specifications only we understand, to insistently arrange our desks this way and this way only.

*   *   *

Compulsions that accomplish this are as bizarre and varied as the human imagination.

A few years ago a sixty-five-year-old man came to the attention of a mental health clinic in Amsterdam because, for sixteen years, he had felt an irresistible compulsion to whistle carnival songs. His wife had contacted a mental health clinic "close to desperation from listening to the whistling of the same carnival song for nearly 16 years," Dutch psychiatrists wrote in a 2012 paper in the journal *BMC Psychiatry*. "It would go on for 5 to 8 hours every day" and got worse when he was tired. Mr. E., as they called him, had been treated with the antidepressant clomipramine, which cut the carnival-song whistling to a mere three to four hours a day, but the side effects were intolerable. When the psychiatrists visited his home, they were "immediately confronted with the clear and perfectly in tune whistling of the same song, almost without interruption." The doctors probed for the possibility of obsessive-compulsive disorder, but Mr. E. assured them that no obsessive thoughts instigated his compulsive whistling. "He did feel annoyed and anxious if he was asked to stop," however.

If compulsive whistling, why not excavating? Britain's "Mole Man," William Lyttle, felt compelled to dig massive, winding, deep tunnels under his house in East London, tunnels sixty feet long and some as deep as twenty-six feet under the house he inherited from his parents. "I first tried to dig a wine cellar, and then the cellar doubled," he told reporters just before his 2010 death. After local authorities, fearing the house would collapse, evicted Lyttle, engineers removed thirty-three tons of debris from inside the tunnels, including three cars and a boat.

Such extreme disorders might make one think compulsive behavior is something that afflicts other people, a mental illness that few of us have to worry about. But data show otherwise. As many as 16 percent of U.S. adults (38 million people) engage in compulsive buying, Stanford University scientists found in a 2006 analysis. Between 2 and 4 percent (up to 9 million people) are compulsive hoarders.

Over any twelve-month period, 1 percent of us suffer from obsessive-compulsive disorder (OCD), the dark prince of anxiety disorders.

Even more of us find ourselves in the grip of a compulsion that falls short of something disabling enough to qualify as a mental disorder—in fact, some compulsions are downright adaptive, helping us lead our lives or perform our jobs more effectively and efficiently (or so we tell ourselves). You probably don't know anyone who whistles carnival songs compulsively, tunnels under his house, or feels compelled to have repeated CT scans. But I bet you know many people who feel compelled to reach for their smartphone as soon as they wake up in the morning . . . or even, as one high-powered literary agent did, to demand his smartphone the moment he came to after open-heart surgery. Our compulsive behaviors can be so mild as to go unnoticed by everyone except those who observe us most closely and astutely.

You may also know people like Amy, who was a graduate student in neuroscience and the organizer of a compulsive-behavior support group when we met at a cafe. As I neared the restaurant I didn't look twice at the woman standing at the corner of 73rd Street. Having glanced at her gorgeous brunette mane, I figured she couldn't be the person who had agreed to tell me about her compulsion to rip out her hair.

Yet that's who hesitantly introduced herself.

"Sharon?"

"Amy?"

Over the course of a meal, Amy explained that the hair pulling started when she was twelve. "It became a way to regulate the anxiety," she said, such as from the pressure to excel academically and win acceptance to one of New York City's stellar science high schools. She wore hats to cover her bald spots. For ten years she gave up swimming because she didn't confine the pulling to her head—her legs and arms were also fair game—and eventually had no more body hair than a snake. Despite the ridicule she suffered from her trichotillomania—a syndrome marked by pulling one's hair out so excessively that sufferers can become bald—it worked for her, relieving her omnipresent anxiety. "I'm wired for anxiety," she said. "It builds up, and then I pull and it's extremely rewarding. You feel normal again, like going back to your baseline instead of being at this heightened level of stress."

One member of Amy's trichotillomania support group is a cop who used to love playing golf but had to stop. "Every time he looked at his hands holding the club he had to pull out the hair on his wrists and the back of his hands," Amy said. Another member, a rabbi, is consumed with guilt—not over the hair pulling itself but over the fact that he was doing work (hair pulling counts as work) on Shabbat, the day of rest when observant Jews will not so much as turn on a light.

While it is always fascinating to tour the fringes of human behavior (if only for the *there but for the grace of God go I* factor), these stories of severe compulsions brought a realization: that I was seeing shadows of myself, family, friends, and colleagues in them. We might not live at the extremes, but they illuminate the broad middle of the spectrum of human behavior where most of us do live. Over the years of research and reporting for this book, I came to see how much of what we do, although falling short of pathological and diagnosable, is driven not by the need for joy and not by curiosity, not by a sense of duty or even ego, but by a drive to quell anxiety. Maybe it's keeping old books and papers because not having them around makes you feel as tense as if your bedroom walls had vaporized. Maybe it's throwing yourself headlong into a project because it allays corrosive anxiety about the many dangers that could happen—to you, to your family, to the world—if you don't. Maybe it's shopping for groceries with military precision, or demanding that towels be hung just so, or expecting that household chores be executed according to a choreography that would make Balanchine roll his eyes.

Are We All at Least a Little Crazy?

The danger in immersing yourself in any subject is that you tend to see the world through a prism it creates and thus see examples of it everywhere. Behavior that once seemed ordinary acquires an aura of pathology. By the time I finished the reporting for *Can't Just Stop*, every time I saw my colleagues furiously BlackBerry-ing in the elevator, unable to travel the few seconds from the nineteenth-floor newsroom to the sixteenth-floor cafeteria without checking for texts and emails, I thought, *compulsion*. I looked back on my decision to hitchhike to work after Hurricane Sandy in October 2012 (when the public transit system was down) as more than a bit compulsive, too. I couldn't look at my husband's book collection without seeing hoarding, especially when my idea of a good time on a Saturday afternoon is "Let's give away some of these old books!" (Maybe that 1966 page-turner, *Ecology and Field Biology*, which he hadn't looked at in decades?) Anxiety (about missing something, like a message about one's job), anxiety (about the consequences of missing work), and anxiety (about losing part of one's past) again.

In other words, much of what we do, for good or ill, grows from the same roots as pathological compulsions. By seeing our and others' behaviors through that lens, what had seemed inexplicable, frustrating, self-destructive, or just plain idiotic (*Why is she making a federal case over how I load the dishwasher? Why can't she start working until she rearranges her desk? Why can't he resist scrounging the red bows on the Christmas wreaths that the neighbors leave at the curb every January?*) becomes understandable. And what I came to understand above all is that compulsive *behavior*, per se, is not a mental disorder. Some forms of it can be, and people in the clutches of true compulsions suffer terribly and need to be diagnosed and helped. But many, many "compulsions" are the expressions of psychological traits as commonplace as the drive to be loved and connected, to matter and to make a difference.

Most of us have probably told ourselves we could break free of our compulsions if we wanted to, that we could turn off the smartphone for most of our waking hours, resist the box of Thin Mints, or stroll past the "Huge Savings" sign in the window of our favorite store without a single muscle twitch propelling us toward the entrance. But a little voice asks, "Are you sure?" Venturing inside the heads and the worlds of people who behave compulsively not only shatters the smug superiority many of us feel when confronted with others' extreme behavior. It also reveals elements of our shared humanity.

CHAPTER ONE

What *Is* a Compulsion?

A GENERATION OR SO AGO, it became trendy to describe all sorts of excessive behaviors as addictions, meaning an intense appetite for an activity, as in "I'm addicted to shopping" . . . or to weaving, yoga, jogging, work, meditating, making money (as a 1980 book called *Wealth Addiction* argued) or even to playing Rubik's Cube (a 1981 story in the *New York Times* deemed it "an addictive invention"). Once neurobiologists discovered that the same brain circuitry underlying addictions to nicotine, opiates, and other substances is also involved in, for instance, a chocoholic's craving for Teuscher truffles, pop sociologists were off to the races. Suddenly, we were all addicted to email and working and Angry Birds playing and Facebook posting and . . . well, everything that some people do in excess became an addiction. The only significant scientific barrier to this trend—psychiatry did not recognize any behavior as addictive in the formal sense of the term—fell in 2013. That spring, the American Psychiatric Association published the latest edition of its *Diagnostic and Statistical Manual of*

Mental Disorders, widely regarded as the bible of the field, and for the first time it recognized a behavioral addiction: gambling.

Gambling made the cut because it met the three criteria that, for decades, have been the defining characteristics of an addiction. First, the behavior (or substance) is intensely pleasurable, at least initially, and sinks its claws into soon-to-be addicts the first time they experience it. Second, engaging in the addictive behavior produces tolerance, in which an addict needs more and more of something to derive the same hedonic hit. And, finally, ceasing to engage in the addictive behavior triggers agonizing withdrawal symptoms on a par with those that torture the addict who is trying to kick a heroin habit.

By these criteria, "addictions" to the electronic crack of the twenty-first century don't look like addictions, and they don't feel like it either, most crucially because they lack the defining hedonic quality. For me, at least, compulsively checking for emails feels more like what people with obsessive-compulsive disorder experience right before the urge to wash their hands or straighten a picture or step on the magical fourth sidewalk crack (because if they don't their mother will die). It feels like something you have to do, not something you want to do; something that alleviates anxiety (*Is an elusive source finally getting back to me, but about to try a competitor unless I reply in the next five seconds?*), rarely something that brings pleasure.

They are compulsions, not addictions.

What's the difference? The two terms are often used interchangeably in casual conversation ("compulsive shopping" vs. a "shopping addiction") with a mention of "impulsive" often thrown in for good measure. But since this is a book about compulsions and not addictions, let me explain how experts understand the differences.

To wit: surprisingly, alarmingly, disappointingly, exasperatingly poorly.

A Taxonomic Odyssey

Without ratting out people who were kind enough to sit still for my persistent questioning, I'll simply note that they did not fill me with confidence about the solidity of the scientific foundation underpinning the understanding of compulsive behaviors. "Well, a behavioral addiction is governed by things like neurons and hormones," one tentatively began. "But a compulsive behavior is psychological, but is governed by physical mechanisms." Huh? The muddle was captured nicely, if inadvertently, by a 2008 paper in which the authors invent something they name "impulsive-compulsive sexual behavior" and define it as "one type of addictive behavior." Trifecta: a behavior that's impulsive, compulsive, and addictive.

The lines dividing a compulsive behavior from an addictive one from an impulsive one seem to shift like tastes in fashion, and the confusion between and among them was practically codified by the many iterations of the American Psychiatric Association and its *Diagnostic and Statistical Manual.* Over the decades, the editions of the mega-selling *DSM* have rotated *addiction, compulsion,* and *impulse* through the definitions of syndromes, including eating disorders and anxiety disorders, as if the three were interchangeable. The *DSM* hasn't even managed to draw clear boundaries around OCD, which you'd think would be firmly ensconced as a compulsive disorder by virtue of its name, if nothing else. But no: early editions of the *DSM* described obsessive-compulsive disorder as marked by recurrent and persistent *impulses* to do this or that. When the APA's experts began working on what would become the *DSM-5,* their working names for pathological Internet use and pathological shopping were "C-I Internet usage" and "C-I shopping"—where the *C* stood for compulsive and the *I* for impulsive. The idea was that the excessive behaviors have features of both: impulsivity is the proximate cause, but a compulsive drive makes the behavior persist.

To get a sense of how muddled the taxonomy was, consider tricho-tillomania, which afflicted Amy, whom you met in the Introduction. In 1987 it entered that year's *DSM* (edition III-R) as an impulse-control disorder, along with kleptomania, pyromania, and intermittent explosive disorder, among others. That reflected the common meaning of impulsivity as "rapid, unplanned behavior with little foresight of or regard for the negative consequences," as Yale University psychiatrist Marc Potenza defined it one day when I visited his office in downtown New Haven, Connecticut. But the 1994 edition, *DSM-IV,* added two criteria for diagnosing trichotillomania: "an increasing sense of tension immediately before pulling out the hair or when attempting to resist the behavior," and "pleasure, gratification, or relief when pulling out the hair." Both of these are exactly what defines a compulsion. Yet trichotillomania sat among the impulse-control disorders until 2013, when the *DSM-5* (it switched that year from Roman numerals to Arabic) plucked it out of the impulse-control disorders and stuck it at the end of the chapter on OCD as a "related disorder." Oh, and the *DSM-5* eliminated the criteria that hair pulling be preceded by tension and lead to relief—and yet there it sits, in the OCD chapter, a chapter for a disorder whose defining characteristic is the anxiety that spurs an action that relieves said anxiety.

Tric's wanderings in the psychiatric wilderness are nothing compared to those of pathological gambling. The 1994 *DSM* had put *compulsive* gambling (my emphasis) in a grab-bag category called "impulse-control disorders not elsewhere classified," along with kleptomania, pyromania, and others. Again, that reflected the thinking that someone might impulsively decide to play the ponies and then, through some poorly understood mechanism, segue into doing so compulsively. In 2013, gambling also pulled off the trifecta: having previously been called compulsive and classified as impulsive, it became the first behavioral disorder to be formally categorized as an addiction.

At least the new classification made sense, in that it hewed to the traditional three-part understanding of addiction (initial hedonic hit leading to intense desire for the substance or, now, the experience; tolerance; withdrawal) in the context of drugs. For starters, pathological gamblers experience cravings as powerful as a junkie's. While it's obviously tricky to quantify a subjective experience like craving, there is some empirical evidence that the brain mechanisms underlying an addiction to gambling overlap with those in an addiction to alcohol, nicotine, pain pills, or illegal drugs: when pathological gamblers watch videos of people playing craps or roulette or another casino game, the regions of their brains' frontal cortex and limbic system that spike with activity are nearly identical to the regions that go haywire in cocaine addicts who watch videos of people doing lines. In addition, pathological gamblers build up tolerance to gambling just as alcoholics do to booze or junkies to heroin: to get the same pleasurable rush from gambling, they have to make larger and larger bets. And finally, pathological gamblers experience psychological withdrawal when they try to quit or even taper off, again akin to what substance abusers suffer. Cravings, tolerance, withdrawal: pathological gambling qualifies as an addiction.

In part, *addiction* and *compulsion* get mixed up because both words are used in ordinary language as well as clinical terminology, said Tom Stafford, a cognitive scientist at England's University of Sheffield who studies compulsive video-gaming. "Many people are cavalier about saying they're addicted to sports, or to shopping, or to their iPhone," he told me. "There isn't a clear line between an addiction like alcohol and a behavior they are very compelled to do, but I'd rather use the term compulsion for these behaviors."

It isn't just casual use of the terms that causes confusion. "It's a real scientific controversy, how and in what ways addictions are or are not like compulsive behaviors," James Hansell, a professor and clinical psychologist at George Washington University and coauthor of a popular textbook on abnormal psychology, told me. Hansell paused, as if trying to find properly diplomatic language: "There is a primitive quality to this, trying to define what is a compulsion and what's an addiction."*

Indeed, many researchers feel that the understanding, not just the nomenclature, of excessive behavior "has been shifting under our feet," as psychologist Carolyn Rodriguez of Columbia University said when I visited her office at Columbia University Medical Center. "Terms we had been using—like addiction, compulsion, and impulse control—are being looked at in a new light." Is there any hedonic hit from executing a compulsion? Rodriguez flipped through her mental Rolodex of patients. "In talking to them, I wouldn't say it feels good," she answered. "It just relieves anxiety." That relief might feel good, but it's a different kind of good than the pleasure that giving in to an addiction brings. Executing a compulsion brings an ebbing of the tide of angst, a lifting of the cap from a shaken soda bottle about to explode. People who feel compelled have a mental itch they need to scratch, like a poison ivy of the mind. One of Rodriguez's patients, she told me, "has intrusive thoughts about the name *James*. It makes him so anxious that if he ever sees it—like in the newspaper—he has to write *Edward* to cancel it out, and use Visine to wash away the sense that 'James' has contaminated his eyes." Rodriguez paused. "These people really suffer."

Fortunately, a growing number of experts have begun to grapple with the failure to clearly distinguish addictions from compulsions from poor impulse control, and not merely to classify behaviors correctly for the sake of tidiness. There is a practical motivation, too: if therapists aren't sure whether the behavior that has hijacked your life is a compulsion, an addiction, or a manifestation of lousy impulse control, they're not likely to identify the most effective therapy. The treatment for a behavioral addiction is very different from that for a compulsive behavior, which in turn is different from the treatment for

---

* Soon after we spoke, Hansell died suddenly in 2013 at age fifty-seven.

an impulse-control disorder. "You do need to get it right to determine effective treatment," Yale's Potenza said.

What finally emerged is this three-part taxonomy:

An addiction begins with a flash of pleasure overlaid by an itch for danger; it's *fun* to gamble or to drink, and it also puts you at risk (for losing your rent money, for acting like an idiot). You like how you feel when you win or when you get a buzz on. The addict-to-be takes a drag on a cigarette and finds that the nicotine hit makes him feel energized or mentally sharper. But eventually the substance or behavior ceases to bring pleasure, not only at the original levels of use but even at the extreme levels that typically characterize an addiction. Smokers lament that the forty-third cigarette of the day just isn't as pleasurable as the third smoke used to be. What once brought the high no longer does, necessitating ever-increasing doses, in substance abuse and in a gambler's greater bets. Despite the diminishing hedonic return on investment, so to speak, to cease engaging in the addictive behavior causes abject misery and, often, physical withdrawal pains like the shakes, irritability, or moodiness. Pleasure, tolerance, withdrawal: the Big Three of addiction.

Impulsive behaviors involve acting without planning or even thought, driven by pleasure seeking and an urge for immediate gratification. They have an element of risk seeking—*Hey, I bet it would be a blast to swan dive off this cliff!*—where the risk is expected to lead to a feeling of reward. Pyromania and kleptomania are classic impulsive behaviors because they're all about seeking pleasure and excitement. As a result, impulsivity can be the first step toward a behavioral or substance addiction. Something (a stimulus) triggers a response, and the pathway from the stimulus to response does not pass through the cognitive or even the emotional brain, at least not consciously. Instead, an urge zips from your most primitive brain center to your motor cortex—*Claim that wonderful sofa someone left at the curb; grab that luscious-looking cherry cheesecake from the dessert cart*—without so much as a pit stop in regions that control higher-order cognitive functions

(*Where the heck would you put another couch? You know you'll feel guilty if you eat that*). You do it reflexively. Like addictions, impulsive behaviors "have a hedonic quality," Jeff Szymanski, executive director of the International OCD Foundation (IOCDF), told me when we met in his hotel suite during the Foundation's 2013 annual meeting. "'I stole and got away with it,' 'I lit this fire and got all these cool fire trucks to show up'—very much like, 'I gambled and won.' It's not about reducing anxiety." We give in to impulses because we expect to be rewarded with a feeling of pleasure or gratification or excitement. Impulses make us grab the 500-calorie muffin when we were *sure* when we entered the store that all we wanted was a skinny latte. Like addictive behaviors, impulsive ones offer the allure of something pleasurable. Impulsive behaviors become impulse-control disorders when you repeatedly give in to your urges and suffer detrimental consequences.

Compulsions, in contrast to addictive and impulsive behaviors, are all about avoiding unpleasant outcomes. They are born in anxiety and remain strangers to joy. They are repetitive behaviors we engage in over and over and over again to alleviate the angst brought on by the possibility of negative consequences. But the actual behavior is often unpleasant—or at least not particularly rewarding, especially after umpteen rounds of it. At its simplest, the anxiety takes the form of the thought *If I don't do this, something terrible will happen.* If I don't check my BlackBerry constantly, I'll miss seeing emails the millisecond they land, and will therefore not reply in time to an urgent invitation or demand from my boss, or will just feel like *I don't know what is going on.* If I do not check my fiancé's Web history, I will not know whether he is cheating. If I do not religiously organize my closets, my home will be engulfed in chaos. If I don't shop, it will be proof that I can't afford nice things and am headed for homelessness. If I don't hang on to each precious object and instead bow to my family's wishes that I shovel out the clutter, I will feel exposed and vulnerable, like my most treasured memories have been buried in a landfill.

Underlying every compulsion is the need to avoid what causes you pain or angst. "A compulsive behavior is one that's done with the intent of decreasing an overwhelming sense of anxiety," said Szymanski, who before becoming executive director of the foundation in 2008 treated patients at McLean Hospital's Obsessive Compulsive Disorder Institute. Unlike addictions with their frisson of risk taking, he said, "a compulsive behavior is risk averse," driven by the need to avoid harm and executed with the goal of reducing the anxiety triggered by the thought of that harm. *I must do this to quell my fear and anxiety.* The roots of compulsion lie in the brain circuit in charge of detecting threats. This circuit, receiving a message from the visual cortex that a stranger is lurking in the dark doorway up ahead on the deserted street where you're walking alone, screams, *danger, danger!* "*That's* anxiety," said Szymanski. "It's the feeling that something is not quite right and that you may be in some sort of danger. You have a crushing emotion that you would do anything to get rid of."

Soon after interviewing Szymanski, I trekked up to the Bronx to meet Simon Rego, a psychologist at Montefiore Medical Center who specializes in OCD. "As long as the function is to relieve distress or anxiety or prevent a catastrophe that you firmly believe will otherwise happen, it's a compulsion," he said. "People will do a compulsion until 'it feels right.' Compulsions come from a sense that if I can't do this, I'm terrified about what will happen. The relief from distress can be pleasurable, if you think that calling a halt to smacking your head against a stone wall is pleasurable, but not in the same way that an addictive behavior is pleasurable."

Thus, a compulsive behavior is one that you engage in to squelch anxiety. That's clearest in OCD, where a compulsion is paired with and preceded by a specific obsession, an anxiety-provoking thought that you can't shake. You are obsessed with the thought that your hands are dirty and so you compulsively wash; you are obsessed with the thought that you left the stove on and so you keep returning home to check; you are obsessed with the belief that stepping on a sidewalk crack will bring a world of tragedy down upon your family and so you meticulously pick your way across the concrete.

The examples of the self-destructive rituals that OCD sufferers resort to in order to alleviate anxiety are legion. David, whom I visited in his Brooklyn apartment, apologized that he had not showered before I arrived. The reason, he said, was that when he showers he feels so compelled to scrub every square millimeter of his skin, and so certain he has missed a spot, that he will spend hours and hours under the pounding water, which would have made him late for our appointment. Others with a similar shower compulsion have it even worse: they use up the building's hot water and put them at risk for hypothermia when they can't leave the stall despite the freezing-cold water pouring onto them.

By the end of my taxonomic odyssey, I had settled on this: A compulsion differs from an addiction because the initial impetus is alleviating anxiety, not finding pleasure, and because how much you need to engage in the compulsive behavior in order to do that does not escalate, as it does with an addiction. A compulsion is a driven behavior where the emotion behind the wheel is a psychic itch, a sense of distress, even a sense of foreboding which grows worse and worse if you do not give in. "Compulsive behavior is a form of self-medication," as James Hansell put it. "There are painful emotions being numbed or soothed or avoided by means of the compulsive behavior. There is anxiety underneath it." The compulsive behavior keeps pain at bay. It's a form of self-reassurance—*Everything's okay now that I've checked the BlackBerry in the elevator leaving my office all of fifteen seconds after I checked the email on my desktop, but boy, I feel much better. Oh, wait, maybe a new one has arrived* . . . Compulsions become habit-forming because they work so well: my worries about being out of the loop by failing to read a text the instant it lands melt away when I check compulsively. So I'll just keep doing it.

Complications Ensue

Just when I thought I had it all sorted out, Scott Caplan, a psychologist at the University of Delaware who studies excessive online gaming and Internet use, warned me, "Remember, 'addiction' and 'compulsion' are just words that people came up with. They may not track nature perfectly."

Among the imperfections: an addiction can become a compulsion in the sense I'm using it. Over time, a behavioral addiction that began with thrill and pleasure seeking, driven by an overpowering desire for risk and reward, can segue into being all about assuaging the anxiety, agitation, and overall misery that come from tolerance and withdrawal. The addict uses the substance or engages in the behavior compulsively even though the reward waiting at the end of the rainbow is pleasurable only in the sense that when you stop hitting yourself over the head with a hammer it feels pleasurable. Deep into an addiction, said psychologist Nicole Prause of the University of California, Los Angeles, "a reward state changes into an aversive, craving state, and you begin to take a substance or engage in a behavior to decrease negative affect. You don't want to do it, but you have to in order to get yourself back to baseline, emotionally and psychologically." What had been an addiction morphs into a compulsion.

Another wrench thrown into this neat taxonomy is that the same behavior can be a compulsion for one person, an impulse-control disorder for another, and a behavioral addiction for a third. One over-shopper hits the mall because of a failure of impulse control: she can't keep herself from steering into the parking lot while driving home, can't keep from "just checking to see if there's anything good on sale," and can't keep from buying. Again. But for other over-shoppers the behavior is a compulsion: if they are not engaging in it, their anxiety rises to an intolerable level, and engaging in it assuages that anxiety.

Compulsive exercising illustrates the difficulty of trying to fit complicated, messy human behaviors into neat pigeon holes. When research on excessive exercise took off in the 1970s, about the time the jogging craze spread across the United States, scientists struggled to define what, exactly, they were studying. To some, the phenomenon of exercising to excess was "exercise addiction." To others it was "obligatory exercise," "compulsive exercise," or even a noble-sounding "commitment" to exercising arising from a competitive drive, a devotion to fitness, or the love of a challenge.*

The terminological mishmash underlined the fact that scientists did not know whether they were dealing with an addiction (motivated by pleasure) or a compulsion (driven by an anxiety that only exercising could quell) or something else. A 2002 review of eighty-eight studies on excessive exercise, published over the previous twenty-nine years, found that the research had been hampered by "inconsistent or nonexistent control groups, discrepant operational criteria for exercise dependence, and/or invalidated or inappropriate measures of exercise dependence," as researchers at the University of Florida concluded in *Psychology of Sport and Exercise*. In other words, attempts to study extreme exercising were so lacking in methodological rigor they were practically junk science.

But the problematic studies, in asking people to articulate why they exercised, did offer at least a glimmer of an empirically based taxonomy. People may punish their body through exercise for all sorts of complicated psychological reasons, research has shown. Some are motivated by the need to feel they are in control of at least part of their destiny, namely, their fitness and physiology. Others are driven by a need to demonstrate they can rise above common physical needs ("rest is for the weak") or that willpower can vanquish baser desires (to

---

*By whatever name, excessive exercising is not as prevalent as one might think from the gyms full of people taking spin classes or sweating on ellipticals. Even among the physically active, the population from whom studies typically seek volunteers, the prevalence of excessive exercise is around 3 percent.

self-indulgently laze around). Still others, who take up exercise to improve their fitness, are driven to ever-longer and more frequent bouts of running or using a treadmill because it brings them pleasure—the hedonic-hit model of addiction. Others exercise for extrinsic rewards such as medals and the admiration of others. In none of these cases, however, do the extreme exercisers feel like their brain is about to explode if they can't exercise.

In contrast, compulsive exercisers tend to exercise for intrinsic, mood-altering or -stabilizing reasons. They view exercise as the focus of their lives. It is the only way to relieve unbearable anxiety, and they suffer that anxiety if unable to exercise. They might have once been motivated by the pull of fitness, but eventually they do not so much enjoy exercise as find it the only way to quell the angst they feel when they are not exercising. "We know people have various motives for starting to exercise," said Danielle Symons Downs, a kinesiologist at Pennsylvania State University who developed an exercise dependence scale so therapists and individuals can assess whether the exercise is excessive. "And there are multiple reasons" why people do it to excess; "doing it to avoid intolerable anxiety is plausible." These are our compulsives, people like Carrie Arnold.

Granted, the boundaries between addiction and compulsion can be fuzzy, since being deprived of an activity you deeply enjoy and want can trigger anxiety, too. But an addiction is *born* in joy and pleasure, a compulsion in anxiety. Compulsive exercisers experience "higher levels of anxiety when not running compared to non-obligatory runners," as the 2002 review put it. They feel antsy or worse if they miss a workout. The purpose, as is definitionally true of any compulsion, is "alleviating negative emotions," researchers led by Caroline Meyer of England's Loughborough University wrote in a 2011 study in the *International Journal of Eating Disorders*. "A key feature of compulsive exercise is a negative mood, such as experiencing feelings of anxiety, depression, and guilt when deprived of exercising."

Where does that come from? The psychological and personality traits that put someone at risk of "developing a compulsivity towards exercise," as Meyer put it, include perfectionism and other elements of obsessive-compulsive personality disorder. In particular, compulsive exercisers tend to express much greater concerns over mistakes than other people do, have sky-high personal standards of achievement and morality, and feel chronic doubts about their actions—all reminiscent of the extreme conscientiousness that characterize mild compulsions.*

"Perfectionism was among the best predictors of compulsive exercise," Meyer reported. The inevitable falling short of perfection provokes anxiety, which only exercise can quiet—and the result is a compulsion to work out to a self-destructive extreme.

*   *   *

To a man with a hammer, everything looks like a nail; to a reporter immersed in the science and phenomenology of compulsions, everything we do seems driven by anxiety, and every quirky extreme of behavior seems compulsive. In reporting the prevalences of the various forms of compulsion, I used the most credible numbers I could find, usually from a source such as the National Institute of Mental Health. But the recent surge in diagnoses of mental illness might not be what it seems. For one thing, psychiatrists and others have been relentless in spreading the message that we have a vast, underdiagnosed epidemic of mental illness. As a result, millions of people have taken it to heart, convinced they have a mental disorder and seeking professional confirmation of that. A loosening of diagnostic criteria is likely also fueling the reported rise in the incidence of mental disorders: over the years psychiatrists have decreed that you have to feel a certain way or experience certain symptoms for only three months instead of six, or

---

*Mild compulsions are typical of obsessive-compulsive personality disorder, which itself is often driven by perfectionism, as I describe in Chapter 2.

have six symptoms rather than nine, to qualify for a formal diagnosis. The "epidemics" that the mental health industry cites reflect "changing diagnostic fashions," psychiatrist Allen Frances, who chaired the *DSM-IV* task force, told me. "It's not that more people are mentally ill, but that what counts as a mental illness changes." Remember, too, that there are no brain scans, blood tests, or other objective biomarkers for mental disorders. Rather, to make a diagnosis, psychiatry and psychology rely almost entirely on patients' self-report of how they are feeling. It isn't hard to meet criteria for one or another *DSM* diagnosis, especially because the experts who devise the criteria worry more about missing cases than about diagnosing as "mentally ill" people who are not. To a certain extent, it seems, we're as mentally ill as we think we are.

In speaking to people in the grip of extreme compulsions, I often felt as if I was looking into suns so bright they overwhelmed the planets and the stars. Even after I understood that compulsive behaviors so extreme as to derail lives, loves, and careers stemmed from a desperate need to keep anxiety at bay, it was hard to see that these were just the hypertrophied versions of ordinary, everyday quirks; they were too jarring, too off-putting. But just as the dimmer celestial denizens invisibly populate the daytime sky as well as the night's, so less extreme versions of compulsive behaviors are all around us . . . and, if we look carefully enough, within us. So much of what we do, for good or ill, arises from the same spring as compulsions. By seeing our and others' behaviors through that prism, what had seemed inexplicable becomes understandable. And what I came to understand above all is that compulsive behavior is not necessarily a mental disorder. Some forms of it can be, and people in its clutches deserve to be diagnosed and helped. But many, many compulsions are expressions of psychological needs as common within humankind as to feel at peace and in control, to feel connected and to matter. And if those are mental illnesses, then we're all crazy.

CHAPTER TWO

Obsessive-Compulsive Disorder, or Is Fred in the Refrigerator?

F ROM THE human logjams at the doors, it seems as if every one of the 1,100 attendees at the annual meeting of the International OCD Foundation is filing into the ballroom at the Atlanta Hyatt on this July morning, but once they fan out to the rows and rows of folding chairs they aren't exactly riveted by the proceedings. The public-service award to the elderly couple who launched an OCD group in New Jersey . . . the research award to scientists who did pioneering work on hoarding . . . the crowd is paying more attention to neighbors and phones than the speakers.

But then Shala Nicely strides across the stage, and it's as if an electromagnetic pulse has cut everyone's wireless connection. "It was a hot summer afternoon in 1975," Shala says, pacing across the stage like a caged jaguar, "and I was four. Mama and I were standing at the side of a road, waiting to cross, and I was hoping we were going to go feed the ducks." Suddenly, out of nowhere, a car smashed into them, crushing them so horrifically that Shala's broken legs looked like raw steak rolled in gravel. "We almost died that day," she says, "and my brain learned that the world is a very, *very* dangerous place. My brain decided that to protect me it had to show me all the dangers out there."

The nightmares started soon after. In her dreams Shala saw her parents lying on a guillotine with the blade about to fall, and once she awoke she knew—*knew*—that only she could save them . . . by concentrating on an image powerful enough to vanquish the image of the guillotine: of a horseman galloping to their rescue. Sometimes, though, after conjuring the chevalier, Shala remained terrified that her parents might still be in danger. So urgent, so compelling was the feeling that she could only compare it to what it must feel like if terrorists invaded your home and took your family hostage and pointed a gun at your child or mother or father or sister or brother and said if you don't do *this* I'll pull the trigger. "It's a hot, sick, molten feeling that grows and expands and fills your whole core with fear," she says. "You do whatever he says," where the *he* was the message from her brain that something catastrophic would befall her parents if she didn't . . . well, the thing she had to do changed over the years. But what did not change was the certainty that she couldn't tell anyone: "You don't tell what you see in your head because if you do you will make it happen. I kept it all to myself."

The "it," Shala figured out in her twenties when she finally saw a therapist, was obsessive-compulsive disorder. It drove her to execute rituals that seemed as senseless as they were impossible to resist. Senseless rituals like fours. Shala counted to four, did things in fours, and arranged her toys and books and stuffed animals in fours to ward off the disasters poised to engulf her parents. If the anxiety kept its grip on her throat, she pulled out the big guns: sixteen. Even thirty-two.

Shala was working thirteen, fourteen, fifteen hours a day as a sales representative and marketing manager. The brutal hours were the only way to stifle the thoughts, since when she was mentally engaged her brain didn't see danger everywhere. Therapists were no help. When she revealed her fours compulsion to one and then another and eventually several during a nearly Homeric odyssey in search of help, "they told me to just stop having these thoughts," she said. (On average, people with OCD struggle with the disorder for fourteen to seventeen years before receiving an accurate diagnosis; they see at least two therapists before finding one who knows how to treat it, according to the IOCD Foundation.)

"Just stop!" is the most common response to someone in the grip of a compulsive behavior, with "you're crazy" a close second. But stopping was the last thing Shala felt able to do. While she was driving to work, her brain regularly asked if she was certain—totally, completely certain—that the *ka-thump* she just heard was really a pothole. Maybe it was someone she had just run over, so shouldn't she turn around and check, but wait that's ridiculous, no if she goes back *right now* she might be able to save them; okay, turning around; *sh***, where was it? . . . until eventually Shala was late for work. The compulsions, like some fetid miasma rising from a horror-movie swamp, were "destroying my life," Shala says.

One day in her late thirties, Shala heard OCD whisper, *I think your cat Fred is in there, freezing to death.* Oh, come on, the non-OCD part of her brain retorted; how could Fred have gotten into the refrigerator? But of course, it doesn't hurt to look; such a tiny effort for such enormous peace of mind! There; no Fred. *I think you should check one more time.* Definitely no Fred. Shala stood there opening the refrigerator, poking around until she had assured herself that Fred was neither in the crisper nor hidden behind the jug of orange juice—and then looking compulsively again, and again, and again, a hostage to the OCD. During one of these sessions, Fred sauntered by and into the living room. Shala got an awful thought: maybe Fred teleported himself into the freezer just as she lost sight of him. So she checked again. "I'd say to myself, I know this is ridiculous," she told me later. "I knew Fred wasn't in the refrigerator. But I couldn't walk away."

Intrusive Thoughts, Overwhelming Desire to Act

Before the 1980s, OCD had an estimated prevalence of 0.05 to 0.005 percent, so in a Times Square crowd of twenty thousand on a busy summer Friday you might have one to ten people with OCD, making it one of the rarer mental disorders. Yet over the next thirty years the prevalence seemed to explode. There is bitter controversy about why (overdiagnosis? previously missed cases?), but the National Institute of Mental Health now estimates that 1.6 percent of Americans will develop this neuropsychiatric disorder sometime during their lives and that 1 percent of U.S. adults, or 2 million to 3 million people, have OCD in any given year, with men and women equally at risk. The disorder is half as prevalent in kids, setting up shop in the brains of one in two hundred of those under eighteen. If OCD is going to develop, the most likely ages for it to appear are around ten to twelve or in late teens and early adulthood. Both are periods when the brain is engaged in a frenzy of growing neurons and forming connections and then pruning back those connections, ridding the cortex of extraneous synapses, processes that offer ample opportunity for something to go wrong.

The basic description of OCD is pretty simple. To meet the American Psychiatric Association criteria, you must have distressing, recurrent, persistent thoughts or mental images—obsessions—that feel intrusive and (almost always) "ego dystonic." The last phrase means the thoughts, rather than emerging as part of your true self, feel as if they have invaded the mind from outside thanks to a malevolent puppeteer pulling the neuronal strings of your brain. They clash with your ideas of who you are and what you know to be true. Ego dystonia also means a part of the brain knows the thoughts—most commonly, that you are covered in a slime of germs, that something is "not right," or that some horror is poised to strike those you love—have only a tenuous connection to reality.* As a consequence, while giving in to the thoughts' demands relieves the attendant anxiety, it brings no joy and little satisfaction: you feel you are obeying the command of that puppeteer. You have lost the battle for control of your own mind.

The feeling that the intrusive thoughts originate from outside the part of the brain that makes you *you* does not defuse their power, and arguably makes the disease that much crueler. It may seem as if there is nothing worse than, say, the early stages of Alzheimer's, when someone knows she is losing her memory and her mind but can do nothing about it. OCD comes close: patients know their thoughts are mad, yet awareness of the madness brings no power over it. The vast majority of people with OCD recognize that a cat that just walked by can't really be inside the refrigerator, or that the stove they already checked five times isn't still on, or that failing to scrub their hands raw will give them AIDS. Yet they feel that while the thoughts have an infinitesimal probability of being true, *infinitesimal* does not equal zero. The resulting doomsday fear can be alleviated only by executing an action, so they give in, and give in, the sane part of the brain observing the madness with all the horror of a driver helpless to control a car skidding over a cliff.

This is the second element of OCD: the compulsions, repetitive and often ritualized behavior people with OCD feel driven to perform because they suspect, think, or worry that if they do not then the frightening things that obsess them will come true. They carry out the compulsion the obsession commands because, unless and until they do, the anxiety has them by the throat and cortisol is coursing

---

*About 2 percent to 4 percent of people with OCD lack the insight that their thoughts are illogical or irrational. They therefore carry out compulsions in the belief that the thought that triggered them is true. In these cases, ego dystonia is absent.

through the brain like the toxic overflow from a Superfund site. The specific compulsions that someone with OCD feels driven to execute range as widely as the most gothic imagination. Based on reports from OCD clinics, washing (triggered by obsessive thoughts of germs and other contamination) and checking (driven by an obsessive thought that something is dangerously wrong, like a stove left on) are the most common.

For Americans of a certain age, the best-known OCD sufferer was Howard Hughes, the industrialist, movie producer, and late-life recluse. He became deathly afraid of germs and therefore of human contact, and used his billions to feed his compulsions. His instructions to his staff on "preparing canned fruit," for instance, ran to nine tortuous steps, the third of which directed that the can be washed before opening, the label soaked and removed, the cylindrical part scrubbed "over and over until all particles of dust, pieces of the label, and, in general, all sources of contamination have been removed," and the "small indentations along the perimeter" attacked with copious quantities of soap lather. Step five: "While transferring the fruit from the can to the sterile plate, be sure that no part of the body, including the hands, be directly over the can or the plate at any time. If possible, keep the head, upper part of the body, arms, etc. at least one foot away."*

Washing compulsions are normal behaviors that have become hypertrophied in the OCD brain, which likely explains why they are so common. Checking compulsions, too, reflect normal drives that OCD has ratcheted up to irrational proportions, producing a "something is dangerously wrong" obsession that tortures its victims until they perform an action—checking the door or the stove, or doubling back in the car to see if the *ka-thump* really was a pedestrian they hit that—brings a "phew, danger averted" feeling. Many of us, for instance, ex-

---

*Psychiatrist Ian Osborn described Hughes's compulsions in his 1998 book *Tormenting Thoughts and Secret Rituals.*

perience the occasional nocturnal worry "uh-oh, did I bolt the door?" but Tom Somyak felt it invade his mind multiple times every night, starting in his twenties when he was first living on his own. He felt compelled to heave himself out of bed, haul himself downstairs, and check the locks and deadbolts on the front and back doors, again and again until sheer exhaustion stilled the demons rampaging through his brain.

When Somyak left for work every morning, the desperate need to check again overwhelmed his mind—*Did I lock the door?*—forcing him to turn around and reassure himself that he had. As with his nighttime compulsion, the daytime version would not be quieted with a single check, and on some mornings he turned back eight times. "It was a feeling that something wasn't right," Somyak recalls of this period almost twenty years ago. "So I didn't try to resist it. I just gave in and checked." And checked again. And again.

The birth of his son was the sort of life-altering event that can convince the mind that there are more dangers than were dreamt by Somyak's earlier OCD. He was making the boy's preschool lunch one morning when he got a mental twinge: *I just touched the refrigerator door and now I'm handling these slices of bread for his sandwich; what if I just covered them with germs?* So he washed his hands. But he would then touch a utensil, and who knew if that had been properly cleaned—so he washed again. And he would pick up a juice box, whose previous handlers at the grocery store were anyone's guess, so he washed again, lest he transfer deadly pathogens to his child's food. "It was an all-consuming compulsion to keep things clean for him," Somyak recalled. "I knew he was crawling on the floor and picking up all sorts of dirt and germs, but it didn't matter: I had to do this to keep him safe." Making lunch took an hour. "I knew something was wrong with me, but I figured it would pass," he said.

His symptoms abated for a few years, which is not unusual with OCD. Also not unusual is that when his OCD returned, it took another form. In 2001, someone mailed anthrax spores to media figures and politicians in New York and Washington, killing five and causing an additional seventeen people to contract anthrax poisoning in the worst bioweapons attack in American history. Somyak was in Austin, Texas, where he runs an OCD support group—and which there was no reason to think was on the anthrax mailer's target list. But the case remained unsolved for nearly a decade.* Who knew what and where the terrorist might be plotting?

Somyak did what he had to: he wouldn't let anyone else bring mail from the box at the end of the driveway into the house. When he did so it involved a complicated, ninety-minute ritual of putting on old clothes and gloves, Cloroxing every surface the mail came into contact with, getting special bags to deposit the envelopes in . . . "What if we got mail that had gone through the same sorter [that the anthrax letters had been through]?" he asked me. The question had an element of rationality: that is how ninety-four-year-old Connecticut resident Ottilie Lundgren received a lethal dose of anthrax, and how several others became sickened. But Somyak had taken the concern to a pathological extreme. "It's like you're a night watchman in a warehouse and you hear an alarm go off," he said. "You look for the reason. That's what it's like to people with OCD: you feel this anxiety welling up in you, and you look for a reason."

* * *

Like checking compulsions, just-right compulsions are driven by the feeling that something is amiss or awry. But while most people would agree that the target of a checking compulsion poses a threat (like an unattended stove left on or the front door of an empty house left unlocked), only someone with OCD sees the objects of "just right"

---

*And maybe longer, depending on whether you believe that the FBI got its man: their suspect committed suicide before his guilt could be proven.

compulsions as needing to be fixed. Irrational rituals consume them like a supernatural pyre, compelling them to count the doors they pass walking to work, to alphabetize the cans in their kitchen, to touch certain objects in a magical sequence before leaving home.

The "something is wrong" feeling takes a more inchoate form than obsessions with germs, triggering the belief that they walked or spoke or thought in a way that will lead to an unbearable tragedy. Shala Nicely's obsession that Fred was trapped in the refrigerator is one of the more imaginative variations on the just-right obsession: a feeling that something is amiss in the world seizes the brain and anxiety insinuates itself into what feels like every pore in your neurons, triggering a sense of throat-gripping terror about what will happen if you do not obey its commands. In milder forms, the just-right compulsion arises from the feeling that objects are arranged wrong, where "wrong" is in the eye of the anxiety-laden observer.

Megan's earliest just-right compulsions came when she was four. When it was time to put away her toys—especially Legos and Duplos—she didn't simply dump them into a box. She took a deep breath, surveyed the littered bedroom landscape of reds and blues and greens and other hues, and the cornucopia of shapes, and tentatively picked up, say, a red four-dot block. And put it precisely *there* to start a pile. And then she picked up a four-dot blue . . . but wait, does it go with the four-dot red, or should it go with its fellow blues? Paralyzed with indecision over the exactly right place in the universe for that and every other toy, Megan would try one organizing principle and then another, arranging and rearranging, as the insistent messages pummeled her brain: *Wait, are you sure that's right? It might not be.*

"If it wasn't just right I wouldn't put it away," Megan told me. "My parents thought I was obstinate. But it wasn't that: it was this powerful 'just right' compulsion. It was better to leave the toys out and scattered all over than to put them away wrong. I've never known a time in my life when the just-right anxiety wasn't present."

Megan, who was working in a biology lab at a large midwestern university when we spoke, now confronts her compulsion by using the "only handle it once" regimen, which teaches people compelled to arrange things "just right" to organize them into broad categories and then move on. If someone else decides where to put away lab equipment at the end of the day, she can manage; knowing someone has figured out the organizing principle seems to keep the just-right anxiety at bay.

* * *

OCD is the best-known form of compulsive behavior, but familiarity doesn't breed understanding. Popular culture often depicts the disorder as sort of cute and cuddly and charmingly eccentric, like the detective Adrian Monk in the television show *Monk* (who needs to straighten pictures, align cutlery on tables, and form symmetrical piles of magazines on tables so everything is "just right"). Every one of the people with OCD I spoke to echoed what Shala Nicely told me: "You never see what's happening inside the person, so you never see the level of fear, of totally debilitating, gut-wrenching anxiety. What most people understand about OCD is what they see outwardly. If someone says, 'oh, I'm a little OCD'? They have absolutely no idea what they're talking about."

If a thought doesn't cause you distress as intense as what you would feel if someone held a gun to your child's skull, it isn't OCD. If it does not make you feel like your blood is about to burst the walls of your arteries, it isn't OCD. If it isn't paralyzing, preventing you from doing anything else until you address the source of the anxiety, it isn't OCD. "It has to be an emotion so overwhelming, frequent, and intrusive that it keeps you from functioning, and so crushing you would do *anything* to get rid of it," Jeff Szymanski of the IOCDF told me.

One diagnostic criterion for OCD requires that the compulsive behavior "cause clinically significant distress or impairment" in social situations or on the job and be "time-consuming." While the idea of being "a little OCD" is therefore both a scientific misnomer along the lines of "a little pregnant" and an insult to those with the disorder, there is no question that OCD, like every mental disorder, exists along a spectrum from extreme to mild.

Although psychiatrists have long believed that the compulsive component of OCD is a consequence of the obsessive part—you wash *because* you believe your hands harbor a jungle of pathogens—new research has raised another possibility. For at least some people with the disorder, a recurring urge to, for instance, wash their hands precedes obsessive thoughts of contamination rather than follows them. It is not clear where that recurring urge comes from, though it could be a habit that hypertrophied. Then, as the brain tries to make sense of the perpetual washing, it seizes on contamination as the most logical explanation: *The reason I'm scrubbing my hands every few minutes must be because they're covered in germs.* In this case, compulsion rather than obsession is both the core feature and the genesis of OCD.

A Small Price to Pay to Avert Disaster

Anxiety is an evolutionarily ancient brain system, one that natural selection favored for the same reason it favors any trait: it increased the chances that those who possessed it would survive and reproduce, passing it along to their descendants unto the nth generation. In this case, a visceral, emotional feeling that something is amiss long before our rational, conscious mind can perceive it served our ancestors well. Our Paleolithic forebears who did not feel anxiety at stealthy footsteps, or who failed to act on it, became evolutionary dead ends: before they could reproduce they were some predator's lunch. But those who felt and heeded the anxiety by seeking its cause survived to reproduce. As a result, in us, their descendants, the default state of the brain is to reflexively obey the diktat of anxiety first and question it later (or not at all).

It is not clear why Nicely and others with OCD have a more acute version of that response. The brain circuitry underlying OCD has been worked out in greater detail than it has for any other form of compulsive behavior, but that explains "how," not "why." The latter, in the sense of the genesis of that circuitry, is still so poorly worked out that all scientists can offer is a mumbled invocation of life experience and genetics.

Here's the thing about anxiety: when it is sufficiently, torturously intense, we will do anything to alleviate it. If the "anything" seems fairly inconsequential, and the relief immense, the brain learns an enduring lesson in what we might call mental cost-benefit analysis. When Shala Nicely gave into her brain's command to open the refrigerator, it seemed but a small cost for the benefit of knowing that Fred wasn't turning into a cat-sicle, a possibility that tore at her mind like a Tasmanian devil with capsaicin under its claws. Of course, when the thought recurred the moment Shala closed the door, the cost of vanquishing it over and over again escalated until the wasted time and misery left her barely able to function. But by then it was too late. The OCD brain learns that executing a compulsion *works*; if following the orders of the terrorist holding a gun to your daughter's brain (in Nicely's analogy) spares her life each and every time, of course you learn to follow orders.

For Dave Atlas, the cost-benefit analysis is obvious: he is regularly bombarded with thoughts that his family is in danger. He does what he must to keep the horror from coming true.

"I have a lot of obsessive thoughts," Atlas told me, "all about keeping my family or me out of harm. I'll see a picture of a shark online, and because it represents a threat I have to knock wood three times and say, 'my family will be okay, my family will be okay.' Or I'll be walking down the street and have a thought that something bad is going to happen to them—this happens twenty or thirty times a day—and I have to hit my head three times to get rid of the feeling. If someone says, 'oh my god,' it also makes me think something bad will happen to my family, so I have to put my hands together and turn my face to the sky," as if to appease a threatening deity.

We were sitting outside a Starbucks in Manhattan's financial district. His OCD had not paralyzed him—Atlas held a job in healthcare IT—but the intrusive thoughts were like an insistent toddler that demanded constant attention, breaking his concentration and distracting him from work. As he described the feeling—a throat-clutching anxiety—a cab driver speeding up traffic-clogged Water Street swerved around a slow-moving van and came to a screeching stop at a red light, three inches short of a pedestrian. Unthinking, I blurted out, "Oh my god!" And Atlas did what he had to do to keep his family safe. He turned his face skyward, pressed his palms together, and then gave his head three quick punches.

*   *   *

After speaking with Atlas I walked uptown, where I met Leah. She had just graduated from college and was about to start a job at a daycare center. As we made our way across 42nd Street to the atrium of Altria's headquarters, she seemed to be picking her way unusually carefully, watching the Tennessee marble floor of Grand Central and then the asphalt street as if she were afraid of tripping, and sort of shuffling along. Once we found a table, she explained.

"I have to make things even," she said. "If I step on one thing, like a piece of paper, I have to step on another one of the same shape and size. Or if I step on a crack, I have to step on another to balance it out. If I don't, my dad will be attacked."

Once when she was in a coffee shop and smelled smoke, firemen suddenly rushed in and ordered everyone to evacuate. In a rush, Leah ran roughshod over cracks and stomped on litter, never once "making things even." And what happened? A manhole cover exploded. "With one part of my brain I knew I hadn't caused that to happen by not evening things out, but it's this 'better safe than sorry' feeling, you know?" she said. "Doing these things has such a low cost," just a little extra attention as she walks and a somewhat odd gait, but really, it seems like a small price to pay to hold off calamity.

So does her subway compulsion. When the train screeches into a station and the conductor blares out the name of the stop, Leah feels anxiety rising up through her body and gripping her windpipe. She feels compelled to touch the nearest pole before she exits, "once with my left hand and one with my right," she told me matter-of-factly. "Just thinking about not doing that is terrifying. If I don't do it, bad things will happen to the people I love."

Anxiety in All Its Forms

For years the American Psychiatric Association wrestled with the taxonomy of OCD, sort of like musicologists debating whether to classify Bob Dylan as folk musician or rocker. The third edition of its *Diagnostic and Statistical Manual*, published in 1980, lumped OCD with anxiety disorders such as generalized anxiety and panic disorder, since like those it is marked by an overwhelming sense of fear and apprehension and is often accompanied by sweating, elevated blood pressure, and a racing heart. For the *DSM-IV*, published in 1994, OCD remained an official anxiety disorder.

By the early years of the new millennium, however, as scores of expert committees worked on the *DSM-5* (published in 2013), some psychiatrists had come to doubt that classification. The debate became somewhat esoteric, but it started with revisionists questioning how central anxiety is to OCD. One camp argued that anxiety is the *cause* of the obsessive thoughts and compulsive behaviors. The competing camp held that anxiety is a *symptom* of the obsessions, the emotion that acts as a bridge between them and the compulsions: a thought such as "huh, the world is covered in germs" triggers anxiety and that anxiety drives the brain to seek any way of defusing the aversive feeling—namely, by executing a compulsive behavior. The second camp won. The recognition that anxiety is not the *primum mobile* of OCD but, instead, an intermediary force that arises from obsessions and drives compulsions became an argument for wresting OCD out of the "anxiety disorders" category and making it a standalone one.

The committee was also swayed by the fact that anxiety disorders and OCD arise from different brain circuitry. Most anxiety disorders involve the amygdala, which generates our sense of fear, and related circuitry. OCD, in contrast, reflects overactivity in what has been dubbed the "worry circuit," which (as I explain more fully in Chapter 11) includes the frontal cortex and the striatum, structures that in healthy brains play a role in ritualized behavior as well as error detection. Crucially, this hyperactive circuit is not seen in any other mental disorder. Thanks to recent discoveries like these, the psychiatric association kicked OCD out of the anxiety disorders and designated it a separate mental illness.

With washing and checking compulsions, the content of the anxiety (Fred might be freezing beside the sherbet!) leads logically to how to defuse it (open the door of the Sub-Zero). But other compulsions, especially those you're sure must be performed in order to keep things right and your family alive, have no logical connection to the content of the anxiety. These are odd rituals such as touching things or stepping in a certain way, or mathematical compulsions that your brain has convinced you will ward off catastrophe. "Magical" compulsions like these are often invisible to the outside world: thoughts trigger the intolerable anxiety, and only thoughts can counter that anxiety, in a neurological cage fight—as Carli showed me.

Mental Compulsions

Carli had emailed me that she'd be the one in cut-off jeans and robot T-shirt, so she was easy to pick out of the crowd approaching the corner of Bryant Park, where we'd arranged to meet that Friday evening in July. Climbing the stairs to the snack kiosk, I asked her, "What will you have to drink?" Which made her think, *twenty-two*. After a few seconds, she managed to ask for bottled water, to which I asked, "Still or bubbly?" Which made her mind seize on thirteen. And when I said, "I bet we can find some chairs up there," she thought, *thirty*.

Those are the numbers of letters in the words I spoke to her.

A writer and editor, Carli was diagnosed with OCD when she was sixteen, but it had burrowed into her brain years before that. In fourth grade, she told me, she began counting the words in sentences people spoke to her, doing the calculation as automatically as people who sight-read music translate images on a page into finger positions on a piano. Soon she began counting the letters. The chorus of Jon Bon Jovi's "I'll Be There for You"? Ninety-three characters. Apostrophes count as one. There are rules to these things, needless to say.

She also feels compelled to make lists of "alls"—all the states, all the campuses of the University of California (Berkeley, Irvine . . .), all the public colleges in Ohio, all the episodes of a television show (she can name the 117 of *The Brady Bunch*), all the dorms at the Massachusetts Institute of Technology, all the majors MIT offers, each of which is numbered and which she proceeds to reel off for me (Environmental Engineering is 1; Mechanical Engineering is 2; Materials Science and Engineering is 3 . . .). When she forgets one she feels an anxious incompleteness that begs to be filled in. If she is not at a computer to look up the single missing item? She's frozen. "Once when I couldn't remember the seventh of the Seven Sisters, I lay in bed half an hour and couldn't do anything until I remembered Vassar," Carli said as we fended off panhandlers popping out of the dusk like fireflies. "If I don't think of it my cat will die."

As best she can remember, there was no acute triggering event. Instead, her mental compulsions arose from the conviction that something awful would befall her or her family if she did not count words and then letters in spoken sentences, or items on a list. It was "just a thing nagging at my brain," she said, an anxiety that would build to a crescendo if she didn't execute the compulsion. Counting words and letters in the sentences she heard in school made it as hard to learn math, history, and the rest as if she were trying to swim while playing bongos. She got through college on the strength of her writing talent and sheer force of will.

It isn't just counting. Reading or hearing the word *cancer* triggers anxiety that someone she loves will develop the disease, producing an irresistible compulsion to counteract the power of the dread word by invoking a magic eraser: after Carli Googled "thyroid cancer" when a friend was diagnosed with it, she immediately had to Google "ulcerative colitis." The less-awful disease erases the power of cancer, she believes (yes, it has to start with *c*). Now that the color pink has become the symbol of breast-cancer awareness, whenever she sees it her eyes have to drink in any other color, to wipe away the pink. "October—when breast-cancer awareness month makes the whole world look like it's swathed in bubble gum—is, you will not be surprised, a tough time for me," she said. "Every time I see pink I have to do a quick 'colitis.'"

For sufferers of OCD, new compulsions come, and sometimes old ones go, for reasons experts cannot explain. There is little research on why someone feels driven to execute one compulsion and not another. Typically, OCD attaches itself to something already there, either from one's own life or from something seen only fleetingly. For Mark Henry, it was a film.

Soon after he and his family moved to another state when Mark was eleven, he happened to watch the 1973 movie *The Exorcist*. Before long, he began to think the unfamiliar, creaky new house was haunted. But he knew just how to keep the demons at bay: look into a mirror in a certain way whenever he passed one. If he was rushing out of the bathroom and failed to do so, the anxiety welling up in his throat seemed to fill every molecule of his body, and he had to run back and perform the mirror magic.

Soon, mirrors were not enough, and Mark had to add to the demon-deterring rituals: walking through a door a certain number of times, until it felt right; putting on his clothes a certain way until he felt that the supernatural had been averted for another day. This last was considerably more onerous than the mirrors and doors, and Mark frequently found himself taking off his school clothes, underwear and all, so he could do it right: he had to think "positive thoughts" while dressing, and if the tiniest negative thoughts strayed into his consciousness he had to start again. "It was an ambiguous but clear feeling of dread," he said. "My heart would pound and I had to pace back and forth."

One morning, performing his clothing ritual, he couldn't finish. He was frozen to the closet floor. The next day he was in a psychiatric hospital, his frantic parents beside themselves with terror over what had befallen their son. Mark stayed until the family's insurance ran out, but he received little more than custodial care; treating OCD requires intense sessions of cognitive-behavior therapy, and few hospitals offer that.

In his midthirties, Mark found himself in the grip of yet more compulsions. He was cleaning out some heating ducts in his new apartment when he developed, out of the blue, a compulsive need to de-germ everything in sight. He became convinced that his clothing was irredeemably infested with fiberglass particles, so he threw out every last shirt, sock, boxers, and jeans. The feeling that his hair follicles were packed with particles so overwhelmed him that he shaved his head, the better to give the contaminants an unobstructed path out. He couldn't look at his sheets and blankets without seeing microscopic asbestos fibers dance before his eyes; they went in the trash, too. He felt his car was contaminated, so he sold it. The apartment itself seemed to be crawling with contaminants, so he moved into a hotel, changing rooms once he felt the contaminants build up. The only clothes he could stand to have against his skin were silk, which somehow felt less contaminated. "I was like a runaway freight train, with one compulsion running into another," he recalled of that time.

Mark, who runs an OCD support group, knows the theories about what causes the illness, how there's likely a genetic component and that traumatic experiences can push a susceptible person into the abyss of OCD. Shala Nicely's brush with death taught her brain that the world is a deeply dangerous place, and that to survive she needed to see danger everywhere. Mark's brain processed danger somewhat differently. One evening when he was about seven, he wanted to watch Pink Panther cartoons at the same time that an older relative was settling down for the evening news. A sharp "No!" wasn't enough for him. He grabbed Mark by the ankle, dragged him like a felled deer up to his bedroom, and beat him with a belt. "As a child, you can't process what's happening to you," he told me. "OCD makes you feel there are some things you can control. When I was doing my mirror ritual, or my clothing ritual, for those brief moments I felt, yeah, I had done this thing and I had managed to keep the house from being possessed. The anxiety that came over me and made me do the ritual felt no different from an actual, visible, physical threat like the terror that I was going to be beaten again. I couldn't stop the actual threats, but I could make the terror I felt from the other ones go away."

Like Mark, most people with OCD go years before receiving an accurate diagnosis. That seemed odd; how hard can it be to identify a desperate need to wash your hands every few minutes or check the door locks hourly as OCD? But of course, OCD isn't always this stark. Both primary care doctors and clinical psychologists do pretty well identifying contamination- and symmetry-driven compulsions as OCD, but when the disorder takes a different form, especially one driven by "just right" obsessions, the rates of misdiagnosis are as high as 50 percent in primary care. Clinical psychologists don't do much better: a 2013 study by researchers at Yeshiva University in New York found that when a random sample of 2,550 American Psychological Association members were given OCD vignettes and asked how they would diagnose someone with the symptoms it described, 39 percent failed to detect OCD.

Scrupulosity

Not to minimize the torment of feeling that fiberglass particles have infiltrated your scalp, as Mark believed, or that your mother is one uncounted letter in a sentence away from cancer, as Carli did, or that the world is one untouched subway pole away from mishap, according to Leah. But then there's burning in hell for all eternity. In the form of OCD called scrupulosity, the triggering anxiety involves religion or morals, and the resulting compulsions are of a whole other magnitude of misery: they are meant to avert not piddling little worries like whether you left the door unlocked, but the certainty that if you do not do *this* particular compulsive act exactly right you will be condemned forever to the fires of Hades.

At the OCD meeting in Atlanta, Ted Witzig, a pastor and clinical psychologist at Apostolic Christian Counseling and Family Services in Morton, Illinois, led an informal session on scrupulosity. He asked the thirty people sitting in a circle what had brought us to his session. One man recounted how he felt compelled to drive the twenty miles home in the middle of a workday to ask forgiveness from his wife; he had told her the weather forecast called for sunny skies, but he just saw a fluffy white cloud float overhead. The thought that he had lied to her—and yes, he was convinced it was a lie—"feels as real as real and as urgent as urgent," he said. The young man next to him was convinced that if he did not attend mass every Sunday and follow every dictum of Catholic law, he was going to hell, probably sooner rather than later. The middle-aged woman was paralyzed with anxiety that she "would do something against the Bible or the Church," and so read and re-read it so she would not forget to, for instance, say the proper number of Hail Marys.

Scrupulosity is an equal-opportunity demon, preying on people of every religious background. That determines what form it takes. A Catholic tormented by scrupulosity may become paralyzed with anxiety that he took communion incorrectly or didn't say the right number of Hail Marys. A Jew might become felled by the angst of fearing that she read the wrong Torah portion on Saturday morning, a Muslim by the conviction that he deviated from Mecca by an infinitesimal degree of latitude. Unlike people who engage in religious rituals out of faith (or habit), people with scrupulosity do so to avert the anxiety and distress they would otherwise feel. The person becomes narrowly focused on getting it right.

Some of Witzig's patients have been terrified that they are praying to Satan rather than God. Others worry that they did not repent "correctly," are not fasting properly, or are encountering numbers like the satanic 666 much too often for it to be coincidence. Others see deceit in their most innocent actions (getting the weather forecast wrong), or feel the slightest deviation from truthfulness is a cardinal sin (some even feel compelled to read and understand every word in those interminable online agreements before clicking the "I agree" box). People Witzig has counseled told him they had committed themselves to Jesus and wanted nothing in life but to follow God's will—only to become tied up in mental knots when they became uncertain what His will was. They need a sign, some rock-solid proof of God's will, but OCD has a way of undermining that. No matter what they see or feel, the OCD will whisper, *Wait, are you* sure *that lightning bolt when you picked up the phone to call your fiancé was a sign from God?* Just as it whispers, *Are you* sure *you turned off the stove?*

Just ask Jane. If you had chanced to see her walking to school in the mid-1980s, when she was seven or eight, you might well have thought she was awfully careless, always doubling back as if she had dropped something, or perhaps unusually curious, retracing her steps to check out a funny-looking bug on the ground. In fact, the little girl was besieged by "horrible, horrible" images of pentagrams and tombstones with her name incised on them and images of the fires of hell consuming her, and by profanities and blasphemies that she knew would speed her trip there.

Jane knew precisely what to do to keep the satanic images from coming true and the blasphemies from being heard (and counted against her) by God: retrace what she was doing when she envisioned or thought them, like a burglar stomping on prints he had left to obliterate all traces of his path. Her steps were not always visible, but Jane knew where they were—she went back precisely five steps, or nine, or twelve, however many she took during the time the thought and vision unfolded in her mental theater. She felt compelled to walk over the steps, and walk over them again, as if to rewind time and resume her life from the point before the damning thoughts and images.

After some fumbling attempts to describe to adults the vivid, terrifying pictures and thoughts that were popping into her head, Jane vowed that the safest course was to keep quiet about the visions that compelled her to perform the rituals. "I really did think I was an evil person, so that kept me from telling my story," she told me. She resigned herself to executing the behavior that, her gut told her, was the only way she could keep the visions from coming true. "It's just five or ten seconds of your time versus burning in hell forever," she said. "There was a part of my brain that knew it wasn't true, but there is a feeling in the core of your body, an anxiety that makes you do the compulsion." And what if the thought or vision she desperately needed to erase occurred while she was sitting in a chair or lying in bed? "I had to shift to a different position," she said. "That was the rule. That would erase it."

But soon Jane became caught in loops. "While I was retracing, that thought would happen again, so I had to erase those footsteps, but while doing that I had another burn-in-hell vision, so I had to erase again, and again, and pretty soon it was taking five minutes, or twenty, not five seconds," she said. "There were times when I couldn't make the thoughts stop."

As Jane got older the religiously inspired thoughts and images gave way to more worldly ones. If she thought even momentarily about failing an upcoming calculus test, she had to erase the footsteps she made during the seconds the idea took to unfold. If she had a "bad" thought during a test she felt compelled to erase what she had written until then, which was a disaster in timed tests. She was late for classes and dates and appointments; better that than failing to erase the visions. It was only as a college sophomore that Jane figured out she had OCD and began seeing a therapist; when we spoke she was on her fifth. It has helped to some degree. She knows, when the thoughts force their way in, to slow down rather than double back to erase her steps. Occasionally she is able to resist at least for a few seconds, which is sometimes long enough to fully occupy her brain with thoughts of something safe and allow her to move on. "I probably feel the urge to do a compulsion every hour of every day," Jane said. But she nevertheless managed to graduate from college, get a master's degree in conservation biology, and land a job at an evolutionary genetics lab at a large public university. "Something is still going on in there and it's not me," she said. "I'm afraid of being alone with my brain."

Paradoxically, perhaps, the crazier the belief that compels a behavior the more likely it is to yield to therapy. The two most successful treatments for OCD harness the power of the mind to treat, and perhaps cure, itself. When either treatment—cognitive behavior therapy and mindfulness, which I'll discuss more fully in Chapter 3—succeeds in diminishing or eradicating the compulsions of OCD, it is because the person recognizes that the belief driving the compulsion is demonstrably, empirically false. With some part of their brain, smart, successful people like Jane know that "erasing her steps" doesn't erase a thought, let alone change the future, just as Dave Atlas knows that turning his face to the sky is not keeping the grim reaper from knocking at his family's door. The ego-dystonic nature of OCD can be harnessed to treat it.

The paradox is this: the premises of much milder compulsions tend not to be demonstrably untrue. And that makes rescuing people from the resulting compulsions—to do the laundry in a certain way, to hang the tea towels or set the table or even walk through their front door just so—harder than treating people with severe compulsions. In their way, milder compulsions are even more exasperating to those who love or live with or work with the compulsive person than extremes are. The former come wrapped in a veneer of reasonableness and logic that makes pushing back against them seem churlish and futile. Indeed, my encounters with people with mild compulsions underlined even more strongly how bad psychiatrists and psychologists are at drawing hard boundaries between mental illness and eccentricity.

CHAPTER THREE

With Treatment, from Blood in a
Snowbank to Hollywood

E THAN SMITH's first spoken words were *fly* and *bug*, and not because his parents were entomologists. Instead, even as a toddler he had a palpable fear of swallowing something small and alive and six-legged which, he believed with the certainty born of a child's understanding of physiology, would cause his head to explode. He also had forays into garden-variety obsessive-compulsive disorder, such as when he was convinced the only way to keep from vomiting while asleep was to blink in time with the flashing dots separating the hour and minute on his digital clock (dots on: eyes closed; off: eyes open). That turned out to be an excellent way to lie miserably awake for hours. But by the time Ethan was six, in the early 1980s, he had settled into his very own form of tortured compulsion: to check himself for signs of serious illness over and over and over again.

He started off by suspecting a brain tumor in every headache and meningitis in every fever. By high school he was carrying at all times three thermometers (one might break, and so might two; hence a back-up for the back-up) and checking his temperature as frequently as his friends checked their chins for the first facial hair.

In his twenties, Smith managed a successful acting career in South Florida, starring in national commercials and landing supporting roles in television and film. But by his early thirties, his OCD completely overtook him. "My compulsion became CT scans," he told me. He kept having throat-clutching thoughts that he "might" have hit his head on something and have a cranial bleed. He was 99 percent sure he had, and the 1 percent of doubt from the rational bits of his brain didn't stand a chance. The risk seemed so real, he started going to emergency rooms and claiming he had in fact hit his head, just to get a CT. At one point it got so bad that when the scan was finished he'd sit up and think he might, just *might*—who could be sure?—have bumped his head against the machine itself, which triggered such a panic that he screamed at the doctors, *"I need another one right now!"*

Researchers aren't sure what to make of the compulsion to seek medical treatment absent signs of illness. Some symptoms, such as the dizzying anxiety triggered by the belief that one is seriously ill, overlap with panic disorder. Others, such as the obsession with checking for symptoms and the compulsion to get treated, overlap with OCD. In the last few years, however, research has been converging on the idea that a compulsion to seek medical tests and treatment is actually its own disorder. The American Psychiatric Association calls it "illness anxiety disorder," defined as an occupation with serious illness despite not having symptoms of such. At any given time at least 1.3 percent of U.S. adults, the association estimates, have it, but the prevalence seems to be rising: anxiety about health affects most of us at some point, and a 2015 study in the journal *Mindfulness* estimated that it becomes clinically significant for up to 5 percent of the general population at any one time.

Studies have found that just a small percentage—perhaps 8 percent—of patients with illness anxiety disorder (formerly called hypochondriasis) also have OCD. That's a higher prevalence of OCD than in the general population, but nevertheless shows that illness anxiety is a distinct compulsion rather than a manifestation of OCD. Instead, people with illness anxiety disorder are more likely to have generalized anxiety disorder (73 percent, found a 2000 paper in the journal *Psychiatric Clinics of North America*), major depression (47 percent, twice the rate in the general population), or phobias (38 percent versus 23 percent of everyone else). The key reason why a compulsion to seek medical care is not a form of OCD is how each disorder feels. While patients with OCD generally view their anxieties as unrealistic (the ego-dystonic nature of the obsessions) and try to resist them, people with a compulsion to seek medical care are usually convinced they have a severe disease. Ethan certainly was, and the feeling that drove his behavior places it squarely in the realm of compulsions: a desperate anxiety compelled him to undergo screenings and diagnostic tests such as CT scans, and it was only by doing so that he was able to reduce that anxiety—albeit, as with all compulsions, only temporarily.

When I asked Smith whether his compulsion to seek medical care came from a traumatic childhood illness or accident, he suppressed a laugh. No, the only thing he could remember was the terror of swallowing a bug and having his head explode. That jibes with new research on this kind of compulsive behavior. For decades psychiatrists had assumed that its roots lay in previous experiences with illness, if not one's own then that of a loved one, seen up close and terrifyingly. But as a team of German psychologists wrote diplomatically in a 2014 paper, "empirical research [on that belief] is insufficient." In fact, when they studied 240 volunteers (roughly one-third were healthy, one-third had illness anxiety, one-third had a different anxiety disorder), they found that more patients with illness anxiety recalled having been seriously ill during childhood, and of experiencing other trauma during childhood, than the healthy controls. But there was no difference between patients with illness anxiety and those with other anxiety disorders. In other words, childhood illness and trauma were risk factors for later anxiety, but not specifically for anxiety about illness.

Smith didn't care about the roots of his compulsive behavior. After doctors told his parents that he should be admitted to a psychiatric ward, probably for the rest of his life, he eventually washed up at the OCD Institute of McLean Hospital outside Boston. He was confined for two months. During one therapy session in January 2011, Dr. Jason Elias asked Smith to smack his own head as hard as he could: this was a form of exposure-and-response prevention, or ERP. A standard OCD therapy, it involves exposing patients to what triggers their compulsion (if it's germs, they might touch a doorknob in a public building), with the trigger becoming more and more intense (after mastering doorknobs the patient might try to touch toilets in a public bathroom), but preventing the patient from executing the compulsion (washing his hands). Since Smith's compulsion was to seek medical treatment, his therapy was to experience a minuscule, meaningless smack upside the head . . . and then try, just try, not to run to the ER and demand a CT scan.

"I refused to hit myself, and they said if you don't we're going to call security," Smith recalled. Desperate, he finally smacked his head, delighting his therapists with his "progress." Smith, however, was filled with a sense of misery as profound as any he had experienced, and staggered out of the therapy session onto the frozen streets of Boston.

Uncompelled

Simon Rego is bent over double, whacking his hand on the carpet where his office door swings open. "How about here? Could you touch here, where no one ever walks?" He springs up and touches a light switch on the wall. "How about this?" he asks. "Or the back of this seat? Or the seat itself, where people put their *behinds*!" "How about the inside of the door; I'm the only person who touches it? Or the outside of the door—does that seem more contaminated, since it faces the waiting room?"

Rego, a clinical psychologist, is darting around his office at Montefiore Medical Center in the Bronx on the first day of summer, having said goodbye to his three p.m. patient and settled in to persuade me that exposure-and-response-prevention therapy is not the horror it seemed to Ethan. ERP dates to the 1960s, when British psychologist Victor Meyer applied to humans what worked with frightened animals: if rats were exposed to what scared them for a prolonged time and prevented from leaving the situation, they became less scared. Meyer, who had served as a fighter pilot for Great Britain in World War II and been a German prisoner of war after being shot down over France, first tried ERP in 1966 with a patient at Middlesex Hospital in London whose severe contamination fear caused her to spend most of the day cleaning. After shock treatment, drugs, and psychotherapy failed to help, Meyer and his nurse exposed her to objects that triggered her anxiety—and, crucially, prevented her from washing or cleaning. They actually turned off the water in her room. After four weeks of this, her anxiety began to ebb. After eight, her cleaning was still compulsive but less all-consuming, though she was by no means cured. ERP is still the predominant form of therapy for OCD today.

The psychological basis for ERP is that obsessions convince people with OCD that catastrophe is imminent and can be averted only through a specific action (checking that the door is locked, tapping a subway pole, washing a city's worth of germs off your hands . . .). Since executing the compulsion drains away the anxiety, the brain learns that compulsions are singularly effective at alleviating intolerable anxiety and becomes trained to execute the compulsive behavior as quickly as the rest of us would act if we saw a toddler teetering on the edge of a fire escape.

ERP forces you to watch the toddler, do nothing, and hold out long enough to see that the little tyke crawled back to safety. *See? You did not follow your compulsion, yet everything turned out fine.* Therapists don't actually put toddlers at risk, of course, but in patients' eyes they come close. ERP gradually exposes a patient to the situations or objects that trigger anxiety. But the patient is supposed to resist carrying out the related compulsion—and, in theory, wait for the anxiety to dissipate on its own. That teaches him that it can and will. With exposure and response prevention, when anxiety levels rise *but nothing disastrous happens*, the brain notices. "You confront the danger your brain tells you is imminent and life-threatening, but you don't do anything to protect yourself," said Jeff Szymanski of the International OCD Foundation. "By having the strength to find out what happens or doesn't happen—you don't get sick from not washing your hands after touching a doorknob—you train your brain to realize that the probability of this terrible thing occurring is low."

Therapists using ERP construct a scale of horrors. If someone is obsessed with the ubiquity of germs, the therapist picks something well short of having the patient wipe her hands inside the bowl of a public toilet. The patient describes how anxious she feels touching, say, a doorknob in the therapist's office: 10 (I am going to die), 9 (I could die), 8 (maybe I won't die just this one time), 7 (this feels horrible), 6 (this feels bad), 5 (I don't like how this feels), and so on down to 1 (I'm not feeling any distress) and 0 (peace and serenity). The therapist refrains from giving reassurance; no "it's okay, you know there aren't lethal germs there." The patient is supposed to experience throat-clutching anxiety, because that is the only way to become desensitized and habituated to it—much like (to pick an example from my own household) keeping the thermostat at 50 degrees inures you to cold.

That's what got Rego jumping around the room, touching the light switch and spots on the carpet and sides of the door as he would ask a patient to do. On the ten-point scale, "You want to get high enough so you learn something," he explains. "Okay, you say the seat of the chair is a four for you, so when you're ready, put your hand on it. Keep it there. What are you feeling? What are you experiencing? Hold it there long enough so you feel the anxiety increase and decrease. If you pull it away, what led you to pull it away? What were you feeling up until the moment you did that?"

A typical course of treatment is sixteen weekly sessions of about forty-five minutes, supplemented with homework: the patient practices ERP at home, ideally daily. Preferably, she varies the kind of exposure she subjects herself to. Someone obsessed with the fear that she ran over a pedestrian will drive on side streets and highways, at night and during the day, in rain and sun, with passengers and alone—each time going over, say, a speed bump and preventing herself from doubling back to check. "That variation teaches the brain to generalize," said Szymanski, and gradually it learns to quiet the anxiety triggered by an obsession and stifle the drive to execute a compulsive behavior.

It worked for Shala Nicely. With a therapist's help, she trained herself to stare at the refrigerator, feeling her anxiety about Fred rise and rise, but not giving in to it by opening the door. She also practiced what you might call extreme ERP, forcing herself to grab door handles in public places even if she was not going to open the doors and ordering herself to eat off the floor several times a week to tame her contamination compulsions. "It's worth it to get a cold or something" from assertively exposing herself to germs "to keep the OCD in check," Nicely said. "I still have OCD. But while it used to bother me all the time, now it's a blip on the screen."

People with OCD consult, on average, three therapists before they find a competent one, and spend some fourteen years between when OCD first creeps into their brain and finding effective treatment. None of the OCD specialists Carli (the woman with the compulsion to count syllables, among other things) consulted seemed familiar with exposure and response prevention—and this was in New York City, hardly a psychiatric desert. One uses hypnosis, for which there is no evidence of efficacy. And when I chatted with random therapists attending the IOCDF meeting in Atlanta, easily half—including those who said they treated OCD patients or wanted to—had no clue what exposure-and-response-prevention therapy is, let alone how to do it. "There is no licensing test for treating OCD," said psychologist Jerry Bubrick, an OCD specialist at the Child Mind Institute in New York City. "Clinicians pick up a manual for OCD and study it for a while, and then claim they know how to treat it. There is no standardization and virtually no accountability," especially since many patients who don't get better blame themselves and not their therapist.

Even those who find a competent therapist aren't necessarily on the path to cure. Between one-quarter and one-half of people with OCD decline exposure and response prevention, in some cases before they start; they simply can't stand it. Studies show that ERP responders' symptoms decline by 60 percent to 80 percent. Note that those are percentages for *responders;* it excludes those who can't stomach even one session of ERP. That raises the disquieting possibility that those helped by exposure and response prevention are the most tractable cases, people able to stomach what ERP demands of them.

And the others? Absent qualified therapists, many people with OCD wind up getting treated by primary care physicians, who rarely do more than write a prescription for Paxil, Zoloft, Prozac, and other selective serotonin reuptake inhibitors. As any patient will tell you, however, this sledgehammer approach can take a grim toll, often leaving them drowsy, nervous, nauseous, insomniac, and with their interest in sex evaporating like a puddle on a hot tin roof.

An alternative to drugs or ERP is one that many people with OCD find to be both more effective and more tolerable: mindfulness-based cognitive therapy. Originally a meditation technique, mindfulness entails mentally stepping outside yourself and observing the contents of your mind, dispassionately and without judgment or emotion. The "cognitive therapy" part refers to the essence of mindfulness, namely, evaluating your own thoughts. In a mindfulness technique pioneered for OCD by neuropsychiatrist Jeffrey Schwartz of the University of California, Los Angeles, for instance, patients learn to tell themselves that their obsession is just an errant brain signal, not a true indication of danger. "Mindfulness leverages the ego-dystonic nature of the obsession," said Szymanski of the IOCDF: since for some 97 percent of OCD patients the "something is wrong" message they're getting from their brain is contrary to what they know to be true, they have a head start when they monitor those thoughts, making it easier to dismiss them as aberrant neuro-noise. That makes mindfulness sound simpler, and easier to accomplish, than it is. But Schwartz and others have documented that the technique produces changes in brain function comparable to those seen when medications work: a quieting of activity in regions that are overactive in, and arguably the proximate cause of, OCD. And in head-to-head comparison of cognitive therapy and ERP for illness-anxiety compulsions like Ethan Smith's, researchers led by psychologist Florian Weck of Germany's University of Mainz found that cognitive therapy and ERP both produced remission rates of 55 percent after twelve months, they reported in a 2015 study in the *Journal of Nervous and Mental Disease*.

In our current age of cyberchondria, when Googling your symptoms can be enough to persuade you that you have a horrible, incurable illness, that comes as welcome news. Mindfulness-based cognitive therapy has proved remarkably successful at quelling the worry, rumination, and hypervigilance to body sensations so easily triggered by finding that your rash looks an awful lot like one from the Zika virus. In one case described by psychiatrists at Oxford University, a forty-something married man had experienced health anxiety since having a serious heart operation a dozen years earlier. He routinely monitored his breathing and interpreted anything out of the ordinary, even simply breathlessness, as an impending stroke or other catastrophe that only immediate medical attention could avert. But through mindfulness-based cognitive therapy, he learned to recognize that "his mind was creating catastrophic scenarios," the researchers explained in a 2015 paper in the journal *Mindfulness*, but that he could train his mind to recognize them as baseless fantasies and the triggering sensations as just a little pain or discomfort. Over eight weekly two-hour sessions, he began to realize "that the thoughts that were coming into his head were 'just thoughts' and that he could accept them, let them come into his mind and 'not get carried away,'" they reported. "He was physically present in the 'here and now' rather than in that scenario." After eight weeks, many of his health anxieties had disappeared.

Which brings us back to Ethan Smith, fleeing his exposure-and-response-prevention session.

Convinced he would die without immediate medical care but frantic that McLean would kick him out if he sought it, Smith grabbed a sharp rock lying beside a sidewalk and gouged his head. In a panic, he began fabricating a story that he had fallen on the ice and badly injured himself, but as he practiced what he would tell the EMTs he realized he needed to sell it: for good measure, he plunged headfirst into a snowbank. He lay there, hypothermia creeping through his limbs, for twenty-five minutes. Finally a passerby called 911. Smith got his CT.

He did get kicked out by the OCD Institute, which saw through his ruse and decided that tough love was the only hope for helping him. His parents went along; they told him if he showed up at their Florida home they'd have him arrested for trespassing. Reeling, Smith found a dingy apartment in a crack house in South Boston and lay in bed for six days.

I don't mean he lay in bed except for going to the bathroom, to the kitchen for a snack, or even to the front door to pay the pizza guy. No. Smith lay in bed for six days without eating or drinking; he peed into the mattress. "Death seemed like my only way out, but I didn't want to die," he said. He figured the only way to not die was to get out of bed and go to the corner market. Somehow the will to live overcame the death grip that his illness had on him. Survival became more important than his compulsion. His doctors at McLean took him back, he endured ERP three days a week, and began to function again: he got a job at a guitar store, met a girl, and started living. In 2011 Smith went to Los Angeles, where he works as a writer, director, and producer. He was the 2014 keynote speaker at the International OCD Conference in Los Angeles.

He's not cured, but he's no longer paralyzed by the compulsion to get CT scans. Somehow what he learned at McLean, and on the streets, kicked in, and he learned to separate the being who is Smith from the pathology that was his CT compulsion, and he has held on to it for dear life.

CHAPTER FOUR

In the Shadow of OCD: Carrying Conscientiousness Too Far

AT FIRST, Bianca hadn't the slightest clue about why she feels compelled to keep her sprawling three-story house in a state of organization, tidiness, and cleanliness. Certain chairs must stand in certain places and no others. Towels in the bathroom must be arranged and folded just so, light-colored ones on the outside of stacks and dark-colored ones on the inside. The dishwasher must be loaded according to a strict and undeviating system: utensils business-side up, large plates (always loaded first) toward the back, smaller plates in front, cups and glasses on the upper rack in descending order by size from back to front. In the kitchen, tall glasses must be stored on the right of an upper cabinet shelf directly over smaller ones, with medium glasses on the left; identically colored mugs hang in one place while nonmatching ones are banished to a closet. Bianca is not fanatic about keeping the house looking like a still life, however. When visiting children, stepchildren, and grandchildren leave rooms in disarray, she doesn't feel the intolerable anxiety experienced by someone with OCD who's faced with a dining chair that's not at a perfect 90-degree angle to the table. "I know that I can put it back together again the way it should be, so I don't feel too anxious," she said. "But I definitely feel a strong need to get that done. I put everything back exactly as it's supposed to be. I used to ask, *What will the world throw at me next? What will be the next shoe to drop?* These systems let me have control over things within the four walls of my home."

The targets of Bianca's mild compulsiveness have, over the years, extended beyond domestic affairs. During the years she worked as a piano tuner, she felt driven to re-test every note, anxiously returning again and again to notes she had already tuned, unable to leave them alone. A standard tuning takes sixty minutes, but Bianca regularly spent two and a half hours; the possibility that a note had sneakily become slightly flat or sharp irritated her brain like a cortical mosquito bite. Her morning routine is also mildly compulsive. She rises at six a.m. every day, practices yoga for forty-five minutes, then bicycles around her neighborhood for seventy-five minutes. "The routine makes sense to me," Bianca said. "But more than that, I just like my habits. They comfort me."

As we spoke, the emotional origins of her deep need for control came tumbling out. Growing up in Europe in the 1950s and 1960s, she had little say over her own life, even on such mundane decisions as what she would wear, how her hair would be cut, or what furniture would fill her bedroom. "Even my friends and my activities were picked for me," she said. The feeling of her fate being in the hands of others was disquieting enough, but it was made even more stressful by never knowing "which mother I would have when I woke up each morning": her mother's moods swung unpredictably from white-hot anger to warm caring to cool aloofness. It all made Bianca feel at sea, lacking the emotional anchor that a predictable parent provides.

She coped as best she could, developing a strategy that crystallized during childhood idylls. Her family spent summers at an old farmstead whose house had to be aired out, dusted, de-cobwebbed and otherwise made habitable, and the lawn mowed and raked, every time they arrived. One day the mountain of tasks overwhelmed her mother. "She became so depressed about what had to be done, that I said, 'We don't have to do all of it right now. We're tired after the long trip. Let's just clean up a little bit of lawn, and put out some chairs and a table so we can have a nice haven,'" Bianca recalled. "That was when I realized, even if I can't fix everything, as long as one little place is in order, as long as there's one little island where I can think clearly, it's okay."

That drive to create an island of order and calm in a sea of chaos and tumult grew stronger when Bianca left Switzerland for the United States in her early twenties. A divorced, single mother struggling to make her way in a new country, she seized on any chance to grab the reins of her life. "It became important for me to have things where they belong and to do things in a certain way, even little things like arranging chairs or hanging coffee cups in the right place," Bianca said. "It gives me a sense of peace, a feeling that there are some things I have control of. If I can't get it all the way I want it, I can live with that, as long as there's one little place in perfect order"—one little place like the patch of grass outside the farmhouse. "If I let things go, I feel a lot of stress and anxiety until I put them back in order," a reminder to herself that she is no longer the little girl whose life was steered in ways large and small by the caprice of others.

Shadow Syndromes

Around the turn of the millennium, many psychiatrists began to see mental illness wherever they looked. People who are fixated on finding the perfect expression of, say, diver scallops over quinoa, or the platonic ideal of a *ciabatta toscano*, were not simply foodies; they were suffering from "gourmand syndrome," one team of researchers contended. Divorced dads who forgot to send child support were not deadbeats and jerks, proposed another, but men with "environmental dependency syndrome," unable to focus on anything not in front of their eyes. People who failed to file income tax returns on time were not just disorganized procrastinators; they suffered "from an unrecognized adult form of attention deficit disorder," the 1997 book *Shadow Syndromes* argued.

The titular term was popularized by the book's coauthor, psychiatrist John Ratey of Harvard Medical School, to mean mild forms of mental illness, based on the theory that human behaviors, thoughts, and emotions once considered quaint, eccentric, odd, or simply unusual are in fact expressions of psychiatric disorders. As the number of named afflictions exploded, it began to seem that psychiatry was trying to make us believe that we're all a little crazy.

Not surprisingly, that spawned a backlash. Critics saw it as an effort to drum up business for therapists ("There is money in madness," Harvard psychologist Richard McNally wrote in his 2011 book, *What Is Mental Illness?*). One of psychiatry's most eminent figures, former *DSM* editor Dr. Allen Frances, lamented in a 2010 essay in *Psychiatric Times* that "what was once accepted as the aches and pains of everyday life is now frequently labeled a mental disorder and treated with a pill. Eccentrics who would have been accepted on their own terms are now labeled as sick." Not all idiosyncrasies and quirks, even those driven by the acute anxiety that underlies compulsions, are signs of a mental disorder, he and others argued.

Critics of expanding the boundaries of mental illness pointed out that the dividing line between mental health and mental illness is prone to shifting with the cultural tides, casting doubt on the supposedly scientific underpinnings of shadow syndromes. In 1850, for instance, a Louisiana physician named Samuel Cartwright told the state medical association he had discovered a hitherto unknown disease. He proposed to call it drapetomania, from the Greek *drapetes* (runaway slave) and *mania* (craze). It meant the mental illness that causes "Negroes to run away" from their slave masters, he explained in a New Orleans medical journal, because only a crazy person would attempt to escape slavery. Flight was the primary symptom of drapetomania, but secondary symptoms included dissatisfaction with being another man's property and a general sulkiness. And before we laugh (or cry) at the ignorance that pervaded a nonscientific age, remember that until 1973 the American Psychiatric Association considered homosexuality a mental disorder.

Efforts to see mental illness in every eccentricity foundered once and for all on a criterion that psychiatry had long insisted on: for behaviors to qualify as symptoms of a mental illness, they had to cause distress and dysfunction. For many of us, our little compulsions do the opposite. They help us function, and they allay anxiety, the defining characteristic of a compulsive behavior. They're soothing, not distressing; beneficial, not dysfunctional. That alone would disqualify Bianca for a diagnosis.

Although the "we're all a little crazy" campaign largely failed, the idea that mental health is a continuum survived. In large part, that realization reflects discoveries in both neurobiology and genetics. While neuroimaging has identified patterns of brain activity and circuitry that underlie a number of mental disorders, those patterns are not clear-cut. Similarly, the genetics revolution of the last twenty years has revealed that multiple genes contribute to the risk of developing one or another mental illness; with rare exceptions, it's not the case that the presence of a single gene causes a mental disorder while its absence prevents same. "The idea of a continuum represents a major cognitive breakthrough for genetics," Stanford University neuroscientist Robert Sapolsky once told me. "It suggests that a middling genetic load [of genes related to behavior and emotions] gives you a personality disorder, a lighter one gives you a personality quirk, and a still lighter one gives you mainstream America." A dozen or so genes, for instance, may contribute to the trait that psychologists call "novelty seeking," but it's rare for someone to have all twelve. Someone with ten, however, might be a heroin addict, while someone with one or two might grow antsy at watching the same movie twice, or might be a bit fickle, excitable, quick-tempered, and extravagant—humankind's explorers, innovators, and iconoclasts. Similarly, a number of genes have been linked to neuroticism. Parents who nervously check their watches when their teenager is out late may well have one or two of them,* but the dysfunctional agoraphobe might have a dozen.

The original shadow-syndrome proposal labeled all of these people mentally ill, either mildly (the explorers and the worried parents) or seriously (the addict and the agoraphobe). Today, psychiatry recognizes that although no mental condition is an island—they all sit on continua where the boundaries between pathological and quirky, disordered and eccentric, mad and mundane shift with the fads of medicine and culture—the term "mental disorders" should apply to only a small part of the continuum. Countless common, everyday behaviors tiptoe up to the boundaries between illness and health without crossing them. To argue otherwise is to plunge into the *reductio ad absurdum* of labeling "mentally ill" a good fraction of the population— people like Bianca and others who have mild compulsions but whose behavior falls well short of a clinical diagnosis.

Numerous studies have shown, for instance, that anxiety can compel people to create a minuscule piece of their world over which they have some control, but let me choose just one. Martin Lang, who at the time of the research was a graduate student in anthropology at the University of Connecticut, and his colleagues told volunteers (students at Masaryk University in the Czech Republic) they had a challenging task ahead of them: give a five-minute speech to a panel of art experts

---

*Especially since genes for slightly neurotic vigilance, by making our brain pay attention to potential threats, are likely adaptive.

about a decorative metal object sitting on the table in front of them. Other volunteers were instructed to simply look at and think about their objet d'art. Fitted with a heart-rate monitor and an accelerometer (to measure movements of each wrist), the sixty-one participants got to it. After three minutes, the researchers asked everyone to polish their object with a wet cloth until it seemed clean. Finally, the give-a-talk volunteers were let off the (fictitious) hook, with the explanation that the art experts were unavailable.

Volunteers who had anticipated giving a presentation told the researchers they felt more anxious than the just-think-about-it group did, and the heart-rate monitors confirmed that: their pulses had quickened. The accelerometers were even more telling. The most anxious volunteers, those anticipating speaking before a panel of experts, cleaned their object differently than those who felt no such pressure. The former cleaned more repetitively, predictably, meticulously—dare we say compulsively, Lang and his colleagues reported in a 2015 paper in the journal *Current Biology*. "When facing a complex, uncontrollable, and unpredictable situation," they wrote, the mind becomes anxious about its inability to know what will unfold. To cope with that fraught mental state, people feel driven to actions that might be completely unrelated to the source of the anxiety yet help them "regain a feeling of control over the situation," Lang and his colleagues concluded. "[T]his regained sense of control might result in anxiety alleviation."

You probably haven't faced an assignment of impressing experts with your understanding of an objet d'art, but perhaps you have felt anxious about an upcoming negotiation—and, since you can't control that any more than you already have through hours of preparation, you compulsively rearrange your bedroom drawers. Or perhaps you are anxious about meeting your partner's parents, and you compulsively scrub the bathtub. You likely know people with compulsions like these, for you can find them across the street, in the adjacent cubicle, in your yoga class, on the other side of the bed . . . and probably in the mirror.

Conscientiousness on Steroids

According to psychology's widely used Five Factor Model, a quintet of traits defines every personality. Larger or smaller doses of agreeableness, openness (to new experiences), neuroticism, extraversion, and conscientiousness combine to form the myriad of personality types that describe the human menagerie. While psychologists debate the validity of the system, it captures the fact that each individual has greater or lesser amounts of each personality ingredient. The ingredient most relevant to compulsions is conscientiousness.

Manifested most clearly by a tendency to be disciplined, deliberate, and dutiful, especially in matters of ethics and responsibility to family and society, conscientiousness is also characterized by a striving for competence, a preference for order, and a drive to achieve. Low conscientiousness, in contrast, is marked by being carefree, impulsive, spontaneous, and hedonistic, as well as irresponsible, uninhibited, and negligent. The highly conscientious among us are dedicated to work and have strong, often unyielding, moral principles and opinions. Those in the middle might step up to register voters for a local election that no one else cares about or finalize a client presentation as everyone else troops off to happy hour. They are the significant others who are adamant about the ideal way to sort the recycling. Toward the more-extreme end of the spectrum, they are people whose preference for order has been ratcheted up into a preoccupation with rules and lists, whose striving for achievement has become the compulsive devotion to career and productivity known as workaholism, and whose drive for competence has hypertrophied into perfectionism. At that extreme, conscientiousness steps over the boundary into obsessive-compulsive personality disorder (OCPD).

Now there's a discontinuity in the spectrum. Extreme conscientiousness may be OCPD, but extreme OCPD is not obsessive-compulsive disorder. OCPD is not OCD Lite. For one thing, to the surprise of laypeople and experts alike, few people with OCD also have obsessive-compulsive personality disorder or vice versa. That is, few people with OCD are particularly conscientious, disciplined, and dutiful, while few people with OCPD are seized by the throat-gripping anxiety that characterizes OCD. In the early 1980s, research found that fewer than 20 percent of adults with OCD also had OCPD, while barely 20 percent of those with OCPD also had OCD, psychiatrist Steven Rasmussen of Brown University Medical School and colleagues reported. Even when psychiatrists loosened the diagnostic criteria for obsessive-compulsive personality disorder in the late 1980s, only 30 percent of those with OCD also had OCPD. An obsessive-compulsive personality is not even the most common personality diagnosis in people with OCD. As far back as 1993 psychiatrists made the counterintuitive discovery that when people with OCD have a personality disorder, it's unlikely to be OCPD, researchers led by psychiatrist Donald Black of the University of Iowa Medical School concluded in the *American Journal of Psychiatry* that August.

In fact, compulsive personality traits are not unique to or even more common in people with obsessive-compulsive personality disorder. Instead, they're strewn around the population like rice at a wedding. Chronically insisting that people submit to exactly your way of doing things, for instance, characterizes about three-quarters of people diagnosed with OCPD. No surprise there. But that trait is present in an even higher percentage of people diagnosed with narcissism and passive-aggression.

Another distinction shows the disconnect between OCD and OCPD: the compulsions of OCPD are worlds away from those of OCD. With enough effort, you can demonstrate that the fears of someone with OCD are empirically wrong. You can swab her hands and show they are not covered with pathogenic germs. You can have him step on a sidewalk crack and show him that his mother is still quite alive. And of course you can show Shala that Fred is in the living room, not the refrigerator. In contrast, the compulsions of someone with OCPD typically have a firm grounding in reality: hanging up bathmats after they're used *does* reduce the chance they'll get mildewed, turning off lights in unoccupied rooms *does* reduce energy waste. Heck, you can find virtually all of these "rules" in one or another list of *50 Ways to Save the Planet* (run the dishwasher only when it is absolutely full; turn off the faucet while brushing teeth) or *10 Tips for a Germ-Free Home*. If an insistence on organic foods, distilled water, careful handling of raw chicken, or fifty minutes of daily exercise is a manifestation of OCPD, then most of upper-middle-class America qualifies.

Most importantly, the compulsions of OCD feel like actions you are executing under the orders of an outside force. The feelings behind the compulsions are ego dystonic. In obsessive-compulsive personality disorder, however, the compulsions are ego *syntonic*: they feel rational, obvious, and reasonable, an expression of your core beliefs, values, and needs. It's just the rest of the world that thinks they're nuts. Because of the ego-dystonic vs. ego-syntonic distinction, OCD and OCPD (not to mention compulsivity that falls short of OCPD) feel totally different. While people with OCD feel that their compulsions arise from a neural interloper, those with OCPD or extreme conscientiousness feel their compulsions are an expression of their very self.

Liza Jane practically defines herself by her compulsive conscientiousness. If you need a computer repaired, she's your woman. When a laptop seems shot, she told me, "other people would say, 'screw it, I'll just reformat the hard drive.'" Reformatting is a quick solution to a machine that seems beyond help—one with the blue screen of death, for instance—but it wipes out saved documents, settings, and programs, leaving the customer to reconstruct his cyberexistence from scratch. "I wouldn't do that," Liza Jane said. "It was a source of pride. I couldn't stop myself. I'd insist on going in there and finding the virus or whatever the problem was. I spent way too much time doing it—I probably wound up making about twenty-five cents an hour—but I never blow things off. I kill myself to get something done, and done the right way."

That attitude make bosses "love you to pieces," she said. It also underlines the benefits of a compulsive personality: being meticulous and organized, setting high standards, and striving for excellence. That combination is nevertheless a mixed blessing. "You end up doing a lot of things yourself" because no one lives up to your standards, Liza Jane said. Despite the downside, she can't dial back a conscientiousness that feels like a well-thought-out, carefully considered expression of her values and intelligence. "It's hard for me to think this isn't the right way to be," she said. The thought of letting her standards slip unleashes the anxiety the compulsions were developed to quash. "It's so normal to someone like me to live with the constant anxiety. I'm just trying to do things the right way or make things right," Liza Jane said.

The "Crazy Rules"

While we all have personal preferences and habits, someone with OCPD regards these choices as being the *only* rational ones and as having the moral, scientific, or logical force of the Ten Command-ments and Newton's laws of motion rolled into one. They are not choices. They are imperatives. Someone with OCPD feels her be-havior is not merely justified, but is so hands-down superior to the alternative way of doing even mundane tasks that when someone deviates from her prescription she can neither understand nor tolerate it. A person with OCPD has "extensive intellectual backup for his be-havior," explained the pseudonymous Paul, who runs an online forum about OCPD. It's the thinking man's OCD: people with a compulsive personality back up their imperatives with a Ph.D. thesis's worth of logic, rationalizations, and ethical arguments.

Julie sees that every day. When she dated the man she eventually married, he seemed "very fastidious," she told me. But after years of marriage, fastidious doesn't begin to describe him. A technical writer, he has a "system" for everything under the sun: the best way to roll up a towel to block the light from seeping under their daughter's bedroom door at night; the best way to handle garbage (don't throw away used tape; it might make the sides of the garbage bag stick together); the best way to tuck away venetian blind cord so as not to strangle anyone. "He says he's spent forty-five years working out the best way to do things," Julie said. "When you don't do it his way you're an idiot—and, worse, if you don't do things right he can't stand it."

The reason the compulsions of OCPD morph from sensible choice into imperatives is that anxiety is at their root, just as in every compulsive behavior. OCPD sufferers believe there is a clearly right way and an obviously wrong way to do just about everything, and theirs is the right way. Moreover, if they do these things this way, they will be safe, but if they do not then things will go to hell in a handbasket. Following rigid rules offers the halcyon promise of imposing order on the chaos that is rampant in the world, of keeping disaster far from your door. But flouting them triggers throat-constricting anxiety.

People with compulsive personalities fall into either of two camps: those who impose their standards on themselves and leave other people alone, and those who try to make everyone conform to their notions of how to behave. OCPD people call those notions their "crazy rules." A sampling from Paul's online forum:

> When loading forks and knives into the dishwasher, you must put them point-down.

> The remote control must always be put on top of the TV, even though you need it when you're on the couch.

> Never order the same thing at a restaurant as your companions. Doing so robs everyone of the opportunity to sample as many dishes as possible.

The garden hose must be wound up after each use,
with the spray handle facing the "correct" direction.

"Straighten out" the curves on the road by crossing over the
double yellow line to maintain as direct a line as possible.

Having a few crazy rules doesn't necessarily qualify someone for a diagnosis of OCPD. Passing the *DSM-5*'s diagnostic threshold for the disorder requires meeting four of eight criteria: the preoccupation with rules and lists; perfectionism that keeps you from completing tasks; such "excessive" devotion to work that you reject leisure activities and friendships; ethical inflexibility and over-scrupulousness; hoarding; miserly spending; inability to delegate tasks (since no one else can do anything right); and/or general "rigidity and stubbornness."

Somewhat more user-friendly is the Cammer Test for OCPD, which asks respondents to answer how well twenty-five statements describe them: never, for which you give yourself one point; sometimes, worth two points; often, three points; or almost always, four.

1. I prefer things to be done my way.
2. I am critical of people who don't live up to my standards or expectations.
3. I stick to my principles, no matter what.
4. I am upset by changes in the environment or the behavior of people.
5. I am meticulous and fussy about my possessions.
6. I get upset if I don't finish a task.
7. I insist on full value for everything I purchase.
8. I like everything I do to be perfect.
9. I follow an exact routine for everyday tasks.
10. I do things precisely to the last detail.
11. I get tense when my day's schedule is upset.

12. I plan my time so I won't be late.

13. It bothers me when my surroundings are not clean and tidy.

14. I make lists for my activities.

15. I worry about minor aches and pains.

16. I like to be prepared for any emergency.

17. I am strict about fulfilling my obligations.

18. I expect worthy moral standards in others.

19. I am badly shaken when someone takes advantage of me.

20. I get upset when people do not replace things exactly as I left them.

21. I keep used or old things because they might still be useful.

22. I am sexually inhibited.

23. I find myself working rather than relaxing.

24. I prefer being a private person.

25. I make a budget and stick to it, not living beyond my means.

If some of these items made you think, *Wait, what's wrong with that?* (6, 12, 16, 17, 21, 23, 24, and 25 did that for me), then you see the flaw in the shadow syndromes argument. Just because a long list of symptoms is needed to qualify for a diagnosis of a mental disorder, it doesn't mean that a few of those symptoms define a milder form of that disorder. Obviously many of the self-descriptions in the Cammer Test are beneficial, even the foundation of a functioning society.

In fact, a score of fifty to seventy is standard. Notice how many things you can be compulsive about and still fall short of obsessive-compulsive personality disorder, which requires a minimum of 75 points: if you answer "always" to, say, 1 through 7 (28 points) and "sometimes" to the other 18 (36 points)—a combination that, to the layperson, sure looks like a compulsive personality—you fall short. Nevertheless, the National Institute of Health's 2001–2002 National Epidemiologic Survey on Alcohol and Related Conditions, which interviewed 43,093 U.S. adults, found that 7.9 percent (or nearly 15 million people at the time) had obsessive-compulsive personality disorder, making it the most common personality disorder. That estimate held up a decade later, when psychiatrists led by Jon Grant of the University of Minnesota Medical School used face-to-face interviews, also with thousands of adults, and concluded that the lifetime prevalence of OCPD was 7.8 percent. Men and women were about equally likely to develop it. It was less common in younger adults, Asians, and Hispanics, and significantly more common in people with a high school education or less.

My own compulsiveness manifests itself in grocery shopping, where any idiot can see there's an optimal way to operate. Obviously you buy only items on sale, you buy the size of the item that has the lowest unit cost, you use coupons, and you certainly do not impulsively purchase anything that's not on the shopping list. On those rare occasions when my husband does the family grocery shopping there is hell to pay, for invariably he violates one of the shopping commandments. My compulsiveness arose from anxiety that we'd run out of money. Logically, I knew an extra seventy-nine cents my husband spent on Swiss cheese because he stupidly bought Kraft rather than the store brand wasn't going to tip us into foreclosure. But I had convinced myself that unless we watched every penny it was just one short step to eating cat food.

> The air freshener can has to be on the right side of the
> toilet tank and has to be laid on its side when showering.

> Shirts must face left in the closet.

> The car must never stop until you reach your destination.
> Turn right on a red light even if a right turn is not the
> direction you want to go.

> Don't walk the same path to and from the bathroom,
> or the carpet will get smashed down.

All paper currency must be flat, facing the same way, with
the portrait on top, and sorted by denomination from ones
at the front of the billfold followed by fives, tens, etc.

By the time Bev left her boyfriend, the number of shower-related
rules—which had begun with a simple, reasonable, request to turn
on the exhaust fan—had grown to a dozen. She was regularly repri-
manded for leaving the shower door eight inches ajar rather than the
prescribed six (the perfect distance to balance the need to air out the
stall but not obstruct someone in the bathroom), not hanging up her
towel perfectly, not returning the bath mat properly. When they dined
out, she wasn't even allowed to choose what to order, so certain was her
boyfriend about what she would "really like." He was mystified that she
could not see the logic of this. "People with this disorder really don't
get that you're a separate person they can't control," Bev said, "even to
the point of expecting you to like the foods they like." They have made
such a careful study of the options that their conclusion, to them, has
the authority of a *Consumer Reports* refrigerator recommendation.

Such extreme conscientiousness is always justified by the utmost
rationalization. The ways people with a compulsive personality have
chosen to live their lives seem so right to them, so much better,
smarter, more efficient, less wasteful, than other choices. "Sometimes
it feels like it's due to a love of beauty and elegance," as one member of
the online OCPD forum put it. "Finding the most elegant solution to
something, or doing day-to-day things in a very thoughtful and careful
manner, is just really, really satisfying. It's creating order and harmony,
reducing entropy and chaos. Other times it seems like a totally irrational fear of incompetence, in oneself or in others." "The rules may be
crazy but they are there to help us cope with the world," said another.

For one man with OCPD, the sight of someone dog-earing the
pages of a book provoked angst and anxiety on a par with what others
would feel upon seeing someone methodically gouging chunks out

of Michelangelo's *David*. Dog-earing, he explained, "messes up" the orderliness of a book and "changes the status quo," something that should never be done lightly. It also "changes the book into an object that is less than perfect, and that is unacceptable."

The lawn has to be mowed in a different direction every week.

When pumping gas, top it off until the dollar amount is a round number, or at worst a half dollar or quarter-dollar. In a book used only for this purpose, note the date, mileage, amount, price per gallon, total amount spent, and where purchased.

Organize food in the cupboards by time zones, starting at Hawaii (pineapple), moving on to the United States (hot dog buns) and Italy (pasta) and ending at Japan (soy sauce). Turn the packages so all the labels face front, forming a de facto world map.

All knobs or dials in the vehicle—temperature, fan, or stereo volume—must be left in the middle, or vertical, position, upon exiting the car.

Let me insert a caveat here. OCPD gets applied to behaviors and personalities like a twin-size quilt trying to cover a king-size bed. Lots of behaviors may have elements of OCPD, but they are something else entirely. Specifically, insistence on adhering to rules and explosions of anger when they're broken have strong elements of the controlling behavior and contempt for others that marks narcissism and even psychological abuse.

What can we make of a man who decrees that his girlfriend's friends and family are not allowed to phone her during what he designates as his "quality time" with her—after 8:30 p.m. six nights a week and all day on weekends? This guy is not invoking the consci-entious, perfectionist, order-making rules of someone with OCPD, but the controlling domination of a narcissist. So, too, with many of the "OCPD rules" that wives and husbands told me about. If the rule is "agree with everything I say without exception," "keep everything the way I like it because that is the right way," "not have friends who take up your time, because I might need you and I always come first," and always "have the children at the front door like little soldiers when I arrive home from work, as my mother did": again, not the anxiety-driven compulsions of OCPD, but the egotistical, dictatorial orders of narcissism and coercive control.

Is obsessive-compulsive personality disorder a mental illness? It's not as if the minds of people with "crazy rules" and extreme conscientiousness aren't working properly. They're not seeing visions or hearing voices, they're not dysfunctional, and they're often not dissatisfied with their beliefs and compulsions. But psychiatrists do classify OCPD as a mental illness, and have since the time of French neurologist Philippe Pinel (1745–1826). Best known for reforming the treatment of mental illness, Pinel literally unchained the patient-inmates at Hospice de la Salpêtrière. Established by Louis XIV in the mid-seventeenth century on the former site of a gunpowder factory,* it housed ten thousand paupers and prostitutes but also people with mental disabilities, epilepsy, and other neurological and mental illnesses. Seeing the breathtaking number of ways the mind can go off the rails, Pinel proposed that one can have a mental illness without being mad, "mad" in this case meaning the experience of delusions or hallucinations, intellectual impairments, or other defects of reasoning. Lucidity of thought could exist alongside "defects of passion and affect," Pinel argued, so that one's power of reason might be intact at the same time that the emotions are deeply unbalanced. And voilà: certain personalities became "disorders."

----

*Hence the hospital's name: saltpeter, or potassium nitrate, is a key ingredient in the manufacture of gunpowder.

In the early twentieth century, American and European psychiatrists had a field day coming up with forms of personality pathology. Being shallow, cocksure, or undependable all qualified. So did being "excessively" critical of others, querulous, impulsive, insecure, moody, fractious, callow, cold, rigid, or obstinate. Every edition of the *Diagnostic and Statistical Manual* has included personality disorders, starting with the first, in 1952. Over the years, it became easier to meet the diagnostic criteria for OCPD. The *DSM-III* of 1980 required a person meet four of five criteria, while the *DSM-III-R* of 1987 required meeting five of nine. That loosening of the standards had the effect of doubling the incidence of OCPD, psychiatrists Bruce Pfohl and Nancee Blum of the University of Iowa noted in a chapter in a 1995 book, *The DSM-IV Personality Disorders*. But, they continued, "it is not clear whether this represented an improvement." Indeed. The debate over whether any personality can be disordered reached a crescendo in the debate over conscientiousness in the service of work.

Work, Work, and More Work

Compulsive working, manifested as excessive devotion to job and productivity to the exclusion of relationships and downtime, is one of the eight diagnostic criteria for obsessive-compulsive personality disorder. "It's a very insidious kind of compulsion because you get rewarded for it," said Michele, who runs a website firm in Austin, Texas. Society dangles the promise of riches and renown in return for hard work. It is the rare company that asks its employees not to work hard; the rare parents who tell their high-schooler to dial back on the Advanced Placement courses and resume padding. To the contrary. To pronounce oneself a workaholic and a multitasker is a badge of honor in twenty-first-century America. "In this culture," Michele said, "trying to recover from workaholism is like trying to stay sober in a bar."

In those who feel intense anxiety when they are doing anything but working, the seeds were likely sown in childhood. Especially in a certain demographic (at least middle class, with educated parents, and usually in a suburb or city), "kids have to be in an activity and productive constantly," Michele said. "It's almost frenzied"—signing up baby for infant yoga and music "appreciation," arranging play dates and museum visits and science-center outings. "It continues into high school, where activities take over these kids' lives." It's only rarely that the activity is done for its own sake, let alone for any joy it brings. (Remember that when anxiety rather than joy or other positive emotion becomes the impetus for a behavior, the behavior qualifies as compulsive.) If you find yourself at a recreational soccer or baseball game, ask some of the kids—especially the benchwarmers—why they're there. "I love soccer" or "I love baseball" is usually a distant runner-up to "I have to do extracurricular activities to get into college." If the parent feels more driven to get the child to take music lessons, do volunteer work, make a sports team, captain the debating squad, and edit the yearbook than the child, it's anxiety once removed, or compulsion by proxy.

Michele's anxiety-driven compulsion to work began in grade school. "I was constantly trying to get attention by getting great grades. I got the message that you're worthwhile if you produce. In college I worked as a waitress, where the faster you move the more you get done and the more you make." To minimize downtime, which made her so anxious it felt as if her body were trying to jump out of its skin, she scheduled appointments too close together, forcing her to speed from one to the next. "I was constantly moving," she said. "If I sat down to watch a movie I immediately jumped up again. I couldn't sit and relax. I couldn't watch TV unless I was also doing something else. I couldn't read unless it was work-related or I was learning something—unless I felt I was accomplishing something. Even on vacation I made sure we were constantly scheduled—I was always saying *Come on, come on, we have to go to the beach or the tennis court or on the tour.*" For Michele, the "just right" feeling that drives people with OCD didn't come from aligning photo frames or intoning magic numbers. It came from plunging into work.

Absent work, anxiety fills the compulsive doer's every pore, as I heard one sunny September morning. I had driven up to West Point to meet Bruce for brunch at the historic Thayer Hotel, an impressive pile of stone overlooking the military academy's track and field facility. We settled into a table with a breathtaking view of the Hudson River.

Even as a child, Bruce worked compulsively, driven by a need to best his brother and get the attention of his parents and other adults. "Whatever he did, I had to do better," he said. It started when his brother was a Cub Scout. Bruce missed the age cutoff by a few weeks, which goaded him. When the den held a paper drive—yes, there was a time before recycling when Boy Scouts collected papers—Bruce's unofficial hoard dwarfed everyone else's; he still has the photo showing him perched atop a nine-foot-high pile. By high school he was running community youth groups, church fellowship groups, political groups, Boy Scout troops, "and every school group except the Girls Athletic Association," Bruce told me, all driven by his own Age of Anxiety: an almost existential angst that came from wondering, *Does my life matter? Is there any record that I was here?* He lettered in baseball, football, and basketball; his photograph appears in his high school yearbook sixty-six times. He had figured out how to make his life leave an impression.

After law school, he took a job in a district attorney's office in a rural community. "I could stay at the office until two or three in the morning every night, and I did," Bruce recalled. "I'd go into the empty grand jury room and put twenty-three stacks of legal files on the twenty-three empty jurors' chairs, working on twenty-three cases at a time. . . . It gave me a real status in the legal community. I prided myself on working longer, harder, smarter, better, and faster than anyone else in the office." Striving to gain recognition and money "was what

I had been all about since I was eight," he said. "I created the vision of a super-competent, overachieving, powerful, highly respected worker. And I achieved that vision."

Even after his compulsion to work led his wife to divorce him, "I'd bring home briefcases full of papers," he recalled. "When my second wife said we have to move far away enough from my office that I couldn't work until ten every night and go in every weekend, I'd work the property: my mind had to be fully engaged, even if I didn't get any kudos for clearing a three-acre field. It wasn't about the praise; it was keeping my mind working all the time. I had to keep mentally active. If I didn't, I felt like climbing the walls." An almost palpable twitchiness flooded him when he was not working, as if slacking off even slightly would erase his existence.

Batter Up . . . and Other Superstitions

It is the same twitchiness that drives some of society's most public compulsions: those on athletic fields. George Gmelch, who played first base in the minor leagues for the Detroit Tigers organization in the 1960s, became interested in anthropology after he retired, and so combined his two loves: studying rituals in baseball the way other anthropologists study the rituals of exotic tribes. Gmelch was especially struck by a classic study of the Trobriand Islanders, who inhabit the Kiriwina Islands off the coast of New Guinea. Anthropologist Bronislaw Malinowski had studied how the Trobrianders fished in both an inner lagoon, where fish were plentiful, and on the open sea, where yields were unpredictable. The islanders rarely invoked magic before lagoon fishing, where they believed their haul reflected their knowledge and skill, Malinowski observed in his 1922 opus *Argonauts of the Western Pacific*. But in the open sea, they used every magical ritual their ancestors had handed down to them, believing it would ensure their safety and increase their catch.

Gmelch saw parallels to the Trobrianders' fishing rituals in baseball. Pitching and hitting each involve both a high degree of skill and a considerable amount of chance. A pitcher's best pitch may be walloped out of the park, while his worst pitch may be smacked on a direct line to a fielder's glove for a double play. Similarly, a hitter might get great wood on the ball only to see the laser shot caught by a speeding outfielder, or the opposite: barely make contact with the ball yet see a bloop fall in for a three-run double. Pitching and hitting are thus a bit like fishing in the open sea. Fielding, in contrast, is (save for the occasional bad bounce) almost pure skill—baseball's version of fishing in the lagoon. And just like Trobriand fishermen, Gmelch found, baseball players call on magic in situations where Lady Luck can smack down talent like a typhoon can wallop the best fisherman: in hitting and pitching, not fielding.

For years third baseman Wade Boggs, who hit for both average and power during his years with the Boston Red Sox and then the New York Yankees in the 1980s and 1990s, ate chicken before every game, Gmelch wrote in his 1992 essay "Superstition and Ritual in American Baseball,"* which appeared in *Elysian Fields Quarterly*. Chicago White Sox shortstop Ozzie Guillen didn't wash his shorts after he had a good game at the plate. After every win San Francisco Giants pitcher Ron Bryant added a stick of bubblegum to the stash in his back pocket. Minor league pitcher Jim Ohms of the Daytona Beach Islanders added a penny to his jock strap after each win, so that by the end of a successful season his every dash to first base to run out an infield grounder was accompanied by a bizarre jingling. One minor league catcher had a three-hit game one evening, kept wearing the shirt he had on, and had a pretty good week at the plate. "Then the weather got hot as hell, eighty-five degrees and muggy, but I would

---

*Superstitions are the beliefs, usually related to the supernatural, that drive rituals. Rituals are the practices. But rituals can arise from something other than superstitions.

not take that shirt off," he told Gmelch. "I wore it for another ten days, and people thought I was crazy." Yankee great Mickey Mantle compulsively tagged second base en route to or from center field. Another player was more precise: he tagged third base as he jogged back to the dugout, but only after innings that were multiples of three. Outfielder John White told Gmelch that he was jogging out to center at the start of a game and picked up a scrap of paper. He hit well that night "and I guess I decided that the paper had something to do with it. The next night I picked up a gum wrapper and had another good night at the plate . . . I've been picking up paper every night since."

Pitchers have a reputation for being both cerebral and neurotic, and who can blame them, playing a position so painfully dependent on backup from eight other guys? Minor league pitcher Dennis Grossini, one of Gmelch's teammates in the Tigers organization, got up at precisely ten a.m. every day he was scheduled to start a night game. Three hours later he stopped in the nearest restaurant for two glasses of iced tea and a tuna fish sandwich. He then changed into the sweatshirt and jock strap he wore the last time he won, and an hour before game time put a chaw of Beech-Nut chewing tobacco into his cheek. On the mound, he touched the letters of the team name on his uniform after each pitch and straightened his cap after each ball. After every inning in which the opposition scored, he washed his hands. "I'd be afraid to change anything," Grossini told Gmelch. "As long as I'm winning, I do everything the same. . . . When I can't wash my hands, it scares me going back to the mound. I don't feel quite right."

It isn't just baseball players, of course; rituals are ubiquitous in sports. One reason is that success and failure are unambiguous and close to instantaneous. That makes it easy to associate an action with a good or bad outcome, even if, logically, that action has no effect on performance. When tennis great Rafael Nadal takes the court, he sets up his water bottles according to a ritual known only to him, picks up his towels in a certain order, adjusts his gait with a little hitch or shuffle to avoid stepping on lines and pulls at his shorts before he serves. During changes of side, when the players sit briefly on sideline chairs, Nadal shakes his legs as if he is getting ants off them. When he walks back onto the court he zigzags and then, reaching the baseline, hops like a kangaroo. Through ritual, Gmelch wrote, a player "seeks to gain control over his performance"—just as the regular mortal with a compulsive personality uses crazy rules to gain control over his world.

Whether fishing, taking the mound at Yankee Stadium, or stepping onto center court at Wimbledon, the power and even the rationality of rituals derive from the sense of control and thus confidence they give their practitioner, both of which translate into better performance. A fisherman who believes his amulets and incantations protect him from a rogue wave is, thanks to his sense of control and confidence, less inclined to panic when one approaches and thus more likely to save himself. A hitter who believes in the power of his chicken dinner might see the ball better, igniting a mean hitting streak.

My Rituals, Your Compulsions

In certain contexts, compulsive behaviors are not only far from pathological: they are so commonplace as to go unremarked. We call them cultural rituals. Viewed from outside the culture in which they're entrenched, they may seem . . . well, interesting, in an anthropological sort of way, and perhaps even expressions of OCD, as researchers suggested as recently as the 1990s. In an influential 1994 paper in the American Anthropological Association's journal *Ethos*, Siri Dulaney and Alan Page Fishe argued that features that "typify rituals . . . also define a psychiatric illness, obsessive-compulsive disorder," and that there is a "common psychological mechanism" between rituals and OCD. Indeed, the idea that cultural and religious rituals resemble the rituals performed by people wrestling with a compulsion goes back at least to Freud, who contended that in both cases people suffer qualms when they do not execute the ritual and are extremely conscientious in carrying it out. Rituals, Dulaney and Fishe wrote, "are inherently compelling."

But are they manifestations of OCD? At first glance, there are indisputable similarities. Pick your favorite culture, exotic or familiar. Perhaps the ritual bath, or mikvah, that orthodox Jewish women immerse themselves in to regain their "purity" after their menstrual period or after giving birth—or perhaps just the ritual lighting of the Sabbath candles that even moderately observant Jews do unfailingly at sundown every Friday. Or perhaps the communion that devout Catholics take at mass, or the prayers that Muslims make five times a day while facing Mecca. Farther afield, Sherpas in Nepal attempt to placate demons and induce them to depart by means of a ritual in which they arrange 100 tiny clay shrines, 100 cakes, 100 butter lamps, and 100 effigies made of dough in a precise pattern of four concentric rings. The Hindi-speaking Gujars of Uttar Pradesh attempt to prevent harm from befalling them by executing a precise bathing and cleansing ritual involving offerings of black rice, black sesame, black flowers, black barley, and seven black cows to a deity, after which they circle an image of the deity seven times counterclockwise. One more: in the Shalako ritual that the native American Zuni perform to ask the gods for rain, health, and well-being, participants make ritual offerings at six points around the village, take six puffs on a special cigarette and wave it toward the Zunis' six compass directions, and watch as six masked figures enter six houses to dance and chant to a six-beat rhythm.

I suspect Shala Nicely—who believed that fours, eights, and sixteens had special power to ward off disaster—would know just how the Zunis would feel if they were forced to stop puffing the ritual cigarette after *five* drags or found their chants accompanied by a *five*-beat rhythm. The power of the ritual would deflate as quickly as a popped balloon, leaving its adherents on edge, unfulfilled, anxious, and worse.

Such commonalities between rituals and pathological compulsions led Dulaney and Fishe to argue that if rituals "lacked cultural legitimation . . . they would be symptoms of OCD." Indeed, they add, "every kind of symptom that is diagnostic of OCD" appears in accounts of rituals from every culture.

Except for one key symptom: OCD, you'll recall, is ego-dystonic, its insidious demands so at odds with what the sufferer knows to be true (stepping on a sidewalk crack will *not* make death and destruction rain down upon the stepper's family) that it feels as if they emanate not from oneself but from a neural interloper. The demands of a ritual, in contrast, feel right and, absorbed through cultural immersion and teaching, an unquestioned part of oneself. Even practitioners who harbor doubts about the purpose of a ritual nevertheless find comfort in it. Before she died, my aunt patiently indulged my persistent questions about why she lit Sabbath candles. No, Evelyn certainly did not believe God would strike her dead if she skipped a Friday night or two. "But it would feel wrong," she said. "If I didn't light the candles, then for the rest of the night I would feel that I had left something undone, as if I were watching myself from outside my body and waiting for this person I'm observing to push open a door after she had unlocked it, or hang up a phone after she had said goodbye, or take some other action that's just hanging out there." It felt, she said, like hearing the opening G-G-G of Beethoven's Fifth: you have a desperate need to hear the resolving E-flat. Without her weekly ritual she would feel an anguished sense of incompleteness, a twitchiness that something was amiss.

Ted Witzig, who led the session on the scrupulosity form of OCD that I described in Chapter 2, was adamant that even "extreme observance," as he called the religious rituals that mark the exceptionally devout, arises not from anxiety but from faith and devotion. It is a source of "meaning and purpose," he insisted. I kept pressing him: from watching my own devout family and friends, it seemed that at least some of what they do is driven by the anxiety they imagine feeling if they do *not* do it. Just try getting between a Jewish mother and her Shabbas candles at a minute before sundown. Witzig relented: "Well, if you tell someone she can't do something that is typical of her religious group, then yes, anxiety would be the normal response."

Scientists have found much the same thing in their investigations of rituals. Because rituals instill a sense of control over a chaotic and unpredictable world, they arose over the centuries for a similar purpose as compulsions: to keep anxiety at bay. Their ability to do so becomes clear not only when we follow rituals during the passages that mark our lives—christenings, bar mitzvahs, weddings—but when we seize on them after devastating losses that seem to pierce our world like a lightning strike on a peaceful afternoon. When Michael Norton and Francesca Gino of Harvard Business School had 247 volunteers write about the death of someone close to them or the end of a relationship, with half of the participants writing only about the experience and the other half writing also about coping rituals they'd performed after the death or breakup, the latter group reported feeling less intense grief about their loss. They were less likely to say they feel that "life is empty without" the dead person, for instance, and felt more in control—not so powerless, not so helpless, Norton and Gino reported in *Journal of Experimental Psychology: General* in 2014. One participant recounted playing the song "I Miss You Like Crazy"; another wrote about sitting shivah (the Jewish period of mourning) after his mother's death and saying kaddish on every anniversary of her passing: "She died 21 years ago. I will do this until I die," he wrote. Engaging in such rituals, the researchers wrote, "serves as a compensatory mechanism designed to restore feelings of control after losses." People turn to rituals, compulsively or not, in order to establish or reinforce a feeling of being in control of their fate. At least a little.

And that is hardly pathological, any more than Bianca's compulsion to keep her world in order is. Quite the opposite. The cultural ubiquity of rituals strongly suggests that humans are wired to invent and follow them, much as we are to invent and absorb language. The specifics of the ritual, like the particular language, are determined by the environment in which we find ourselves, but preexisting neurological underpinnings are ready to encode whichever ones we are exposed to. That wiring can be hijacked in a way that leads to true OCD. But to call mild compulsions a mental disorder—to go the route of "we're all a little crazy"—gets it 180 degrees wrong. Like culturally sanctioned rituals, mild compulsions are transformative, giving order to our world and a sense that we have a modicum of control over at least one tiny corner of it. Feeling compelled to behave a certain way in order to defuse anxiety is not evidence of pathology. It is evidence of humanness and, more precisely, of being a human in our age of anxiety.

CHAPTER FIVE

Video Games

VIDEO GAMES are different from other compulsions. Most people do not become hoarders, OCD patients, compulsive eaters or exercisers or shoppers: their psychological makeup does not make them vulnerable to getting sucked into those behavioral black holes because their threshold for unbearable anxiety is sufficiently high. Video games and other electronic Sirens, in contrast, exploit aspects of human psychology that are nearly universal. I've said earlier that just because someone behaves compulsively doesn't mean his brain is broken; to the contrary, that reaction to otherwise unbearable anxiety is adaptive.

Nothing illustrates that more clearly than the seductiveness of video games, which are so compelling because their designers have figured out how to tap into universal aspects of brain function. As a result, almost anyone can feel the pull and feel powerless to resist it. As John Doerr, the famed Silicon Valley venture capitalist whose firm invested in Zynga, told *Vanity Fair* in 2011, "[T]hese games are not for everyone, it's true, but [they're] for more of everyone than anything else I know." I hoped that game designers and a new breed of researchers called game psychologists could explain why. But first, I had to be sure that games have the requisite anxiety-quelling component to qualify as compulsions rather than, say, addictions.

In a 2012 *New York Times Magazine* story, critic-at-large Sam Anderson described his compulsion to play *Drop7*, a puzzle game released by Zynga in 2009 in which players manipulate discs falling from the top of a seven-by-seven grid, somewhat like Sudoku. "I was playing when I should have been doing dishes, bathing my children, conversing with relatives, reading the newspaper and especially (especially) writing," Anderson wrote. "The game was an anesthetic, an escape pod, a snorkel, a Xanax"—a digital antianxiety drug. He found himself self-medicating, turning to *Drop7* "in all kinds of extreme situations," such as "after an intense discussion with my mother; shortly after learning that my dog . . . was probably dying of cancer." One online commenter confirmed that, for him at least, video games have the sine qua non of a compulsion: they "reduce my anxiety, so I justify playing *Bejeweled* that way," the commenter explained. "I wasn't really concerned about how much I was playing *Bejeweled* until I found myself playing it on the exercise bike at physical therapy" and fell off. Or as Neil Gaiman put it in his 1990 poem *Virus*, "You play through the tears, the aching wrist, the hunger, after a while it all goes away./ All of it except the game . . . /There's no room in my mind any more; no room for other things."

Tens of millions of us can relate. In May 2013 Dong Nguyen, a previously unknown game designer based in Hanoi, Vietnam, released *Flappy Bird*, which, he told reporters the next year, was "pretty much the simplest idea that I can think of." It was the epitome of what serious gamers had begun dubbing "stupid games," whose absence of narrative, aesthetics, and programming sophistication was matched only by the utter mindlessness of their goals. In *Flappy Bird*, players tap the screen to make a barely animated bird (it doesn't even move its eponymous wings, which are nearly invisible) fly through a gap between vertical green pipes. Yet despite—or because of—its stupidity, the game struck a chord: in early 2014, it soared to the top of both Apple's and Android's lists of most popular downloads, mystifying even its creator. "The reason *Flappy Bird* is so popular is unclear to me," Nguyen told the *Washington Post*. Ian Bogost, a professor of interactive computing at the Georgia Institute of Technology and a video game designer, wrote that countless players "have expressed astonishment and distress at their simultaneous hatred for and commitment to the game," which inspired a web page on the British gaming site n3rdabl3 .co.uk called "I Hate Flappy Bird, But I Can't Stop Playing It."

Of course, people also play video games to decompress after a tough day, to feel a tiny sense of accomplishment, or simply to relax and zone out. And not every excessive behavior is a compulsion. Excessive use is not proof of compulsivity (even leaving aside the problematic subjectivity of "excessive"). There is a long list of reasons why people play video games to the exclusion of other activities and to the detriment of their work: to relieve boredom or procrastinate, to avoid social interaction or relieve loneliness. But as the anecdotes above suggest, and as analyses of the psychological allure of games show, for some people video gaming is indeed a compulsion and, for some, a destructive one: since the first decade of the twenty-first century "boot camps" in South Korea and China, with names like "Jump Up Internet Rescue School," have treated children unable to shake the compulsion to spend hours and hours playing video games.

That is not to say, however, that that compulsion constitutes a mental disorder. An expert panel deciding which disorders belonged in the latest edition of the American Psychiatric Association's diagnostic manual reviewed some 240 studies purporting to describe "Internet gaming disorder," but declined to include it as a scientifically validated mental illness, agreeing only that it merited additional study. For now, all science can say is that you can be perfectly sane and nevertheless get sucked into compulsive gaming.

Flow, Intermittent Reinforcement, and *Angry Birds*

Nikita Mikros, T-shirt drenched with sweat and helmet tucked under his arm, is walking his bicycle down the hallway toward where I'm waiting to meet him inside an old waterfront warehouse in DUMBO (Down Under the Manhattan Bridge Overpass), one of Brooklyn's hip neighborhoods, lined with cobblestone streets and coffee bars.

Mikros, who has been creating video and arcade games since the 1990s, had invited me to spend a morning with him learning things like why *Candy Crush Saga*, made by mobile-games behemoth King Digital Entertainment, had 66 million players in 2013, why players like actor Alec Baldwin feel so compelled to keep playing Zynga's *Words with Friends* that he gets thrown off a plane waiting for takeoff, and why *Tetris* was voted the most compelling video game of all time. "We've learned a lot about how to make games irresistible," Mikros had told me by email. "Unfortunately, some of it makes my skin crawl."

Mikros ushered me into the offices of his game-design company, Tiny Mantis, two rooms with just under a dozen workstations. He is widely known among gamers for creations like *Dora Saves the Crystal Kingdom*, *Dungeons and Dungeons*, and *Lego Dino Outbreak*. The offices were filled with flat-screen monitors surrounded by plastic Brooklyn Roasting Co. coffee cups, all framed within exposed piping, painted brick walls, holes in the ceiling, and posters of Mr. Spock and a panda. After Mikros excused himself to change into a dry shirt, he reemerged a minute later in a black version adorned with a Mona Lisa dripping blood. I expected to spend the morning watching him blitz through *Diablo* and *Angry Birds*, but instead he booted up a PowerPoint presentation he'd done for me. Rather than ripping the guts out of monsters, we were deep into Mihaly Csikszentmihalyi.

Csikszentmihalyi is a psychologist who invented the concept of "flow," a state of mind characterized by total absorption in an activity. When you experience flow, you are so immersed in what you're doing that the outside world barely penetrates your consciousness, no other thoughts engage your mind, the sense of time evaporates, and even feelings of hunger and thirst fail to register. After a flow experience it's not unusual to feel, *Holy crap, where did the time go, and why am I starving?*

The best game designers, Mikros explained, put players in a flow state. "You experience a loss of self and a transformation of the sense of time," he said. "You start playing a game and before you know it, *bang*, it's morning. The experience becomes an end in itself. But different people have different envelopes of their flow zone. If players are challenged too much they have too much anxiety and they give up, and if they're not challenged enough they're bored and they stop. But if they're in a middle zone they're happily engaged." Flow is so compelling that it produces a sticky experience, one that people can't easily escape.

One way to keep players of different skill levels within the "flow envelope," Mikros said, is by constantly adjusting the degree of difficulty. The 1980s classic *Crash Bandicoot* did that. If a player was pathetically inept at, say, leaping onto moving ledges, the game took pity on him when he lost a life by not sending him too far back toward the start and making it easier to navigate its many obstacle-strewn environments. On the other hand, *Crash* got harder if a player was nailing it. "Some players like that," said Mikros. "They think, 'I'm getting better, so I want tougher challenges or this will be a walkover.'"

Another way to keep players in a flow state is to reward them for, say, defeating a monster by bestowing a new skill on them, and then using that skill exclusively in the next few situations. "Your powers are upgraded so a monster you couldn't defeat before is now beatable," Mikros said. "Good designers channel you through the flow zone by ramping up the difficulty and then giving you something that's a little easier, then ramping up the difficulty some more before giving you another something a little easier."

But designing games to put us in a flow state sounds fairly benign, I said. While I could see how these design features are necessary for a game to be compelling (it has to be enjoyable enough to keep players playing long enough to get sucked in), I didn't see how they could be sufficient. There is no surefire recipe, Mikros said: "If we'd figured it out perfectly, every game would be *Angry Birds*."

Four years after Rovio Entertainment unleashed that game on the world, it had been downloaded two billion times, as people couldn't resist the chance to use a virtual slingshot to fling vexed avians at egg-stealing green pigs. Why? There are lots of explanations for why the game is fun—it's easy, there's no learning curve, and landing a direct hit on a pig makes it blow up, which everyone's inner seven-year-old loves. But the reason the game is compelling lies deeper. When an action is typically followed by a reward, the way that flinging a bird is followed by a pig exploding, it triggers the brain's dopamine system. Although once believed only to create the subjective feeling of reward or pleasure, in fact the dopamine system is more sophisticated: it calculates the likelihood that an action will bring a reward and sets the brain's expectation module accordingly. "Dopamine's presence signals the brain that there is a reward coming, like glass-and-wood houses deliciously flying apart," psychologist Michael Chorost wrote in *Psychology Today* in 2011 (he deleted *Angry Birds* from his phone to stop his compulsive playing). "But the brain doesn't know how *good* the reward will be. Will the bird just glance off the top, or will it score a glorious direct hit? That uncertainty creates a tension, and the brain craves release. It makes you want to do whatever it is that creates the release," such as pulling the virtual slingshot again and again and again.

No wonder many people who can't stop playing *Bejeweled* or even *FreeCell* describe the experience as not all that pleasurable. They feel stuck, unable to extricate themselves from the clutches of the game, compelled to keep playing but deriving very little enjoyment from it except in those rare moments of success. Somehow, video games tap into deep psychological tendencies that make us expect pleasure, deliver an experience that's frustrating, and make us crave the same experience over and over even though we know the disappointing, aggravating outcome will in all likelihood be the same. The reason games can be compelling without being much fun is that designers take advantage of two common psychological quirks: variable reinforcement and intermittent reinforcement.

Intermittent reinforcement refers to a varying probability of reaping a reward; sometimes you are rewarded (with game loot or leveling up, for example) for an accomplishment and other times the same action yields you . . . nothing. Variable reinforcement describes a system in which the value of rewards for a given accomplishment changes. Slot machines are the epitome of variable and intermittent reinforcement. The only action a player executes is pulling the arm of the one-armed bandit—or, now that mechanics has been replaced with electronics, pressing a button. Sometimes you win, sometimes you win big, and most times you lose. The input is identical, the output as varied as a jackpot and a bust. No wonder the stereotypical image of a slot machine player is someone staring at the machine as if hypnotized, feeding in quarters robotically, compulsively, until her cup of coins is empty and she gets back on the bus.

Like a slot machine, "*Diablo 3* uses variable rewards, which is one of the things that make it so compelling," Mikros told me. For the uninitiated, *Diablo 3* is the 2012 release of a game franchise that was launched by Blizzard Entertainment in late 1996. All three iterations belong to the genre known as action role-playing hack-and-slash games. A player/hero navigates through the Kingdom of Khanduras, battling ghouls and other enemies in order to rid the world of Diablo, the Lord of Terror. If she can beat sixteen dungeon levels and reach

Hell, she faces Diablo in the ultimate battle. Along the way the player casts spells, acquires weapons and other loot, and interacts with characters including a warrior, a rogue, and a sorcerer.

At the start of the game, rewards are essentially fixed: kill the monster and something good happens, such as leveling up or winning "experience" (essentially, power). As you progress through the game, however, the likelihood of a drop (being rewarded with a powerful new weapon or other tool that will help you survive and advance) decreases, but its value increases. "You're still looking forward to it but you're not necessarily getting it all the time," Mikros said. "You've already established the connection that killing this demon or this monster is going to give you something good, like gold or a special sword or a special bow. But now, because you don't know if you're going to get anything, you're waiting expectantly, even anxiously."

Game designers call this a "compulsion loop." It has a brain basis, one that gets to the heart of the hybrid nature of gaming: like other electronic catnip such as email and texting, video games are perhaps the paradigmatic example of activities where addiction and compulsion morph into one another like shape-shifting demons.

Enter Dopamine

Addictions run on a desperate need for another hedonic hit. That's because addictions are born in pleasure; the initial experience is rewarding, exciting, fun, risky. Those feelings are produced by what's been called the brain's reward circuitry, which is activated when we experience something pleasurable and consists of neurons running on dopamine. "Run on" means that when an electrical signal reaches the end of one neuron, it jumps across a synapse to the next by triggering the release of dopamine from the first neuron. The dopamine flows across the gap between the two neurons and is gathered in by the receiving neuron like the International Space Station gathering in a

Soyuz supply ship. In neurons, the docking port is called a dopamine receptor. The act of docking triggers the propagation of an electrical signal down the length of the receiving neuron, on and on until the activity is eventually registered, subjectively, as a feeling of reward that we feel from food, sex, alcohol, nicotine, cocaine, and killing monsters in *Diablo 3*—making them all deeply, joyously, deliriously, euphorically reinforcing.

Nothing in the brain is as simple as scientists initially think, however, including the dopamine story. Reward circuitry is actually better understood as an expectation machine: it makes predictions about how rewarding an experience *will* be.

For a deeper explanation of how video game designers exploit the dopamine system, I called Jamie Madigan, who has a Ph.D. in psychology and worked for years at a gaming company. Madigan has made a name for himself in the gaming world through his website "The Psychology of Video Games," where he posts essays on precisely that, including a "dopamine freak-out" that he said he had just barely survived while playing *Diablo 3*.

At the end of *Diablo 3*, "You've completed the story line" of defeating ghouls and monsters to reach and battle Diablo, he told me, "and are just acquiring more and better loot in order to kill more monsters and get still better loot." There are more than a dozen levels, "and the monsters get tougher to beat unless you've acquired better equipment. It never ends. Eventually, I did realize that I was doing the same thing over and over for three hours a night and it was no longer fun. If someone like me, who knows what elements of a game make it compelling, can feel this pull . . ." His voice drifted off.

But what are those compulsion-making elements? Like *Diablo*, Nik Mikros's paradigmatic example of a game that has aced the variable/intermittent reward structure, the immensely popular *World of Warcraft* is also renowned for drawing players in compulsively by offering unpredictable and unexpected windfalls. A massively multiplayer online role-playing game (MMORPG) released in 2004, it has more than 10 million subscribers, each choosing a character and moving through multiple levels of the virtual world on a quest. In *World of Warcraft*, players choose a profession such as blacksmithing or mining, and can master any of four secondary skills (archaeology, cooking, fishing, or first aid). They band together to accomplish tasks, either ad hoc or through enduring associations called guilds, by inviting others to join via player-to-player instant messaging, group-wide "text channels," or, in some games, voice systems. Guilds give players access to features that can help them on quests, the missions that form the narrative spine of the game and earn players experience points, useful objects, skills, and money. *World of Warcraft* and other MMORPGs also offer the escapism of entering a fully formed, complex, intriguing world without hectoring parents or abusive bosses or unappreciative spouses. And they exploit our drive to achieve even when the achievement—conquering foes, killing monsters, rescuing princesses, accumulating wealth or status, and advancing to higher levels—is not quite real.

But that's the benign, psychologically obvious appeal of multiplayer games. Jamie Madigan fell victim to another. One day, he was merrily killing *World of Warcraft* bandits, which earned him a chance at one or more pieces of armor, weapons, or other supplies—"loot"—that would help him in subsequent battles and quests. Loot varies in quality, with the color of the text identifying it indicating its worth: gray is the lowest, white a little more valuable, on up through green, blue, purple, and orange. The character a player chooses as his avatar also has a place in the pecking order: "classes" such as monks, rogues, shamans, warriors, and druids each have a specific adventuring style, defined by the weapons and defenses they can deploy and the skills, powers, and magic they can gain by achieving various milestones. Since his character was fairly unimpressive, and therefore unlikely to score valuable loot, Madigan was "shocked by the loot drop: a rare pair of 'blue' gloves that perfectly fit my class's needs at the time," he recalled. For a lowly character "to find a blue item on a random enemy was actually very rare, and I experienced a huge rush from it," he said. "But more importantly, with that came an acute desire to keep playing the game and to murder more bandits."

Intermittent reinforcement in the form of random loot drops stokes the brain in ways that expected and predictable rewards do not. "It's incredibly effective at making people keep playing because of how the dopamine-based reward circuitry works," Madigan said. Remember that dopamine neurons predict the pleasure hit that will flood the brain from an enjoyable experience, firing even before the reward arrives (such as when the microwave beep alerts you that your yummy Hot Pocket is cooked, Madigan offers). "But this is only part of what makes loot-based games work so well," he continued. "The real key is that while dopamine neurons fire once your brain has figured out how to predict an event, they *really* go nuts when an unexpected, unpredicted gush of dopamine shows up, giving you an even bigger rush. It's like, DUDE! UNEXPECTED HOT POCKET! KEEP DOING WHAT YOU'RE DOING UNTIL WE FIGURE OUT HOW TO MAKE IT HAPPEN AGAIN! So you keep playing."

And don't count on the rational brain to tell you, *enough!* When your emotions are firing on all cylinders, as when you mow down bad guys in an online shooter game or careen through the diabolical race-courses of *Gran Turismo* stoked by squealing-wheel sound effects, you don't remember that you have to get dinner on the table, or prepare for a presentation at work tomorrow, or finish that term paper. "Despite any intentions born of rational thought, you're just not thinking with the same brain after some infuriating punk has bested you in a shooter or you've just pulled off some thrilling act of derring-do in some other game," Madigan explained. "Rationality gets elbowed aside and you look up to realize that it's a quarter to three on a weekday morning. And yet you're still muttering 'Okay, just one more . . .'"

Nik Mikros wasn't happy that video game designers had tapped into the dopamine system. While it seems as if half the basements in Brooklyn are populated by game designers who program compulsion loops into their creations, not all designers are proud of what their field has nailed with such devious effectiveness. "What makes my skin crawl is games that are completely driven by Skinner boxes," Mikros told me as I was gathering up my stuff. "It's not why I want to make games, just to give people pellets—hit the bar, get the pellets. I don't think that's improving humanity."

Home-Brew Neuroscience

I was beginning to feel as if I were on a quest for Easter eggs in *Halo 3*, hoping the next room I entered—the next expert I interviewed—would reveal more secrets of compulsive gaming. My next stop was New York University's Game Center.

Its home at MetroTech Center in Brooklyn was still so new that after its director, Frank Lantz, let me in from the elevator vestibule, the card key for his office didn't work. (A graduate student came to the rescue.) The common room's game screens were still covered in plastic wrap; packing boxes were everywhere. Founded in 2008 as part of NYU's Tisch School of the Arts, the Game Center offers two-year master of fine arts degrees in the design of games.

Lantz is a legend in the gaming world. He co-founded Area/Code (acquired by Zynga in 2011), which created such Facebook games as *CSI: Crime City* and *Power Planets* ("control the fate of your own miniature planet. Construct buildings to make your inhabitants happy and . . . construct power sources to keep your civilization running"). He has created numerous iPhone games, including *Drop7*. *Sharkrunners*, which he made for the Discovery Channel's 2007 Shark Week, lets players pretend to be marine biologists, interacting with living sharks fitted with GPS units that fed telemetry data to the game.

Settling into the chair behind his nearly bare desk (most of his stuff was still in moving boxes), Lantz said that game design was finally being recognized as a legitimate discipline, especially as it incorporated ideas from fields as different as architecture and literature. "Most game designers have creative goals, and that drives them more than the goal of creating a game that people can't stop playing," he told me. But while many designers are driven by aesthetic and other lofty considerations, companies that sell games are more strongly invested in making a game compelling than ever before. Years ago a teenager would lay out $59.95 for *Gran Turismo*, and that was the last revenue Sony would see from him (until *Gran Turismo 2* came out). It didn't matter if players lost interest.

In the 2000s, however, a new business model took hold: instead of paying up front, players acquired free-to-play games at no cost, often as a download to a mobile device, but then incurred "microcharges." In *Farmville*, for instance, you can pay one dollar to magically "unwither" your crops (which are dying because you weren't paying attention; damn homework) or speed up a harvest (allowing you to reap your vegetables before bedtime). *Farmville* keeps drawing players back to their simulated agricultural fields because it has a timer system: your crops die if you do not tend to them often enough. Many people hate to lose what they have gained, a phenomenon so strong psychologists have a name for it: loss aversion.

Other games invite you to pay a dollar or two to leap over an obstacle, access a more exotic part of the game's world, buy cooler clothes for your avatar, or purchase virtual food and drink for your virtual residents of *CityVille*. With the microcharge model, stickiness—being so attractive that players can't put the game down—is all. "The commercial transaction is *in* the game," Lantz said. "That's causing a really deep discussion about game design, because some of the techniques feel manipulative. They're not intended to make the game experience better or fulfill the vision of the designer, but to get you to run up these microcharges. I don't think game developers are coldly applying behavioral psychology to guarantee players stick with their game. Very few game designers think they're designing a compulsion engine. They want people to look back on their experience and say, 'Hey, that was cool, that was fun.' But yeah, they understand that this body of knowledge exists in psychology."

That's putting it mildly. Whether by trial and error or by design, game developers have become frighteningly good at making games compelling. Something as simple as a list of high scores can do it, Lantz said, beckoning us to join and thereby quench our deep thirst for status by playing and playing and playing until we crack the top 100 (or our thumbs fall off). So can "nesting" goals. In the 1991 video game *Civilization*, for instance, players take turns making moves to "build an empire to stand the test of time," as the blurb says. Starting in 4000 B.C., they assume the role of ruler of a particular empire-to-be, starting with a single warrior and people they can dispatch to form settlements. Through exploration, diplomacy, and warfare players advance their civilization by building cities, amassing knowledge (should you invent pottery or an alphabet first?), and developing the surrounding land.

"Why is it so compelling?" Lantz throws my question back to me. "Because it overlaps immediate goals, like dispatching settlers or getting your character successfully through a quest, with medium goals that you might achieve over the next three or four turns, like developing a city, with longer goals over the next ten to fifteen turns," such as achieving the pinnacle of civilization. "There is a rhythm to the play, so as your mind comes to a resting place on an immediate goal you are also thinking about the next few turns ahead. Overlapping, or nesting, short-, medium-, and long-term goals is very compelling. In the real world, often we don't even know what's connected," such as which short-term achievement would lead to something bigger later. The digital world of a video game offers certainty; A really does lead to B.

Another way designers make games sticky is by offering instant gratification. "You do something and a character jumps," said Lantz. "That can be very appealing when, in the real world, a lot of the buttons are broken." That is, you press the button marked "study hard in high school" but it doesn't get you into a selective college, as promised, or you press "go to college" but it doesn't lead to a good job. In video games, the button performs as advertised, "which makes them deeply compelling," he said.

World of Warcraft, which induces compulsive play through its variable/intermittent reward structure, has an additional psychological hook, much like a good novel, detective story, or thriller. "It's why you go back to *War and Peace* every night to read another chapter," said Lantz. "You want to find out what happens next," and not knowing makes you anxious in a way that drives the compulsion to play. "It's a skill to go into it and come out the other end and be able to walk away," to overcome the compulsion.

Not everyone can, as Ryan Van Cleave discovered. Born Ryan Anderson, in 2006 he changed his name to a *World of Warcraft* term, and by New Year's Eve 2007 the extent of his attachment to the game turned tragic. Van Cleave, a college professor, poet, and editor, was laid off from his teaching job because of his gaming compulsion; he was playing up to 80 hours a week, and had almost completely withdrawn from his wife and friends. On December 31, he told his wife he was making a quick cough-drop run but instead drove to the Arlington Memorial Bridge in Washington, D.C., and contemplated jumping. He slipped and nearly tumbled over the edge into the icy Potomac River. Catching himself just in time, Van Cleave dragged himself back from the edge. In 2010, he published *Unplugged: My Journey into the Dark World of Video Game Addiction*, where he describes his descent into video-game hell. It became the most important thing in his life, to the detriment of everything else, and eighteen-hour sessions were not unusual. His wife threatened to leave him, his kids hated him, and his parents wouldn't visit. "I was so plugged in to virtual worlds," Van Cleave wrote, "I'm not sure I recall what truly happened in real life. I missed out on a ton of it."

* * *

Lantz sounds almost mournful that the artistry and creativity he sees in game design can be the cause of a tragedy like that. "I think game design is a sort of home-brew psychology or home-brew neuroscience," he said. "You're crafting an experience, so of course designers think about psychology. Long before free-to-play games there was the goal of designing a compelling experience for players, but that meant designing a proper game and not just a slot machine. Designers are aware that if they scatter resources a player needs—like strength, powers, lives, and weapons—in one out of every four trash cans, for instance, it makes people feel compelled to keep exploring because of the power of intermittent rewards.

"There is so much voodoo involved," he said. "We still don't know exactly why *Angry Birds* is so popular. There's just something ineffable about it." His favorite game? I asked as I packed up to leave. Go, the ancient Chinese game played with black and white stones on a nineteen-by-nineteen grid.

Pharmatronic

For a video game, the compulsion point is like the apex of a narrow mountain. Slide down one side and you're in The Valley of Too Easy. Slide down the other and you're in The Abyss of Too Hard. Games that are too easy or too hard leave us bored or too frustrated to continue, respectively. Designers therefore adjust games to keep them at a player's Goldilocks inflection point. *Tetris* was one of the first to do this. In this quasi-geometry game, blocks in different shapes—Ls, Ts, Is, two-by-two squares—fall from the top of the screen. The task is to rotate them in midair so they form a solid wall at the bottom, as rows at the base disappear with the addition of rows on top.

"It's been called pharmatronic, an electronic with all the mind-altering properties of a drug," said Tom Stafford, a cognitive scientist at England's University of Sheffield. One reason *Tetris* is so compelling, he explained, is that it exploits a psychological phenomenon called the Zeigarnik Effect. Psychologist Bluma Zeigarnik (1901–1988) was in a cafe in Berlin, Germany, one day when she observed that waiters have perfect memories for orders they have yet to take to customers. But once an order has been delivered they forget it instantly. "It's memory for uncompleted tasks," said Stafford, "and this is what *Tetris* does so wonderfully. It's a world of perpetual uncompleted tasks. Every line you complete, more blocks fall from the sky. Every block you put in place creates another terrain within which to slot the next block." Our memory for uncompleted tasks nags us to *finish already* and creates anxiety until we do. It's Compulsion 101.

"The genius of *Tetris*," Stafford continued, "is that it takes advantage of this memory hook for uncompleted tasks and involves us in a compulsive loop of completing and generating new tasks that keeps us endlessly playing, wanting to do the next thing." Once we start something, taking several steps toward a goal, we feel compelled to finish. It is not only the Zeigarnik effect that makes uncompleted tasks occupy the mind, however. Because of the sunk-cost phenomenon, people hate abandoning something after they have invested time and effort in it. If you're part way toward delivering a letter to someone, if that's your quest, you feel compelled to keep going.

Many MMORPGs tap into the desire to recoup sunk costs by sucking us in, hard, from the start. "These games have what's called a rapid absorption rate," said psychologist Zaheer Hussain of England's University of Derby. "When you start playing, the environment is quite pleasing: there are colors and sound effects and quests that are quite simple and relatively easy to accomplish, and that you get rewarded for. That causes players to spend more and more time in a game." So does a feature that taps into something behaviorist B. F. Skinner discovered in the 1950s: when rewards become less frequent and harder to achieve, as happens in many online games, you not only keep playing but do so ever more compulsively, determined to get the damn reward that seemed so easy to score a level or two ago. *World of Warcraft* and other MMORPGs have a progress bar at the bottom of the screen indicating how many quests you've completed and how close you are to the next level or reward, "and that's a motivator to continue playing," Hussain said. To quit *so close* to the next achievement, especially if that means dropping back to the start of a level or quest, is to lose all that time and effort you just invested.

For what it's worth, when the *Guardian* asked readers in 2014 to name the most "addictive"* game of all time, *Tetris* topped the list, named by 30 percent of respondents, followed by *World of Warcraft* (22 percent) and *Candy Crush Saga* (10 percent).

Ah, *Candy Crush*. To understand its evil allure, I went back to Jamie Madigan, my dopamine freak-out victim. I had been intrigued by his analyses of compulsion loops and figured, who better to explain why millions of people become so engrossed in *Candy Crush* that they miss their subway stop, blow off homework and housework and work work, and give short shrift to their kids, spouses, and friends? For any naïfs out there, the game consists of colored shapes that fill the screen, and the goal is to move them around until three identical icons line up. (A predecessor, *Bejeweled*, was similar.) At that point the triplet drops out, the surrounding shapes rearrange

---

*As usual, there was no effort to distinguish "addictive" from "compulsive," but since readers were naming games they couldn't stop playing the list is a good first approximation of games people play most compulsively, too.

themselves, and you are rewarded with flashes of colored lights, points, an explosion of sound, and the appearance on-screen of reinforcing words such as *delicious*.

At its most basic, *Candy Crush* taps into the brain's drive to find patterns in seemingly random arrays of objects—the same talent that led the ancient Greeks and Romans to see swans and twins and bears in the random splatter of stars in the night sky. "Our brains evolved to notice something good where we didn't expect it to be, like a source of food that wasn't there before," Madigan said. "So we're predisposed to figure out why. We're wired to make sense of patterns, especially unexpected patterns." *Candy Crush* also appeals to a common drive to put things in their place, restore order, and generally tidy up, which is what you feel you're doing when you face an initially chaotic-looking board that you know you can rearrange so like elements are with like. Result: a game that's appealing and fun.

But lots of activities—watching movies, gardening, cooking, or your own preferred pastime—are fun without being "sticky." What makes *Candy Crush* sticky, Madigan said, is that the rewards not only keep coming but come unexpectedly. Occasionally, when the tiles of the triplet you intentionally formed drop out, the new arrangement has loads of such triplets, all of which immediately fall out to produce a display replete with flashing lights, noises, points, and congratulatory messages all over the screen. That "makes the dopamine circuits freak out," Madigan said. "It's like our hunter-gatherer ancestors knew where food could reliably be found, but if they came across something totally unexpected and rewarding, like a stream with fish or a cluster of berry bushes they hadn't known about, it was immensely adaptive to pay attention to that and remember it. When a reward is unexpected we're wired to *really* pay attention to it and to keep looking for another and another and another. Game design takes advantage of that."

Candy Crush has other psychological levers up its digital sleeves. It has a "lives" system: if you fail to clear a board of, say, 100 purples in a given amount of time or number of moves, you lose a life. Losing five lives gets you kicked off the game, and you can play again only if you wait several hours, spend (real) money, or enlist friends to help you log in again. That exploits a psychological quirk called "hedonic adaptation," in which people get used to pleasurable experiences over time until those experiences—driving a new car, living in a delightful new neighborhood, having a wonderful new job—become nowhere near as enjoyable.

A 2013 study showed how it worked. Psychologists Jordi Quoid-bach of Harvard University and Elizabeth Dunn of the University of British Columbia had volunteers sample a piece of chocolate. Roughly equal numbers of participants were given one of three instructions: some were told to abstain from chocolate until they went back to the lab a week later, some were given two pounds of chocolate bars and told to eat as much as they could without getting sick, and the rest were given no instructions other than to report back in a week. Upon their return, everyone was given another piece of chocolate and asked how much they enjoyed it. "Participants who had temporarily given up chocolate savored it significantly more and experienced more positive moods after eating it," compared to those who were either implicitly allowed to eat as much as they wished or were explicitly told to go on a chocolate bender, the researchers reported in *Social Psychological and Personality Science*. By limiting how much you can play, *Candy Crush* keeps you anxious for more, your anxiety growing until you can assuage it with a killer triplet. "While most of us are used to the option of gorging on a game until we burn out on it and move on, *Candy Crush* cleverly forces us to avoid that behavior," Madigan explained. Kicked off the game, players become twitchy and anxious as they jones for their next session and never succumb to hedonic adaptation.

Risky Personalities

It was time to level up for my next challenge: learning whether personality, age, gender, or other variables affect how vulnerable we are to becoming compulsive gamers.

Research on this has been plagued by many of the problems common to new fields of study. Even things as basic as what makes a behavior problematic, and what exactly the behavior is, are defined differently by different researchers in different studies. "It's not consistent or specific," Scott Caplan of the University of Delaware told me. The changing description of those most likely to become compulsive gamers illustrates the problem. In the early 2000s, when fewer people were online, research on excessive online gaming (as well as excessive Internet use generally) focused on identifying psychological predictors of the behavior. Unfortunately, as even a cursory glance at the research literature shows, studies "found significant associations with a great number of psychological characteristics," Daniel Kardefelt-Winther of the London School of Economics and Political Science pointed out in a 2014 paper in *Computers in Human Behavior.* In fact, he continued, "almost all psychological characteristics . . . statistically contribute to the likelihood" of succumbing to excessive gaming. Or, to put it less diplomatically, the greatest risk factor was having a human brain.

At first, the stereotypical compulsive gamer "was a lonely, socially awkward guy who maybe had social anxiety," Caplan said. "But these were about the only guys playing video games then." Personality traits were therefore a marker for the true, deeper cause of excessive gaming, not themselves the cause. The personality trait of neuroticism is correlated with an inability to tolerate anxiety, for instance, and so shows up in surveys of the traits of excessive gamers. But it's not neuroticism per se that compels people to play online games; it's the anxiety they can't defuse in other ways.

Similarly, researchers found correlations between excessive online gaming and a host of personality traits: loneliness, depression, anxiety, shyness, aggression, difficulty with interpersonal relationships, sensation seeking, and deficits in social skills, for instance. It wasn't so much that these traits put someone at risk for compulsive online behavior, however, but that they characterized the majority of people online at all, compulsively or not. "Now everyone is using the Internet, including on smartphones, so the description of the kind of people who do so compulsively has to change, too," Caplan said.

As with other compulsions, playing video games compulsively is not in and of itself pathological, let alone an indication of a mental illness. The reasons people play online games (or use the Internet, tweet, text, or post to Facebook, as I'll discuss in the next chapter) for hours each day "are the same reasons they do other things excessively: boredom, escapism, competition, and sociability—that's where their friends are," Caplan said. Crucially, online games, especially multiplayer ones, provide social interaction behind the protective persona of an avatar, appealing to people for whom interacting anonymously is easier than interacting with people they know. Psychologically vulnerable people may simply prefer online social interaction because the face-to-face kind is too stressful, or because they're not very good at it; they're more comfortable with a virtual life. Spending massive amounts of time playing video games is therefore, for many people, compensatory—a coping strategy, a way to handle stress or depression, to escape from loneliness or a boring job or any of the other lousy elements of the real world. In a 2013 study, Caplan and his colleagues surveyed 597 adolescents who were regular players of online games. The strongest predictors of whether their gaming was problematic and interfering with the rest of their life was that they were using it to regulate mood (relieving sadness, boredom, or loneliness, for instance) and were unable to do that otherwise. "If I'm lonely and go online, it's compensatory," Caplan said. "It's not a primary pathology." Games offer something we need or want. If the compensation works well and becomes your go-to solution for defusing anxiety, it can become compulsive.

Is everyone susceptible? Not equally. Massively multiplayer online role-playing games such as *World of Warcraft*, you recall, have mastered the slot-machine trick of variable/intermittent reinforcement through ploys like the unexpected high-value drops that hit our dopamine buttons. Being vulnerable to that ploy is a near human-universal, though as with everything there is a wide range of vulnerabilities.

Madigan had one final thought about the compulsion to play video games. In addition to their other allures, casual games like *Candy Crush* and *Angry Birds* can be played in the tiny slices of time that fall between, say, activities at work, between one chore and another, or while we're en route from Point A to Point B. Time was, we'd use those moments to think, plan, scheme, ponder, or just daydream. In the always-on era, for many people the very idea is abhorrent; they'd rather suffer an electric shock than be alone with only their mind. (Literally, as I describe in the next chapter.) Online games, especially those played on mobile devices, piggyback on the compulsion to fill those minutes; unfilled, they make us anxious. "You start by playing a few rounds of *Candy Crush* at breakfast while you're waiting for the coffee to brew," Madigan said. "And pretty soon you're playing every night before bed." If you never download *Angry Birds* you can't be sucked in, of course. Avoiding other forms of digital crack is harder, as we'll now see.

CHAPTER SIX

Smartphones and the Web

I N 1995 Dr. Ivan Goldberg, a psychiatrist in New York City, posted an online announcement of a new support group for "Internet Addiction Disorder," or IAD. The incidence of this mental affliction had been "increasing exponentially," he wrote, prompting the creation of a forum where sufferers could share their stories and therapists could outline effective treatments. Goldberg defined IAD as "a maladaptive pattern of Internet use, leading to clinically significant impairment or distress," and—echoing the format of the American Psychiatric Association's diagnostic manual—decreed that people would have to show at least three of seven symptoms over a twelve-month period to qualify. Perhaps they experienced tolerance, needing to spend more and more time online "to achieve satisfaction." Or perhaps they suffered withdrawal symptoms if they stopped going online, including feeling jumpy and anxious or obsessively thinking "about what is happening" online.*

*You can see Goldberg's original post at http://www.urz.uni-heidelberg.de/Netz dienste/anleitung/wwwtips/8/addict.html.

Goldberg hit a nerve. Fellow psychiatrists diagnosed themselves as having "netaholism," and hundreds of people posted their anguish to the Internet Addiction Support Group he set up as a listserv, describing how they spent twelve hours a day online, saw their "RL (real life)" obliterated by this "electronic takeover," and considered "getting a second home phone installed in order to be able to talk to my family once in a while."

There was only one problem. Goldberg had meant the original announcement of IAD as a joke, a send-up of psychiatry's penchant for turning every excessive behavior into a pathology. People could qualify for a diagnosis if they merely spent "a great deal of time . . . in activities related to Internet use" such as buying books or doing online research, spent more time online than they intended, and spent less time socializing because they were, say, editing the Wikipedia entry on the Krebs cycle rather than attending beer pong night at the campus bar. And as you perhaps noticed, by tweaking Goldberg's criteria for Internet Addiction Disorder to describe other behaviors, millions of us would be classified as compulsive joggers, compulsive book readers, compulsive news devourers, compulsive socializers, compulsive sports fans, or compulsive moviegoers. "I.A.D. is a very unfortunate term," Goldberg told the *New Yorker* in 1997. "To medicalize every behavior by putting it into psychiatric nomenclature is ridiculous."

Indeed. More than any other behavior that people engage in compulsively, the online version—from checking Facebook to texting—shows that just because you're compulsive about something doesn't mean you have a broken brain. And just because a behavior is compulsive doesn't make it pathological. To the contrary: understanding the allure of being online sheds light on some of the mind's most salient, and utterly normal, workings.

Despite the lack of evidence for excessive Internet use as a mental pathology, the idea quickly gained traction. Within two years of Goldberg's proposal, colleges were offering help to students who felt they were using the Internet compulsively (the University of Maryland's program was called Caught in the Net) and the highly regarded McLean (psychiatric) Hospital outside Boston had created the Computer Addictions Service. At the University of Pittsburgh, psychologist Kimberly Young founded the Center for On-Line Addiction in 1995 and called on psychiatrists to include it in the *DSM* as an official disorder, which would make insurance companies more likely to cover it. In 2009, the reStart: Internet Addiction Recovery Program in Fall City, Washington (near Microsoft's Redmond headquarters), became the first in-patient facility for compulsive "chatting, texting and other aspects of Internet Addiction," which affected "anywhere from 6 to 10 percent of the online population," reStart said in its launch announcement. Around the same time China and South Korea designated Internet addiction as their top public health threat. In 2013 Young co-founded an in-patient Internet addiction treatment facility at the Bradford Regional Medical Center in Pennsylvania. It described "Internet addiction" as "any online-related, compulsive behavior which interferes with normal living and causes severe stress on family, friends, loved ones, and one's work environment. . . . [I]t is a compulsive behavior that completely dominates the addicts' life." A ten-day stay in its "secure and dedicated patient unit," starting with what its founders call a seventy-two-hour "digital detox," costs $14,000.

As for Goldberg, who died in 2013 at the age of seventy-nine, by the end of his life he had come to believe that a small percentage of the population has what he called "pathological Internet use disorder." It was a canny phrase, camouflaging the fact that no one knew if the behavior was a compulsion, an addiction, or an impulse-control disorder—or none of the above.

In the years since Goldberg floated the notion of excessive Internet use as a mental disorder, research has not been kind to the idea. Poring over the literature, it is easy to get the impression that the disorder not only exists but is nearly as common as smartphone ownership. In fact, the emerging scientific consensus is quite different: many people go online compulsively, but the behavior falls short of a distinct mental disorder. The coup de grâce came in 2013, when—despite hundreds of papers in psychology and psychiatry journals describing excessive Internet use as an addiction or a compulsion—psychiatrists balked, declining to designate Internet Use Disorder as a distinct mental disorder in the *DSM-5*. A big reason was that excessive Internet use results from mental processes so common that tarring it as a "disorder" makes as much sense as labeling other nearly universal cognitive quirks such as post-purchase rationalization ("I bought it, so it must be good") mental disorders. Another concern was that "excessive" is in the eye of the beholder, and as more and more online activities became socially acceptable, the definition of "excessive" evolved. Internet use may be a compulsion for many people, but that does not mean it is pathological. To argue otherwise is to claim that a widespread behavior is a sign of a mental disorder, of a brain not working as it should.

The studies of researchers who did argue otherwise weren't persuasive enough to clear even the low bar that the American Psychiatric Association set for designating a behavior as worthy of further study to see if it might merit recognition as a mental disorder. Many of the studies were so flawed they should have embarrassed a student in Psych 101. Or as psychologist John Grohol, who founded the mental health news site Psych Central, put it, "'Internet addiction' has poor evidence because most of the research done into it has been equally as poor."

How poor? In thirty-nine studies of pathological Internet use, beginning in the 1990s, different researchers came up with wildly different estimates of its prevalence, found a 2009 analysis by Marina Blanton of the University of Notre Dame and colleagues in *CyberPsychology & Behavior*. For starters, there was essentially no agreement on how to define the supposed disorder. Some studies used a single criterion: how much time people spent online. That, Blanton and her team wrote with commendable understatement, "has severe limitations." For instance, it snares millions of people who feel no great desire to be online but must do so for their work and are therefore no more addicted to the Internet than they are to, say, typing. Other diagnostic questionnaires used thirty-two true-or-false questions, or thirteen yes-or-no questions, or something else entirely, and there was no evidence that if someone "passed" (or failed) on one of the questionnaires they would pass (or fail) on the others, a troubling absence of validation. Virtually none of the studies examined whether the questionnaires capture behavior accurately, and they often recruited participants in a way that caused serious sampling bias. By seeking volunteers who were interested in the Internet, the studies wildly inflated estimates of the prevalence of Internet addiction. It was akin to measuring the prevalence of alcoholism by canvassing barflies.

The main trouble, of course, is that the criteria in most Internet disorder questionnaires can be used to label anything a pathological compulsion. Staying online "longer than you intended," neglecting chores "to spend more time online," forming relationships with fellow netizens, checking email "before something else that you need to do," getting complaints from family or co-workers about how much time you spend online . . . well, substitute any activity that society deems more socially virtuous and you can see how ridiculous this is.

Studies of compulsive Internet use have also failed to separate content from form. Users who go online to watch porn or gamble or shop feel compelled to watch porn or gamble or shop. It's not Internet use per se that they find compelling. Instead, the Internet is how more and more people watch porn and gamble and shop. Similarly, if text messaging is how your friends communicate, then your choices are to become adept at typing with your thumbs or become a social recluse. Again, using digital technology this way is not evidence of compulsive behavior.

I asked psychologist Nancy Petry of the University of Connecticut, who led the expert APA group studying behavioral addictions for possible inclusion in the *DSM-5*, to sum up the case against problematic Internet use as a mental disorder. She didn't come up for breath for eleven minutes. You can't reliably assess it, she pointed out, "and when different diagnostic tests come up with prevalence estimates varying from less than 1 percent of the population to more than 50 percent, there's clearly a problem." The criteria in many of the questionnaires are ridiculous, asking whether you have lost sleep due to going online late at night and whether you have "neglected chores" because of it. "Ninety percent of adolescents would say yes to this"—as would most people who love to read, listen to music, or socialize—"but that's not indicative of a psychiatric disorder," Petry said. "The questions have a very low threshold, asking you to agree to only a few symptoms, with no indication that they're clinically significant. You have to distinguish between psychiatric disorders and mere problems budgeting your time, setting priorities, or generally dealing with life's demands."

*   *   *

It's important to debunk the notion of Internet Use Disorder or Internet Addiction Disorder because the wild claims for its prevalence, and even its existence, have pernicious consequences. One is that they elevate the ordinary to the pathological and thus deny the truly pathological. A tiny percentage of people do have a problematic compulsion to live life online, to the detriment of the rest of their life. Lumping them together with the teenager who sends 300 texts a day—no more than the number of conversational exchanges many people had in person, voice-to-voice, in the old days of the 1990s—trivializes their predicament. Another problem is that, as with video games, there is good reason to suspect that excessive Internet use is not primarily about the Internet but is instead a marker or symptom of something else, such as social anxiety or depression. "If you're spending a lot of time on Facebook, is that really its own psychiatric condition or is it a manifestation of something else, like wanting to keep up with your friends, feeling bored or lonely or shy, or in need of mindless distraction?" Petry asked. To call Internet use the primary pathology is like saying that using hundreds of tissues a day to dry your tears is pathological: it conflates the symptoms with the illness and thus obscures the actual reasons for the behavior. Tagging someone as having an Internet compulsion can therefore be like diagnosing someone as having Kleenex Use Disorder . . . and charging $14,000 to treat it, rather than the depression that is the true illness. "The field has to come to a greater consensus before problematic Internet use can be recognized as a true mental disorder," Petry said.

But as with other compulsions that fall well short of pathology, intense Internet use nevertheless reveals something about how the brain works when it is working normally. One way we know Internet use can be compulsive is by the millions of dollars companies have spent to make it so—and you can be sure they're not targeting a tiny fraction of the online audience that has a psychiatric disorder. No; they believe that with the right hooks, many of them akin to what video game designers have programmed into their creations, anyone can be sucked into compulsive use of a website. The travel website Expedia has a "senior product manager of compulsion," *Technology Review* recounted in 2015, and has hired consultants to "develop compulsive experiences." The intermittent and variable reward structure that permeates video games is only the beginning.

Enter FoMO

To identify what it is about online experiences that makes them compelling to people whose cerebral hemispheres are firmly planted in the land of the sane, researchers are taking a page from video-game cyberpsychology. For just as video games have psycho-logical hooks that make people feel compelled to play, so do online experiences.

Start with the fact that the cost in time and effort of a single online "transaction"—a click, a view, checking Instagram or your Facebook news feed—is so minuscule as to be unmeasurable. It is often so low, in fact (*I'm just waiting to give the barista my order*), as to be negative. That is, *not* texting or checking for texts or reading your smartphone screen feels like a greater burden than doing so. "The timescale on which you work with online technology is central to making it compelling," Sheffield's Tom Stafford told me. "It's always on, and time is sliced into small bits. What else can you do in five seconds that's interesting? So why not check your phone?" This is a large part of why "using the Internet can be compulsive."

That suggests that the drive behind use of the Internet, especially via smartphones, is the result of feelings and thoughts more akin to those in obsessive-compulsive disorder—in particular, compulsive checking—than to addiction. "The underlying motivation to use a mobile phone is not pleasure," as the addiction model says, "but rather a response to heightened stress and anxiety," said Moez Limayem of the University of Arkansas, who led a study on this presented to the 2012 Americas Conference on Information Systems. We feel anxious if we're not making use of every tiny slice of time.

Just how hard—even unpleasant and anxiety-producing—it is to be alone with our thoughts was shown dramatically in a 2014 study. Researchers led by social psychologist Timothy Wilson of the University of Virginia gave volunteers (students) two options: do "nothing" for fifteen minutes or give themselves a small electric shock (which three-quarters had previously told the researchers they'd pay money not to experience). Two-thirds of the men and one-quarter of the women chose the latter, so anxious were they for "something to do." Don't blame millennials: adults whom the scientists recruited from a church and a farmer's market reacted the same way, feeling antsy and anxious when left alone with only the contents of their mind. Milton, as usual, got there first: "The mind is its own place, and in it self/Can make a Heav'n of Hell, a Hell of Heav'n," he wrote in *Paradise Lost*. These days, apparently, the mind regards its own company as more like the second option: "The untutored mind does not like to be alone with itself," Wilson and his colleagues concluded.

Especially when the mind, tutored or otherwise, sees dangled before it a payoff structure common to many forms of social media, texts, and email: the intermittent/variable reward system that we met in video games. Most of what fills your Twitter feed or Facebook updates is digital dross. ("Barbara changed her Facebook picture!") Payoff: zero. But every so often, you find a rare gem—a friend offering two free Bruce Springsteen tickets she can't use, or an acquaintance posting that he'll be in your neighborhood tomorrow and is looking for someone to share a beer. Hopping from one site to another and landing on one that tells you the secret to fixing squeaky wooden floors, or that a Kardashian just blew up the Internet again, makes the many duds and time sucks worthwhile. The Internet's cognitive-reward structure compels many people to jump from site to site (*This one might have the fact that will change my life*), to use social media, to see what YouTube video is trending, lest they miss a life-changing, merely important, or just entertaining bit of information. Our brains want more, and our thumbs oblige. Anxiety that we might miss such treasures in the sea of dross drives compulsive Internet use.

"If I give you a treat *sometimes*, you have to keep checking *all* the time: you don't know when it will come," Tom Stafford said. "No matter how frequently you check, even if you checked only a second ago, a brilliant email might have just come in," or a friend might have posted on Foursquare *only a second after you last checked* that she's in the bar you just passed. "You feel anxiety about possibly missing something." Such low-cost, occasionally high-reward activities are catnip to the brain:

they produce the experiences most likely to reel you in and impale you on the hook of intermittent/variable rewards.

If we're prevented from engaging in a compulsion like staring at our smartphones for texts, the anxiety that the compulsive behavior alleviates comes roaring back. Psychologists have reported that people who are separated from their smartphone often experience an elevated heart rate and other signs of anxiety. In one 2016 study, volunteers who filled out a standard questionnaire about their smartphone use and emotions told researchers that they turn to their phones "to avoid negative experiences or feelings" and "to cope [with] or escape from feelings related to an anxiety-inducing situation." Psychologist Alejandro Lleras of the University of Illinois at Urbana-Champaign described it as a security-blanket effect, absorbing our bubbling-over anxiety. That fits with the growing number of studies finding that people text as a way to escape anxiety; in questionnaire-based studies, something like 70 percent of participants say smartphones and texting help them overcome anxiety and other negative moods. It's become a stereotype that people in awkward (read: anxiety-provoking) situations "turn to their mobile phones as a way to disengage," the Illinois researchers said, and do the same "during times of more intense distress."

To get beyond mere observation, Lleras and a colleague attempted something more rigorous. They gave volunteers a short writing assignment that, they explained (falsely), would be evaluated by two experts. To ratchet up the stress further, the researchers said the experts would also conduct an on-camera interview about the essay with the volunteers. While waiting for that, half the volunteers had access to their mobile phones and half didn't. While 11 of 24 volunteers who were able to text and surf to their anxiety-ridden-heart's content felt intense anxiety, 18 of the 25 deprived of their phones did, Lleras reported in the journal *Computers in Human Behavior*. And 82 percent of those who kept their phones used it for every moment of the ten-minute wait. By giving in to a compulsion to use their phone, they were able to defuse much of their anxiety. "People seem to be less vulnerable to becoming stressed in anxiety-provoking situations when they have access" to their mobile phone, the researchers wrote.

Smartphones "function as comfort objects, antidotes to the hostile terrain of wider society," as British social theorist James Harkin wrote way back in 2003. By making us feel we are always connected to the world, they alleviate the anxiety that otherwise floods into us from feeling alone and untethered. Anxiety-driven use of mobile phones is pervasive enough to have inspired the neologism *nomophobia* (for "no mobile phone") to describe the pathological anxiety, bleeding into fear, that comes from being unable to access our Galaxy, iPhone, or other preferred silicon security blanket. No wonder 40 percent of smartphone owners use their device before getting out of bed, according to a 2013 survey by Ericsson ConsumerLab, an arm of the Swedish technology giant, or that Americans checked their smartphones forty-six times a day in 2015 (up from thirty-three in 2014), according to a survey by the consulting firm Deloitte—and seventy-four times a day if they're college-age.

Kevin Holesh's day always started with a cell phone, usually twenty minutes of swiping through "missed" tweets and emails. He slept with it next to his bed, used it no matter who he was with, constantly checked email, and would no more think of turning it off than a heart patient would consider turning off his pacemaker. "I was afraid of missing out on some big email," said Holesh, a technology designer and developer in Pittsburgh. "Some CEO wanted to talk, and I wanted to be there instantly. It was me imagining this golden ticket appearing in my inbox." In 2013, he developed Moment, an app to track how much time users are on their phone each day. Knowing his own numbers—looking at his phone every twenty-three minutes, on average—didn't quell the anxiety he felt when he tried to resist it, but removing temptation did. He began placing his phone outside his bedroom at night and removed his email from it. That slowly helped him realize he didn't need to reply to every email instantly; it was fine to wait until morning, or even the next day.

A character in the 2014 New York City production of Laura Eason's play *Sex with Strangers* says upon learning there's no cell phone service at a bed-and-breakfast, "People will think I'm dead." People don't like feeling dead. A 2010 study by the International Center for Media & the Public Agenda at the University of Maryland showed how profound an existential dread engulfs people cut off from the online world. The researchers asked two-hundred students at the school's College Park campus to abstain from using their phones and computers (and all other media) for twenty-four hours, after which they were asked to describe their experiences. Those descriptions, in which the students said they felt disconnected and anxious that they were missing out on something or were out of the loop, were full of terms evoking compulsion. *Frantically craving. Very anxious. Extremely antsy. Miserable. Jittery. Crazy.*

It's worth reading some of them:

"Texting and IM'ing my friends gives me a constant feeling of comfort . . . the fact that I was not able to communicate with anyone via technology was almost unbearable."

"I feel so disconnected from all the people who I think are calling me, but really they aren't half the time."

"I got back from class around 5, frantically craving some technology . . . I couldn't take it anymore being in my room . . . alone . . . with nothing to occupy my mind so I gave up."

That speaks to an itchiness on the part of twenty-first-century denizens, to our inability to be alone with our thoughts now that we and our telecom toys have become joined at the palm. Watch solitary diners at an outdoor cafe some summer afternoon. Time was, they would do some people watching, maybe some reading. Now they scroll through their inbox, check constantly for incoming texts, and click away desperately at website after website to be sure they're on the right one.

It's not only being deprived of those variable-interval rewards that makes ditching their smartphone unthinkable for many people. Because it has become our main connection to other people and the world at large, the anxiety that comes from not being able to check it arises, too, from the feeling of being cut off, from missing something, as if the entire population (well, at least your friends and colleagues) is plugged in, connected, on top of things, and you aren't. How does the online world manage to reach into our cortex and make us feel on edge, anxious, jumpy if we're not connected? For starters, by extending its tentacles into virtually every aspect of life, from shopping to dating, from keeping in touch with friends to just plain feeling like you're in the loop. "There are people who feel, *If I'm not there, if I'm not on that site, I'm missing something—something about my friends, or my health, or anything else,*" psychiatrist Dr. David Reiss, who practices in San Diego, told me. "It's driven by anxiety over the risk of missing something if they don't check a site every five minutes." In other words, the Internet exploits FoMO, or Fear of Missing Out.

Coined in the mid-2000s (its first entry on UrbanDictionary .com is from 2006), FoMO is defined as "pervasive apprehension that others might be having rewarding experiences from which one is absent," psychologists led by Andrew Przybylski and Valerie Gladwell of England's University of Essex wrote in a 2013 paper in the journal *Computers in Human Behavior*. It "is characterized by the desire to stay continually connected with what others are doing." FoMO studies in 2011 and 2012 had found that some three-quarters of the young adults polled agreed that they at least occasionally had "the uneasy and sometimes all-consuming feeling that you're missing out, that your peers are doing, in the know about, or in possession of more or something better than you." For some people that desire is compulsive in the sense I've used it throughout this book: thinking you might miss an opportunity to meet up with friends (or simply know that others are meeting up), to know what "everyone" knows, or to be aware of someone's status updates on Facebook triggers an itchy, twitchy, edgy anxiety. Being disconnected is synonymous with missing out.

It certainly felt that way to Cynthia Thompson. In 2010, when she had her first child and started working from home, the London-based writer began finding the pull of the online world irresistible. "It was my way of finding out what's happening," she said. Feeling cut off from the world of work, she went online nearly around the clock, checking her phone to find out what she was missing and feeling uneasy if her phone ran out of battery power. "We're so used to that instant culture, that an hour later, or two hours later, it would be too late. I do feel a bit anxious if I can't get to the phone straightaway." Her constant online checking stems from the omnipresent need to reassure herself that she hasn't missed an emergency message from her son's school or a work-related email.

In their research, the University of Essex team had 1,031 volunteers aged eighteen to sixty-two from the United States, Britain, India, Australia, and Canada—all recruited online (confounding alert!)— answer how well thirty-two statements described their everyday experience. From that, they identified ten statements (which people answered on a five-point scale from "not at all true" about them to "extremely true") that best picked up on individual differences in FoMO:

1. I sometimes fear others have more rewarding experiences than me.
2. I fear my friends have more rewarding experiences than me.
3. I get worried when I find out my friends are having fun without me.
4. I get anxious when I don't know what my friends are up to.
5. It is important that I understand my friends' "in jokes."
6. Sometimes, I wonder if I spend too much time keeping up with what is going on.

7. It bothers me when I miss an opportunity to meet up with friends.
8. When I have a good time it is important for me to share the details online (e.g. updating status).
9. When I miss out on a planned get-together it bothers me.
10. When I go on vacation, I continue to keep tabs on what my friends are doing.

They called it the Fear of Missing Out scale, and it was the first attempt to define the concept in a way that would allow researchers to measure it. Younger men had a greater FoMO than younger women, and younger people a greater FoMO than older ones. Then the researchers matched up FoMO scores on a standard assessment of how well people felt they were meeting three core psychological needs—relatedness, or feeling close or connected to others; autonomy, the notion that we are the authors of our own lives; and competence, the sense that we can exert an effect on and in the world. Conclusion: people who most felt they were falling short in these three were most likely to fear missing out. People high on the FoMO scale were also more likely to feel more unhappy and dissatisfied with life in general. And—the key finding—they were also most likely to use social media such as Facebook, Twitter, Instagram, and other sites that allow us to not only proclaim that we exist but also to keep tabs on others and stay in the loop, assuaging at least temporarily the angst triggered by the thought that something is going on that we're not a part of. "Fear of missing out," the researchers concluded, "played a key and robust role in explaining social media engagement over and above" factors such as age, gender, or even psychological factors such as mood. "Those with low levels of satisfaction of the fundamental needs for competence, autonomy, and relatedness tend towards higher levels of fear of missing out as do those with lower levels of general mood and overall life satisfaction."

And if we do miss out? If we're not connected? "It struck me that part of the reason we always stay jacked in," wrote *New York Times* media columnist David Carr in 2014, shortly before his untimely death the next year, "is that we want everyone—at the other end of the phone, on Facebook and Twitter, on the web, on email—to know that we are part of the now. If we look away, we worry we will disappear." If existence is defined by an online presence, then not being online is not to exist. Human history knows no greater motivation for action than the existential one of raging against the dying of the light, of fighting mortality by leaving a bit of ourselves behind through the children we bear or the works we create or the tiny nudge with which we try to bend ever-so-slightly the arc of human history. Indeed, reality television would not exist absent the deep and powerful human motivation to stand up and say, *See, I exist!* When we are not online, when we are not connected, when we miss out, we do not exist, and that causes the most unbearable and existential anxiety there is.

It is not Internet use per se, nor specifically social media use, that is compulsive. Instead, the compulsion is to avoid feeling lonely, bored, or out of the loop. What many researchers (who, by the way, are usually decades older than the Internet users they study) treat as aberrant is instead a new way of living, playing, socializing, communicating, and working "for which researchers currently have only pathological interpretations," as Daniel Kardefelt-Winther of the London School of Economics and Political Science put it in a 2014 paper in *Computers in Human Behavior.* "To suggest that this is a mental disorder seems to be a stretch."

Compulsive Internet use, then, is best understood as the result of nearly ubiquitous psychological traits. The need to feel connected, which existed long before Facebook was a gleam in Mark Zuckerberg's eye, anxiety over "missing out," responses to variable intermittent rewards, a primal drive to have our existence recognized by friends and strangers—all of these can drive us to go online compulsively. Like gaming, compulsive Internet use is better understood as, at worst, a coping strategy—and all of us need a little help coping occasionally. Just as in other compulsive behaviors, feeling driven by anxiety to constantly check the online world via smartphone or any other device is the result of normal, useful, adaptive, near-universal ways the mind works. That is how we should understand the digital compulsion: not as a pathology, but as the result of the online world's ability to tap into something deep in the human psyche and make many of us digital casualties.

CHAPTER SEVEN

Compulsions Past

WHEN JOHN was but a teenager in the mid-sixth century A.D., he renounced the study of the arts and sciences—in which he was so proficient he earned the honorific "the Scholastic"—for a monastic life in the Sinai Desert, a bleak locale that for centuries had drawn holy men, reputed to be the place where God had given Moses the Ten Commandments. Fearing "the danger of dissipation and relaxation,"* John spurned the great monastery on the summit of Mount Sinai in favor of a modest hermitage on its slopes. There, he "assiduously read the holy scriptures and fathers, and was one of the most learned doctors of the church," and was known for his self-denial, humility, obedience, and devout prayer.

Devotion alone would not have sufficed to bring John to the attention of historians of mental disorders. That required *Climax; or, the*

---

*The quote is from the Reverend Alban Butler's 1815 book *The Lives of the Fathers, Martyrs, and Other Principal Saints.*

Ladder of Divine Ascent (whence he became known as John Climacus), which he began writing at age seventy-five, when he was the abbot of the monastery of Catherine on Mount Sinai. The rules by which souls might achieve Christian perfection happen to include the oldest known account of an OCD-like compulsion: being compelled to think blasphemous thoughts by an "atrocious foe" whose "unspeakable, unacceptable, and unthinkable words are not ours but rather those of the God-hating demon who fled from heaven."

Compulsions, religious or otherwise, presumably did not begin in the sixth century; it's not hard to imagine a Neanderthal compulsively hoarding mastodon bones. But historical references in the centuries after John Climacus are so rare that the exhaustive 1995 tome *A History of Clinical Psychiatry: The Origin and History of Psychiatric Disorders* includes chapters tracing how societies have viewed every mental woe known to humankind—except compulsions. The reason, coauthor German Berrios of Cambridge University told me, was that "we could not find a sociologist who could deal with the theme in any depth."

That hampers what we might call behavioral archaeology, or studying what form compulsions took during different eras and how different societies viewed them. From the rare accounts of compulsions, it seems clear that until the late seventeenth century, compulsive thoughts and behaviors were seen as evidence of Satan's hand and addressed by clergymen. There was no medical establishment to challenge the Church's claim on diagnosing and treating religious compulsions. After medicine finally became a profession in the eighteenth century, on the infrequent occasions when a nonreligious compulsion was reported, it was often viewed as a charming eccentricity, an odd but innocuous point on the spectrum of human variation. Before extreme compulsions could be regarded as a neurological disorder, physicians had to recognize the brain as the organ of cognition and emotion, which didn't happen until around 1800. But even after they understood compulsions as a manifestation of something gone awry in the brain, physicians fought bitterly—or as bitterly as proper Victorians and men of science could—over exactly what kind of disorder compulsions were. It was a fight whose echoes resound today in the continuing debate over where the line between madness and sanity lies, and over how an adaptive emotion such as anxiety can go off the rails.

Enter the Devil

Mental compulsions—thoughts one cannot stop thinking—beset any number of the devout, including many eventual saints, and were "ascribed invariably to the direct agency of Satan," William James, the founder of American psychology, wrote in *Varieties of Religious Experience.* They beset ordinary folk, too, including an Englishwoman named Margery Kempe. Born around 1373, the illiterate Margery dictated the first autobiography in English. She had "many hours of foul thoughts and foul memories of lechery and all uncleanness,"* she wrote, in particular visions of "men's members, and such other abominations." She was unable to put thoughts of "bare members" out of her mind. Read what you like into the fact that Margery had fourteen children.

The compulsion with the best-documented history is hoarding, with reports of pack rats going back centuries. Compulsive hoarding apparently existed in the early 1300s, and was notable enough for Dante to include in *The Divine Comedy.* With Virgil as his guide, Dante reaches the fourth circle of Hell, where those guilty of Greed are punished and two mobs pummel each other. In one are those who squandered possessions, while in the other are those who hoarded them. The "multitudes to every side of me" attack each other, Dante

---

*As excerpted in the 1982 book *A Mad People's History of Madness,* edited by Dale Peterson.

wrote, "wheeling weights"—enormous boulders representing the burden of possessions that they wasted or hoarded in life. "[E]ach turned around and, wheeling back those weights, / cried out: Why do you hoard? Why do you squander?"

Behavioral archaeologists have little to go on until the Renaissance. Part of the intellectual revolution it launched took aim at traditional beliefs, including the idea that strange behaviors (there was no concept of mental illness) are caused by the devil or demonic possession. Renaissance thinkers invoked more naturalistic explanations for religious compulsions such as scrupulosity, the irresistible urge to engage in religious rituals or thoughts, accompanied by continual fear that one has not confessed adequately, performed religious rites correctly, or thought about God properly. Archbishop (and, later, Saint) Antoninus of Florence (1389–1459), for instance, described the "scrupulous conscience" as beset by indecision resulting from wild, baseless fears that one has not prayed or otherwise acted according to God's wishes. As for its cause, Antoninus had one foot in pre-Renaissance thinking and one in the modern world: scrupulosity, he concluded, can be caused by either the devil or physical illness.

Antoninus's belief that scrupulosity sometimes had a physical cause, and not necessarily a satanic one, was one of the earliest documented realizations that maladies of thought and behavior were illnesses necessitating "medicine or other physical remedies," as he put it. He recommended that those trying to escape religious compulsions receive God's grace, study sacred Scripture, pray constantly, and put up a spirited resistance to the urge to pray or confess excessively. He also, however, cited approvingly the views of Jean Charlier de Gerson, a fourteenth-century theologian and scholar, that extreme scrupulosity is like a pack of "dogs who bark and snap at passers-by; the best way to deal with them is to ignore them and treat them with contempt"—an early example of the "just stop" approach to compulsions.

Ignatius of Loyola (1491–1556), founder of the Jesuits, described in his autobiography the scrupulosity from which he suffered, largely centered on an inability to stop thinking particular thoughts. "Even though the general confessions he had made at Montserrat had been quite carefully done and all in writing, . . . still at times it seemed to him that he had not confessed certain things," he wrote. "This caused him much distress. . . . [H]e began to look for some spiritual men who could cure him of these scruples, but nothing helped him. . . . He persevered in his seven hours of prayer on his knees, getting up regularly at midnight, and in all the other exercises mentioned earlier. But in none of them did he find any cure for his scruples."

The first explicit account of a washing compulsion comes from physician Richard Napier (1559–1634), whose patient was "sorely tempted not to touch anything for fear that then she shall be tempted to wash her clothes, even upon her back," he wrote. She was "tortured until that she be forced to wash her clothes, be them never so good and new. Will not suffer her husband, child, nor any of the household to have any new clothes until they wash them for fear the dust of them will fall upon her. Darest not to go to the church for treading on the ground, fearing lest any dust should fall upon them."

When one Hannah Allen, an Englishwoman known for her 1683 autobiography, described people beset by melancholy as "*exceedingly fearful* . . . beyond what there is cause for," she noted, "Every thing which they hear or see, is ready to increase their fears. . . . Their thoughts are most upon themselves, like the millstones that grind on themselves when they have no grist; so one thought begets another. Their thoughts are taken up about their thoughts"—the very definition of the anxiety that underlies, and can only be vanquished by, compulsive behavior. Hannah herself was treated for her insistently anxious thoughts with phlebotomy, another indication that the malady was considered physical and not supernatural. She later sought help from Richard Baxter (1615–1691), a leader of the English Puritan church, who became known far and wide for his healing ability.

Sickness, Not Satan

What makes Baxter notable in the history of compulsions is that he firmly rejected the demonic possession explanation for compulsive behaviors, ascribing them instead to "the involuntary effects of sickness." Someone beset by "doubts and fears and depraving thoughts, and blasphemous temptations" was like one "in a fever," suffering "unavoidable infirmities." Friends and family of someone so suffering, Baxter advised, should "divert them from the thoughts which are their trouble; keep them on some other talk or business; break in upon them, and interrupt their musings. . . . If other means will not do, neglect not physick [medicine] . . . tho' they will be averse to it, as believing that the disease is only in the mind."

Anglican bishop John Moore (1646–1714) preached about the "disorder of mind" that brings unwanted "naughty, and sometimes blasphemous thoughts," especially during worship services. Although such sufferers may "charge themselves with the sin against the Holy Ghost," he said, in fact the compulsion arises from a "disorder and indisposition of the body," a mark of the growing recognition that such travails reflected something physical, not supernatural. The solution? "Neither violently struggle with [the compulsions]," Moore advised, "since experience doth teach that they increase and swell by vehement opposition; but dissipate and waste away, & come to nothing when they are neglected"—to which one might respond, easier said than done.

By the eighteenth century more physicians were taking note of patients besieged by mental compulsions that did not necessarily have a religious component. Dr. John Woodward (1665–1728) described one Mrs. Holmes, who in 1716, at the age of twenty-six and pregnant, chanced to look out a window and catch sight of a large porpoise in the river Thames "and was much delighted with the viewing of it." Two weeks later, she was suddenly "invaded" by a "strong perplexing thought of the porpoise; and a fright, lest that should mark her child." Taking to her bed as her child's birth grew near, Mrs. Holmes "had thoughts of the devil, as tempting and vehemently urging of her to ill; particularly to fling her child into the fire, beat its brains out, and the like." Woodward prescribed "an oily draught; and . . . purge . . . to be taken next morning." He reported that its laxative effects were quite apparent—it produced "at least a dozen stools"—and by the next day her thoughts became less "unruly."

In the *Directorium Asceticum, or Guide to the Spiritual Life*, published in 1754, Jesuit theologian Giovanni Battista Scaramelli (1687–1752) offers one of the earliest accounts of behavioral compulsions, "exterior acts," including people shaking their heads, pressing their hands to their chests, rolling their eyes, praying, and repeatedly confessing. Foreshadowing twentieth-century research, Scaramelli concluded that the cause of compulsions was an "anxious character" and observed that giving in to compulsions reinforced rather than vanquished the anxiety propelling them: "The more the thoughts are driven away the more they return to the mind," he warned. Compulsive prayer, in particular, is particularly self-defeating: "Some persons are greatly distressed in reciting vocal prayers, fancying they have omitted portions, or not pronounced the words plainly, so that they repeat again and again the same words."

The end of the seventeenth century brought a tectonic change in how scholars viewed madness, grounding mental illnesses in the nervous system. One dramatic case of physicians recognizing that behavior reflected something going on in the nerves and the brain came in 1787, when two dozen girls working in a Lancashire cotton mill were swept up in an episode of mass hysteria. It began when one slipped a mouse down the dress of another, who, terrified, had what observers called "a fit" and shook with violent convulsions for twenty-four hours. The next day, three more girls—though mouseless—came down with convulsions, as did six more the following day, and more throughout the week. Girls living or working miles away from the mill were also seized by the hysteria. They "were infected entirely from report, not having seen the other patients," as an account from the time put it, reporting with some astonishment that the girls experienced "anxiety, strangulation, and very strong convulsions" so violent as to "require four or five persons to prevent the patients from tearing their hair and dashing their heads against the floor or walls."

A Dr. St. Clare was summoned from a neighboring town. Rejecting any notions of demonic possession, he had just the thing: a device that generated electric shocks. Cranking it up, he administered this treatment to one girl after another. "The patients were universally relieved without exception," we are told. "As soon as the patients and country were assured that the complaint was merely nervous, easily cured," the epidemic vanished. While the episode stands out as an excellent example of the placebo effect, more significant is what it reveals about the paradigm shift in the understanding of mad behavior: the cause lay not in the devil but in "nerves," and the cure lay in the physical world, not the spiritual.

A second leap forward occurred at about this time. Earlier, the only recognized forms of madness were "lunacy," in which the sufferer has parted ways with reality and which today is called psychosis; "melancholy" (irrationality, not depression); and "idiocy," or mental retardation. These conditions were permanent and all-encompassing; anything that did not wholly engulf the mental faculties was not deemed mental illness, so even severe washing or checking compulsions didn't make the cut. But starting in the eighteenth century, doctors recognized that mental disorders could be partial and temporary, not all-encompassing and permanent—making odd behaviors now fair game for neurologists (who preceded "alienists"—psychiatrists—as the designated experts on all matters of the brain). Previously, having a mild, partial, occasional mental disorder had had almost a cachet, even a certain charm. That comes through in an episode of what, had it occurred in a different social stratum and been more isolated, would surely be diagnosed as a behavioral compulsion: the mania for collecting.

Wunderkammers

For two centuries starting in the 1600s, European royalty, scholars, and apothecaries began to create "cabinets of curiosities," hodge-podge collections of the exotic, beautiful, or rare, collected from the grounds of one's estate or from sojourns to the ends of the earth. In 2013 the Grolier Club, a gem of a museum in Manhattan, presented an exhibit of these collections displayed in drawers and on shelves in *Wunderkammers*, the German term for "rooms of wonder," or cabinets of curiosities. The drive and tenacity—yes, compulsion—it took to collect and assemble, catalogue and display the *Wunderkammers* was as obvious as their contents were marvelously bizarre. The cabinets housed dried, exotic plant specimens as well as tiny animal skeletons; shells and pieces of coral; hardened arteries and kidney stones; antique coins and medals; fossils and rocks; scientific instruments and even a stuffed crocodile, and more, all documented in elaborate ledgers.

The mania for cabinets of curiosities waned, as all manias eventually do, with many of the collections seeding some of Europe's and America's great museums of natural history (as well as not-so-great freak shows and traveling circuses). But while they lasted *Wunderkammers* were a socially approved compulsion. The line between disease and cultural activity was already as blurry as the writing on those centuries-old ledgers, but wherever it lay the stigma of lunacy was replaced by the notion of madness as the inheritance of the more sensitive, refined, educated classes—something absent in "the poorer and less civilized inhabitants of modern Europe," as Thomas Arnold wrote in his 1782 *Observations on the Nature, Kinds, Causes and Prevention of Insanity, Lunacy or Madness*. Madness including compulsive behavior—mild, tempered, well-behaved—was now a marker of civilization, breeding, and intelligence. In the eighteenth century, obsessions and compulsions "move to the fore, to signify a very human essence, and to be a characteristic of genius, good birth, and good character," Lennard Davis of the University of Illinois wrote in his 2009 book *Obsession: A History*.

French psychiatrist Jean-Étienne-Dominique Esquirol (1782–1840) introduced the term "monomania" around 1810, meaning mental imbalance caused by a single train of thought or object of attention. Monomaniacs could think, reason, and behave normally in every regard other than the focus of their mania. Hardly had Esquirol invented the term than monomania became one of the most common diagnoses of patients entering France's asylums. This view found its way not only into how people behaved and regarded others, but also into fiction. In the 1886 novel *The Man of Feeling*, author Henry Mackenzie had his main character visit Bedlam (Bethlem Royal Hospital), England's first psychiatric hospital, finding a mathematician who felt compelled to calculate the paths of comets and a famous schoolmaster compelled to determine the precise pronunciation of ancient Greek verbs. An unstoppable compulsion to collect or create, to calculate astronomical trajectories or plumb the mysteries of an extinct tongue, made this mild form of madness—if madness it was—fashionable, a sign of a sharp mind and a tenacious spirit. To be madly compelled was a mark of intellectual accomplishment.

* * *

By the late eighteenth century, case reports of people compelled to think certain thoughts or perform certain actions were more likely to describe nonreligious rather than religious ones. That's not to say scrupulosity had vanished. But as secular institutions and ways of thinking began to compete with the Church, there were many more ways to be compulsive than to compulsively think blasphemous thoughts or confess one's sins. In fact, people in secular cultures tend to have fewer religious OCD symptoms than do those in highly religious cultures; it is the rare atheist, after all, who feels heart-pounding anxiety if she does not light Shabbas candles. A 2004 study by researchers at the Federal University of Rio de Janeiro compared adults with OCD at the university clinic in Rio with those in other parts of the world. A predominance of religious obsessions was found only in the Middle East, suggesting—the authors wrote in the *Journal of Psychiatric Research*—that "cultural factors may play a significant role" in the compulsions that people engage in.

There was another reason for the shift from predominantly religious compulsions to washing, checking, and the like: as medicine became a profession, people besieged by compulsions tended to seek help from doctors, not priests. It thus became the former—eventually joined by psychiatrists—who wrote down their case histories, and patients figured they could reveal compulsions other than scrupulosity.

One such account came down to us because its subject was Samuel Johnson (1709–1784), the essayist, poet, literary critic, biographer, and lexicographer. James Boswell's *Life of Samuel Johnson*, published in 1791, described how Johnson would walk down the street "and repeatedly touch posts. . . . Upon every post as he passed along, I could observe he deliberately laid his hand; but missing one of them, when he had got at some distance, he seemed suddenly to recollect himself, and immediately returning back, carefully performed the accustomed ceremony, and resuming his former course, not omitting one till he gained the crossing."

Boswell also noted Johnson's "anxious care to go out or in at a door or passage, by a certain number of steps from a certain point, or at least so as that either his right or left foot, (I am not certain which,) should constantly make the first actual movement. . . . I have, upon innumerable occasions, observed him suddenly stop, and then seem to count his steps with a deep earnestness; and when he had neglected or gone wrong in this sort of magical movement, I have seen him go back again, [and] put himself in a proper posture to begin the ceremony."

Frances Reynolds, artist and youngest sister of the eighteenth-century English portrait painter Sir Joshua Reynolds, described Johnson's "extraordinary gestures or antics with his hands and feet, particularly when passing over the threshold of a Door, or rather before he would venture to pass through *any* doorway. On entering Sir Joshua's house with poor Mrs Williams, a blind lady who lived with him, he would quit her hand, or else whirl her about on the steps as he whirled and twisted about to perform his gesticulations."

Scholars as well as ordinary people regarded these behaviors as eccentric, peculiar or curious, not evidence of insanity. In his *Life of Samuel Johnson*, Macaulay argues that Johnson's genius was intimately tied to his "eccentricities," a diagnosis that the good citizens of London apparently agreed with. Seeing the great man touch every lamp-post as he walked down the street, they "thought it was eccentric but without further consequence," wrote Lennard Davis. "No one called an exorcist."

Medicine Takes Center Stage

In the nineteenth century, the medical establishment finally came into its own, and claimed compulsions (and much else that had previously been left to the clergy) as its purview. Physicians in France became the first to recognize compulsions as a medical disorder unconnected to religion, and accounts of compulsive behavior bloomed like crocuses in March. Physicians were just starting to parse the idea of insanity, debating whether compulsions were a disorder of the will, the intellect, or the emotions. With only a few exceptions, French physicians during the eighteenth and nineteenth centuries saw compulsions as disorders of the emotions, while the Germans saw them as diseases of the intellect and will.

The first medical account of compulsive checking comes from Jean-Étienne-Dominique Esquirol—the psychiatrist who coined the term "monomania." Combining clinical acumen with rudimentary epidemiology, he described mental illnesses and estimated their prevalence more accurately than anyone before him. As physician-in-chief at the Salpêtrière Hospital in Paris (originally the Hospice de la Salpêtrière), Esquirol was known for his efforts to bring more humane treatment to the mentally ill, and his *Des maladies mentales, considérées sous les rapports médical, hygiénique, et médico-légal* (1838) is considered the first modern text on clinical psychiatry.

One of his patients, the blue-eyed Mademoiselle F., thirty-four, suffered from what today we would call compulsive checking. "She spends much time in completing the accounts and invoices, being apprehensive of committing some error; of substituting one figure for another; and consequently, of wronging purchasers," Esquirol wrote. Nothing that screams stark raving mad, but enough for him to consider her mentally ill and an "interesting case." Mlle F., who sought treatment in 1834, had contamination-related compulsions as well: "her toilet usually occupies her an hour and a half, and more than three hours" when her symptoms are at their worst, Esquirol wrote. "Before leaving her bed, she rubs her feet for ten minutes, in order to remove whatever may have insinuated itself between the toes or beneath the nails. She afterwards turns and re-turns her slippers, shakes them, and hands them to her chamber-maid, in order that she, after having carefully examined them, may assure her that they conceal *nothing of value*. The comb is passed through the hair a great number of times, with the same intent. Every article of her apparel is examined successively, a great number of times, inspected in every way, in all the folds and wrinkles, and rigorously shaken. . . . If, from any cause, these precautions are not taken, she is restless during the whole day." Like today's OCD patients, Mlle F. was "aware of her condition; perceives the ridiculous nature of her apprehensions, and the absurdity of her precautions," Esquirol wrote. He diagnosed an "involuntary, irresistible, and instinctive activity" that had "chained" the poor woman to "actions that neither reason or emotion have originated, that . . . will cannot suppress."

By this time the most common compulsions related to cleaning and checking, for which we can blame the emergence of the germ theory of disease. Similarly, the expectation of being safe in one's own home was a prerequisite for compulsive checking, which was further egged on by the widespread adoption of conveniences such as stoves that came with built-in threats. "Worrying itself, as indicated by the use of the word 'worry' in the modern sense, came into the English language in the nineteenth century," Lennard Davis wrote.

French physician Henri Legrand du Saulle (1830–1886) christened it "*la folie du doute avec délire de toucher*" (the title of his 1875 book). Contrary to Esquirol's view that compulsions arose from disorders of the intellect and volition, du Saulle saw them as disorders of emotion, which is closer to the twenty-first-century view that they are born in anxiety. What du Saulle termed "the morbid drama" began with the "grip of unceasing anxieties" about contamination, bringing about a "neurosis" marked by "fear of touching certain objects along with a grossly abnormal preoccupation with cleanliness and repeated washing." Sufferers are "aware at every moment of the bizarreness of the behavior," du Saulle wrote, in early recognition of the ego-dystonic nature of what became known as OCD.

Among the twenty-seven case histories du Saulle offered in *La Folie du Doute* was a young woman whose father was one day visited by someone with "a cancerous facial ulceration," he recounted. "[S]he was obsessed with the thought that all the clothes and objects around the house were more or less tainted and covered with cancerous matter. Weighed down by this apprehension, she . . . spent all her time brushing, rubbing and washing. She understood perfectly well that her fears were without foundation, but she was powerless to dispel them."

Years later, now married and a mother, she learned that a rabid dog had wandered into her house. She "could not bring herself to touch the 'rabid dust' on her furniture, on the chimney, the floors, her pockets, other people's clothes, kitchen utensils," du Saulle wrote. "She wiped, scoured, brushed or washed everything she touched, even when at other people's homes, nor did she dare touch the door-knocker at her own home. She bewailed her current state (she was now thirty-six), understood that her anxieties were groundless, and beseeched the doctors to cure her," du Saulle concluded, without indicating whether any, including himself, managed to do so.

In America, Dr. William Hammond (1828–1900), surgeon general of the Union Army in the Civil War, described a "young lady, aged eighteen" whom he treated for compulsive behavior arising from a deathly fear of contamination in 1879. "Little by little the idea became rooted that she could not escape sources of contamination, that other persons might defile her in some way or other," he wrote in his 1883 *Treatise on Insanity in Its Medical Relations.* "When she went out into the street she carefully gathered her skirts together on passing any person, for fear that she might by mere contact be contaminated. She spent hours every day in minutely examining and cleansing her combs and brushes, and was even then not satisfied that they were thoroughly purified." She washed her hands "over two hundred times a day. She could touch nothing without feeling irresistibly impelled to scrub them with soap and water. . . .

"In removing her clothes at night preparatory to going to bed, she carefully avoided touching them with her hands, because then she would not have sufficient opportunity for washing," he continued. "She, therefore, had some one else to loosen the fastenings, and then she allowed her garments to drop on the floor, where she left them. Nothing would have persuaded her to touch any of her under-clothing after it had been worn till it had been washed. . . . When not washing her hands or examining her combs and brushes, she spent nearly all the rest of the day in carefully inspecting every article of furniture and dusting it many times." The young lady admitted "the absurdity of her ideas" to him, Hammond reported, but she nevertheless "could not avoid acting as she did."

Madness or Eccentricity?

By the late nineteenth century, medical opinion was coalescing around the view that compulsions were not a form of insanity, as the era understood it. Instead, as English psychiatrist Henry Maudsley put it in his 1879 textbook *The Pathology of Mind*, they occur when a need "to do some meaningless and absurd act" takes "hold of the fancy and will not let it go," compelling the victim "to repeat the act over and over again, since thus only can peace of mind be obtained."

In 1894, Daniel Hack Tuke kicked off a debate on compulsions with a paper in the neurological journal *Brain*. "I refer to those cases in which a person would not be regarded as insane, although the mental trouble may be as distressing as it is in actual insanity." Compulsion symptoms vary, he continued, and can include "certain ideas or words aris[ing] with painful frequency and vividness." Such mental compulsions, he continued, can be accompanied by physical ones, as in "persons who invariably touch some object in passing it in the course of an accustomed walk (*Délire du toucher*), the antithesis of which is seen in the dread of touching certain objects at all." Tuke also recognized "arithmomania, or the morbid desire to count without rhyme or reason, or to make interminable calculations." He bemoaned the then-faddish tendency of "alienists" to coin terms for every compulsion, fretting that doing so could "distract our attention from the fundamental characteristics common to all," namely, "their automatism, the overwhelming and recurring tendency to be haunted by a certain idea, to perform certain acts . . . with a consciousness of the utter uselessness and absurdity of" the compulsive thought or act.

This was an early explicit recognition that compulsions, despite taking forms as different as checking to see if you ran over someone or pedaling your exercise bike until you drop or frantically swiping your smartphone screen . . . all reflect an underlying mental state: a profound anxiety that can be relieved (albeit temporarily) only by executing the compulsive behavior. Someone besieged by a compulsion is "utterly powerless to resist it," Tuke wrote. The cause? "Undue mental labor, intense emotional excitement"—the key ingredients of anxiety, an emotion found in perfectly sane people. A "slight degree" of the anxiety that triggers compulsions "is not uncommon in perfectly sane people," Tuke argued. A lab worker at an asylum, he said, had recounted how, "after shutting the door the last thing at night and having no doubt that it was shut, he would return once or perhaps twice to satisfy himself that this was the case. In the same way I have known persons open an envelope in which they had placed a cheque and had exercised great care that the date and signature were correct, in order to satisfy themselves that they were so." Even at the dawn of science's embrace of compulsions, the experts of the day acknowledged that they can be so mild as to make calling them madness—or, today, a form of mental illness—absurd.

English psychiatrist Sir George Henry Savage (1842–1921) agreed that compulsions are not manifestations of madness. He called compulsions "very common" and offered that "nearly everyone has some. . . . I have the feeling, which is common I believe, about walking along a pavement. I have an inclination to avoid the cracks and at the same time I have a tendency . . . to touch the iron railings with my stick when I walk along a street. . . . Few of these cases need to be permanent inhabitants of asylums."

This was not a universal opinion, however. English neurologist John Hughlings Jackson (1835–1911), who founded *Brain*, described the compulsions that Tuke and Savage were trying to downgrade from madness as "insane delusions." And thus was teed up a debate that continues today: whether compulsions are a manifestation of mental illness or simply a more intense form of behaviors essentially everyone carries out.

Think of the motivation behind quotidian actions like wiping down your kitchen counters or making the bed, or buying enough food for a few days, or even of studying diligently and holding a job. Isn't there a hint of anxiety—over germs or messiness, starving or failing—that compels us? Human behavior exists along a very long spectrum, and while those on the extremes may seem different from those clustered at the center they are still on the continuum, not tumbling off it like victims of psychosis. In the latter case, the brain has fallen into a mode of functioning that is sharply disconnected from normalcy. But a compulsion to scrub our hands after using the bathroom, or to see if any critical emails arrived since we checked two minutes ago . . . these, and compulsions arising from other anxieties, seize us all at one time or another. As Tuke wrote a century ago, "the difference is one of degree, and . . . it is a most difficult thing to determine when the boundary line has been passed."

Tuke carried the day. By the turn of the last century, a consensus had been reached that compulsions, and the anxieties that command them, are neuroses rather than psychoses—quirks, eccentricities, even peculiarities, but not madness. Even Hughlings Jackson, of the "insane delusions" school, backed down, embracing Tuke's argument that while these are "departures from normal mental states or at least . . . exaggerations and persistencies of mental states," their genesis in the sorts of anxieties that are the common condition of humankind is such that "it would be pedantic to call [them] abnormal."

Compulsions came into their own, scientifically, in 1903, when French psychiatrist Pierre Janet (1859–1947) published a 750-page treatise on obsessions and compulsions, *Les Obsessions et La Psychasthénie*. It was the most extensive discussion to date of what is now called

OCD. Never translated into English, it described OCD symptoms exhaustively, including symmetry compulsions such as when one "chances to view a red object on his right [and then] needs to find one on his left," in Janet's example. He argued that compulsive behaviors arise from a sense that actions have not been completed correctly, from—as we understand it today—anxiety. (In France, OCD is still sometimes called *la folie du doute*, the doubting madness.) Compulsions, he argued, were the result of "lowered energy in the innermost elements of the mental organization"—essentially, the mind was too weak to block the anxiety that led to compulsions.

His suggested treatments were nothing if not imaginative. Janet recommended that people in the grip of a compulsion be prescribed "proper nutrition, sleeping habits, fresh air, and avoidance of fatigue," while "bromides in high doses may be useful." He also believed that getting patients high could do wonders, occasionally prescribing opium "for those suffering from great anxiety," he wrote. William Hammond, who described the young woman with the cleaning compulsions, prescribed sedatives. English psychiatrist Henry Maudsley, in his 1895 psychiatry textbook, recommended opium and morphine three times a day, augmented occasionally with a pinch of arsenic.

Even as experts disagreed about treatment, by the late nineteenth century there was a consensus that compulsions "resulted from disturbances of emotions rather than thinking," German Berrios wrote in *A History of Clinical Psychiatry*. "Anxiety-based explanations became acceptable because great men were espousing them, and because during the second half of the nineteenth century there was a revival of 'affectivity' [and] emotions" as objects of scholarly inquiry. As a result, although compulsions had been explained as a disorder of the will or intellect in the eighteenth and nineteenth centuries, by the turn of the twentieth century "the 'emotional' hypothesis prevailed."

"I Felt the Need to Walk"

Late nineteenth-century France saw a mini-epidemic of one of the odder compulsions in the annals of psychiatry: mad travelers. For reasons that leading psychiatrists of the day debated ad nauseam, clerks, artisans, craftsmen, laborers, and other working-class men were suddenly and inexplicably seized with the compulsion to strike out for parts unknown, by foot and by rail, for weeks and even years at a time, often with nothing but the clothes on their backs and a few francs in their pockets.

The first of the "mad travelers"—the name comes from philosopher Ian Hacking's 1997 Page-Barbour Lectures at the University of Virginia—was one Albert Dadas, a gas fitter from Bordeaux born in the 1860s. As a young man, Albert developed an unusual mental malady: upon hearing the name of a distant city such as Marseilles, he felt compelled to head for it. And so he did, walking as much as forty miles a day. Upon arrival, he overheard conversations about Africa, and he felt compelled to board a ship for Algeria. Later walkabouts, which usually occurred in a state of amnesia about his identity, took him through Belgium and Holland, to Nuremberg in Germany, and points east—far east: Prague, Berlin, Posen, Moscow in 1881, from Bordeaux to Verdun in 1885.

Over and over, recounts Hacking, "the need to go overpowered him." He was, Albert told his doctor, "tormented by a need to travel"—which echoes the anxiety that drives today's compulsions. "I only need to walk," Albert told one physician. "A few moments ago I had a terrific desire to go. I almost left you for Liege." When on the road, he almost always experienced "gaiety," he told his doctors; if he was seized by a sudden sadness, after a kilometer or so of walking "my sadness suddenly disappeared." His distress at being in one place grew unbearable when he saw others depart, as when he saw soldiers board a train to join their regiment. "I could not stand it," he later told his doctor. "I envied the lot of the conscripts who were going to see the country." On such occasions "I felt the need to walk, to go a long way. Every moment I felt the pressure which drives me toward the road."

Albert frequently wound up in one or another hospital, compulsively walking their corridors, and psychiatrists had a field day diagnosing him. A fugue state analogous to the confusion that follows an epileptic seizure, said one school. Nonsense, said another: hysteria treatable with hypnosis. No, *dromomanie,* a neologism (from the Greek signifying racecourse) meaning a state in which one feels compelled to take flight. The physician who studied Albert most closely, Philippe Tissie, diagnosed "pathological tourism," which he deemed a form of madness. This was the era when travel for the masses, not only aristocrats, took off, aided by the rise of iconic companies such as Thomas Cook & Son. But where members of London's merchant class presumably put some thought into which Cook tour they selected, Albert's rambles were "obsessive and uncontrollable," Hacking said, "less a voyage of self-discovery than an attempt to eliminate self." And they "inaugurated an epidemic of mad travel."

Like other instances of mass hysteria, hearing about one person's actions inspired hundreds of copycats. German and Russians doctors documented cases of mad travelers; so did physicians in northern Italy and in regions of France outside Albert's Bordeaux. Regardless of the details of the men's lives (for they were almost all men; women, mad or not, seldom traveled alone in 1880s Europe) or the particulars of their peregrinations, each described to his physician being "taken by an overpowering desire to walk, and off they went, in spite of themselves, abandoning everything in order to justify this need," as an 1892 thesis on eighteen patients stricken with "*l'automatisme ambulatoire, ou vagabondage impulsif*" at Tissie's hospital in Bordeaux put it. Yet mad traveling disappeared as quickly as it appeared. "Compulsive aimless wandering as a medical entity" lasted from 1887 to 1909, Hacking explained, "and then it was no more."

Compulsions on the Couch

And then came Sigmund Freud (1856–1939).

The founder of psychoanalysis deemed what we now call OCD the most fascinating of the mental disorders, and published fourteen papers on it. But he confessed in a 1909 essay "that I have not yet succeeded in penetrating a severe case" of it.

Freud nevertheless relished the compulsions his patients brought him. He interpreted them in a way that represented a sharp break from the past, for he analyzed them as he did dreams, memories, and virtually everything else his patients brought him: symbolically. Take the compulsive bedtime ritual a nineteen-year-old woman described to him, one she could not go to sleep without. She stopped the large clock in her bedroom and removed others, as well as watches; "her tiny wrist-watch was not allowed . . . to be inside her bedside table," Freud recounted. The door between her room and her parents' had to be precisely half-open, which she accomplished by placing various objects in the open doorway. She moved flower pots and other vessels so they would not fall, and arranged pillows to form a diamond shape. The down-filled duvet had to be shaken so the feathers fell to the bottom, but she then anxiously evened out the down by trying to press the feathers apart. "There was always an apprehension that things might not have been done properly," Freud reported. "Everything must be checked and repeated, doubts assailed first one and then another. . . ."

Today, psychiatrists would likely diagnose a "just right" compulsion, probably driven by anxiety if the bedroom items were not arranged just so. But to Freud, the young woman's compulsive bedtime ritual was packed with hidden—usually sexual—meaning. The bedding symbolized her desire to become pregnant (creating a nest for her brood). The timepieces were sexual symbols: clocks and watches have "a genital role owing to their relation to periodic processes" and because "a woman may boast that her menstruation behaves with the regularity of clockwork." And "the ticking of a clock may be compared with the knocking or throbbing in the clitoris during sexual excitement." The woman—whom he diagnosed as "a neurotic" with "agoraphobia and obsessional neurosis"—removed them because she wanted to banish "symbols of the female genitals . . . for the night," Freud explained in a lecture. Vessels such as flower pots and vases are likewise female symbols, he said, and the woman's ritualistic banishing of them before bedtime arose from her anxiety that she would not bleed when her marriage was consummated on her wedding night, revealing that she was not a virgin. The woman initially rejected his symbol-laden explanations, Freud reported, but eventually "accepted all the interpretations" and abandoned "the whole ceremony."

Moving beyond the compulsive behavior of this patient, Freud proposed that obsessions and compulsions generally originated (as did every mental malady) in childhood. When a boy or girl wanted to engage in violence or sexual play but was stopped by a parent, the conflict between unrequited desire and stymied action produced "repression" of the mental energy behind the desire. This energy became bottled up in the unconscious, eventually popping out in adulthood as obsessions and compulsions. Most psychiatrists held to variations of Freud's interpretation of OCD, involving the unconscious and repression and defensive ego maneuvers, well into the 1960s.

In an ironic analogue of the shoemaker going barefoot, Freud exhibited a compulsion of his own. He "lived pen in hand; he writes everywhere, all the time, and has always done so," biographer Lydia Flem recounted in *Freud the Man*. He also worked compulsively, seeing patients from morning through late afternoon and then writing from evening well into the night, typically until two or three o'clock in the morning. Freud admitted that "I really can't imagine that a life without work would be comfortable for me: fantasizing and work are one and the same for me, and nothing else is fun for me." In a confession that resonates with the current understanding that compulsive behaviors are born in anxiety, Freud expressed the terror that words might sometimes fail, and thoughts might refuse to come, and that it is "impossible to stop trembling at this possibility." It has "never been the case" that he could count on "productive capacity at all times and in all moods," but instead had days "when nothing could come" and he was "in danger of losing all ability to work and to struggle." Notice the last phrase, reading which it is impossible not to imagine a compulsion to write and work driven by the anxiety—even the existential terror—that one day he would not be able to.

Freud called obsessive, compulsive illnesses *Zwangsneurose*, echoing the coinage of Austro-German psychiatrist Richard von Krafft-Ebing, who referred to irresistible thoughts as *Zwangsvorstellung*. In England *Zwang*, whose English translation is usually *forced*, was instead translated as "obsession," but in the United States it was translated as "compulsion." *Obsessive-compulsive disorder* emerged as the compromise solution. In other words, although psychiatrists and researchers today take pains to emphasize the dual nature of the illness—obsessive thoughts that trigger anxiety that can be relieved only by executing a compulsive action—its earliest investigators saw it as a single entity.

Dead Souls and Other Hoarders

Freud theorized that there existed an "anal triad" consisting of the personality traits parsimony, orderliness, and obstinacy. He posited that children's realization that they are powerless (against their parents) was a traumatic awakening that some deal with by hoarding, gaining control of possessions—many, many possessions. The notion of an anal, retaining personality (born of psychoanalysts' fascination with the nether regions of the human body and, in this case, the idea that children hold back bowel movements for byzantine reasons only a Freudian could love) became the basis for the diagnostic criteria for obsessive-compulsive personality disorder in *DSM-III*. Hoarding was one of nine diagnostic criteria for the disorder.

That marked a significant break from how society had long viewed hoarding. Literary accounts of compulsive hoarding portray it as quirky or eccentric, and perhaps as a character flaw, but definitely not as evidence of madness. In Nikolai Gogol's 1842 novel *Dead Souls*, the wealthy landowner Plyushkin has in his workshop "all kinds of wood and never-used wares," Gogol wrote, wooden items "nailed, turned, joined, and plaited: barrels, halved barrels, tubs, tar buckets, flagons with and without spouts, stoups, baskets, hampers in which village women kept their skeins of flax and other junk, panniers of thin bent aspen, corbeils of plaited birchbark . . ." The hoard was so overwhelming that "never in all his life could [it] have been used even on two such estates," but "to him it still seemed too little."

Compelled to accumulate ever more, Plyushkin would daily walk the streets of his village, peering "under bridges and stiles" for, to his hoarding eye, treasures. The local *muzhiks*—peasants—called him "the fisherman" for this habit of trawling the neighborhood for "an old shoe sole, a woman's rag, an iron nail, a potsherd." After Plyushkin's daily rounds "there was no need to sweep the streets," Gogol wrote, for if a passing officer had lost a spur it "would immediately be dispatched to the famous pile"; if a woman forgot her bucket at the town well he would carry it off. Gogol ascribed this to greed compounded by Plyushkin's wife dying and his children leaving, usually in a way that disappointed him (marrying an army officer, becoming a gambler). Soon after the publication of *Dead Souls*, "Plyushkin" became slang in Russian for a person who hoards discarded, useless objects, and Russian psychiatry adopted the term "Plyushkin syndrome" for hoarding disorder.

Cultural recognition of hoarding spanned Europe. In Charles Dickens's 1853 *Bleak House*, whose narrative core is an interminable case in England's Chancery Court, Krook is a rag and bottle merchant and paper collector as well as the landlord of a boardinghouse where two other characters live. "In one part of the window was a picture of a red paper mill, at which a cart was unloading a quantity of sack of old rags," Dickens wrote. "In another, was the inscription BONES BOUGHT. In another, KITCHEN-STUFF BOUGHT. In another, OLD IRON BOUGHT. In another, WASTE PAPER BOUGHT. In another, LADIES' AND GENTLEMEN'S WARDROBES BOUGHT. Everything seemed to be bought, and nothing to be sold there. In all parts of the windows, were quantities of dirty bottles: blacking bottles, medicine bottles, ginger-beer and soda-water bottles, pickle bottles, wine bottles, ink bottles."

Ironically, the illiterate Krook obsessively hoards papers: "It's a monomania with him, to think he is possessed of documents," Dickens wrote. "He has been going to learn to read them this last quarter of a century, I should judge, from what he tells me." It was a shrewd observation, that hoarders refuse to part with their possessions out of "just in case" delusion—that a seemingly useless item might one day prove useful. Dickens might have been making a sly comment on the futility of arguing a hoarder out of that belief when he sprang on the reader the fact that, amongst Krook's towering stacks of documents, were papers that could have resolved the endless case of *Jarndyce v. Jarndyce*.

Like Krook, Sherlock Holmes had a "horror of destroying documents," Arthur Conan Doyle wrote in the 1893 story "The Adventure of the Musgrave Ritual," "especially those which were connected with his past cases, and yet it was only once in every year or two that he would muster energy to docket and arrange them . . . Thus month after month his papers accumulated, until every corner of the room was stacked with bundles of manuscript which were on no account to be burned, and which could not be put away save by their owner." (Admittedly, that sounds like the offices of half of academia, at least in the days before computers and thumb drives.) Conan Doyle similarly held on to vast quantities of notebooks, diaries, press clippings, and correspondence, according to biographer John Dickson Carr, and they accumulated throughout Windlesham Manor, his home in the Sussex countryside.

William James argued that acquiring possessions is a human instinct but did not consider whether that instinct can hypertrophy. So psychoanalyst Erich Fromm (1900–1980) jumped in: hoarding, he proposed in his 1947 book *Man for Himself*, is one of four types of "nonproductive orientation" a person can have.* The hoarding orientation, Fromm argued, is marked by an inability to form human attachments and a tendency to displace the drive for attachment onto objects, with the result that the hoarder withdraws socially. It is also characterized by a desire to surround oneself "by a protective wall," Fromm wrote, with the primary aim "to bring as much as possible into this fortified position and to let as little as possible out of it." Hoarding is also driven by miserliness, he contended, not only toward money and material things but also "to feelings and thoughts." To "the hoarding person," he argued, "love is essentially a possession. They do not give love but try to get it by possessing the 'beloved.'"

The hoarding orientation, according to Fromm, thrived in the seventeenth and eighteenth centuries. In that era, tradesmen and shopkeepers and other members of the emerging middle class were "conservative, less interested in ruthless acquisition than in methodical economic pursuits, based on . . . the preservation of what had been acquired," he wrote in *Man for Himself*. To such people "property was a symbol of his self and its protection a supreme value." They had a feeling "of belonging, self-confidence, and pride." In other words, what we today take as mental disorders were, Fromm argued, common attributes of large swaths of society.

---

*The others are "receptive," in which you wait for things to happen to you; "exploitative," in which you aggressively take what you want; and "marketing," in which you see yourself as a commodity whose worth is whatever you can sell yourself for.

Fromm's description of hoarders fell well short of later understanding in several ways. He claimed that hoarders "have little faith in anything new they might get from the outside world"; with their focus on hoarding and saving, "spending is felt to be a threat." He was even more off the mark with his contention that hoarders have characteristic facial expressions such as a "tight-lipped mouth" and gestures "characteristic of their withdrawn attitude." Fromm described hoarders' "pedantic orderliness" and "compulsive cleanliness," which would come as a surprise to anyone treating hoarders today.

Ousting Freud

The only real competition to Freudian interpretations of compulsive behaviors came from Emil Kraepelin (1856–1926), the psychiatrist who named compulsive buying. Kraepelin did not see every odd behavior as the result of unresolved child sexual fantasies. Instead, he argued, many compulsive behaviors are, like phobias, driven by fear—not too different from the contemporary idea that they are born of anxiety. Some patients with "compulsive fears," he argued, are "tormented by the idea that . . . they themselves are soiled or poisoned by contact with others" (more evidence that the washing compulsion has persisted for centuries). Others with compulsive behaviors, he wrote, are driven by anxiety that "in tearing up any scrap of paper they might have destroyed valuable papers" (shades of hoarders who cannot part with scraps of paper from, say, 1979). Others avoid books "as a source of contagion," or "wipe dishes frequently" and "inspect every bit of food" for contaminants, or are beset by the "uncertainty as to whether they have closed a door, or have sealed a letter that they have mailed." Now we are getting into the territory of modern compulsions.

Kraepelin emphasized that compulsive behaviors are driven by an urge that feels external to the mind. They "do not arise from normal antecedent consciousness of motive and desire," he wrote in his 1907 book *Clinical Psychiatry,* "but seem to the patient to be forced upon him by a will which is not his own." Executing the compulsion, Kraepelin asserted, brings a feeling of relief—an idea that still prevails in the idea that compulsions bring relief from intolerable anxiety.

Curiously, the compulsions Kraepelin included are so common it's problematic to call them expressions of a mental disorder. For instance, he argued, some people are compelled to remember a name, and if they cannot "think of it all day long, lying awake nights trying to recall it, and the tension cannot be relieved until it comes to them." Others "feel compelled" to "dwell on figures," perhaps by counting "compulsively the guests about the table, the number of forks, knives, and glasses." Others are compelled to continually ask, "Who is God?" "Where did he come from?" and "How was the universe created?" Kraepelin acknowledged that "incidents of this sort occur even in normal individuals"—a harbinger of the recognition that mild compulsions are quite common, and while they pale beside the torment caused by extreme ones, they, too, spring from anxiety.

CHAPTER EIGHT

Compulsive Hoarding

LOOKING BACK on it all, Bonnie Grabowski thinks the problem began when her husband, Glenn, brought home empty cardboard boxes from work. Large, small, and in between, they were nothing special, just containers for storing odds and ends—magazines she hadn't gotten around to reading, newspaper clippings about enchanted places she hoped to visit one day, her children's toys, fancy dishes she used only for special occasions. But for all their mundaneness, the boxes acquired significance over the decades, something she was able to articulate only years later.

It wasn't an easy marriage. Bonnie had four sons and a daughter, as well as seven miscarriages, including a little girl one Christmas Day. Glenn, her college sweetheart, had served with the marines in Vietnam during the 1970s, and suffered terrifying flashbacks for years afterward. His nightmares were filled with Vietcong snipers firing on his platoon from invisible hideouts, hidden mines exploding as he walked narrow paths through the jungle, and enemies in black pajamas leaping from the fetid underbrush to plunge knives into his buddies. Bonnie could tell when something like this was playing in Glenn's sleeping brain; he would flail around until he found her beside him . . . and then try to strangle her.

Bonnie and Glenn lived on the east side of Cleveland, near where she grew up. By the time her children were in elementary school, she was trapped in a marriage that brought her little joy and many bruises. "I remember thinking, I don't want to live anymore," she told me. She felt she had no one to turn to, and so threw herself into her children's activities. "I set aside my own things," she said. "I thought, some day I'll read that book. And some day I'll get back to knitting."

And so the boxes filled up. Skeins of yarn and needles and books were only the beginning. Bonnie stored materials to make tablecloths and children's clothes and supplies to reupholster furniture. She collected crepe paper and cardboard and construction paper and wood scraps for the Little League parade floats she made, and everything her boys needed to become Eagle Scouts (camping stoves and tents, wooden poles, hatchets, scores of individual merit-badge books, and more). The boxes filled up seemingly overnight, but Glenn brought home more, and somehow they filled up, too. And they kept coming.

The little three-bedroom, one-bath house—the living room measures ten-by-ten, the kitchen eight-by-ten—has no closet on the first floor, and only one in the bedroom the four boys shared. Bonnie and Glenn had no dressers to speak of; it was an expense they avoided. Bonnie, despite being "a neat freak" as a child, kept the family's clothes in piles on chairs or in Glenn's ever-growing hoard of boxes. "But I still had it under control," she said.

When the children grew up and left home, however, Bonnie became more and more anxious, feeling that her life was "winding down." Glenn lost jobs and got new ones, and when he was working Bonnie stocked up on toilet paper and peanut butter and other non-perishables, just in case. At first it fit in her cupboards, but then "things just piled up," she said, the wonderment clear in her voice, as if she wasn't sure how it all spiraled so disastrously out of control.

It wasn't just groceries. "I love information, so I'd stack up newspapers for a week," Bonnie said, "and once a pile was there it just seemed easier to keep piling things on." Mail and other papers filled bags and more bags, as she couldn't face deciding what was important and what could be tossed, "and pretty soon the next day's were on top of yesterday's, and it got worse and worse." And every day Glenn would bring home two or three more boxes. "He never gave me anything else," Bonnie told me. "These were his presents. That's why I saved them." Glenn suffered a fatal stroke in 2012.

And one day she looked up, and realized her house was veined with goat paths—narrow openings through shoulder-high piles of stuff.

Behind the front door, ten huge plastic bags filled with mail teetered precariously; much of it had arrived after Glenn died, and she didn't have the strength to deal with it. More plastic bags rose from floor to ceiling in the kitchen and hallways, filled with dishes for Boy Scout events, magazine clippings, books, small appliances, umbrellas . . . she wasn't entirely sure. Boxes of clothing and books and toys in the bedrooms made it nearly impossible to enter; Bonnie couldn't sleep in her bed, so completely had the clothes taken over.

But she couldn't part with the kids' old clothes; they could be hand-me-downs for a less fortunate family. Going through the bags and piles of papers seemed as daunting as Hercules tackling the Augean stables, but the thought of tossing things unseen and unsorted triggered a heart-thumping anxiety: articles about her youngest son's stint with the marines in Iraq, and her mother's death notice from the local paper, were in there. Somewhere.

She couldn't get rid of the kids' toys, especially the tubs and tubs containing her youngest son's Legos; he had made such wonderful castles out of them. Nor could she part with the wooden train sets, or the extra toasters, or microwave ovens. "We were brought up not to waste," Bonnie said. "I'm not a shopaholic; I never liked going to the store. This is all stuff we needed once, and we just accumulated it over the years. When I look at the kids' old clothing now it brings up good memories. I don't know what it is, just this attachment I feel."

Like many hoarders, any joy Bonnie feels about her possessions comes from keeping them and seeing them around her, not in using them. By keeping the stuff in the eternal realm of near-infinite possibility and rose-colored memory, she never has to confront the reality that some old appliance is of little use, that the newspaper article is not life-transforming, that she will never make another Boy Scout float. Hoarding is all about potential, about keeping actualities at bay.

As we spoke, Bonnie surveyed the piles around her and suddenly realized something else. Many of the boxes stacked to the ceiling were empty. She couldn't bring herself to haul them to the curb on trash day despite city authorities threatening to condemn the house. "They were the only things my husband ever brought me," she told me in a soft voice.

I pleaded with her to find some way to clear out enough of the stuff to satisfy the building inspector. She waved her hands toward the newspaper and magazine clippings about health and gardening and vacation spots, and pictures of beautiful rooms and window treatments, all sorted by topic in labeled boxes. "My problem, I think, is that I dreamed about things," Bonnie finally said. "I had a dream that our life would be nice, that we'd go on vacation, or I'd have a beautiful garden, or a pretty room like in magazines. But my husband never made a lot of money, and it didn't work out. Instead of having the things I dreamed about, or going on the vacation, I became attached to the pieces of paper. Now all I have is the paper."

* * *

There is no question that hoarding shares key features with collecting, just as mild compulsions are shadows of severe OCD. Surely there is an echo of Bonnie's explanation of why she can't rid her home of reminders of happier times in how retired Harvard Law School professor Alan Dershowitz described his feelings when, in 2016, he sold a collection of Judaica that he had been amassing for nearly half a century. "It breaks my heart to have to sell it," he explained. "I want to feel that I'm connected to the past."

Yet collecting is seen as benign, even charming. Neale Albert, a retired attorney, owns more than four thousand miniature books, properly printed and bound yet no more than three inches tall—but sometimes the size of a Chiclet or even a grain of rice. He stores part of his collection in a "cottage" atop his apartment building on Manhattan's posh Upper East Side, as well as in twenty boxes he keeps in storage. But the collectibles are tiny, his home is spacious, and he is organized.

Theater and television set designer Eugene Lee collects objects ranging from old typewriters to art deco sprinklers, canes that he displays in a wicker basket, roll-top desks, and hundreds of flea market paintings and silhouettes that fill nearly every square inch of wall space like rare postage stamps crowded onto the pages of a book. His wife, Brooke, collects tin globes made after 1900, her assemblage of two hundred ranging in size from a few inches to a foot in diameter and packed on shelves on the living room walls. The effect is of a disorganized museum, and while certainly not as cluttered or disordered as a hoarder's rooms, their Georgian mansion in Providence, Rhode Island, is packed to the gills with stuff. "We're not crazy," Brooke told the *New York Times* in 2014.

* * *

But hoarding goes beyond collecting in important ways. This compulsive drive to acquire and keep stuff, sometimes including living stuff (animal hoarding is its own separate hell), goes way beyond what you need or use or even remember you have. Hoarders can't stop purchasing or passively letting stuff enter their lives, and they can't get rid of what they've acquired, not when the belongings have filled their homes, blocked their doors, and forced family members to climb in through a window. Hoarders typically don't know what they have, buy the same or similar things multiple times, and don't necessarily use what they've accumulated. One purpose of hoarding is just knowing the stuff is there. Many are ashamed of what they've done, but not all: to some hoarders, the compulsion to acquire and hold, even to the extreme of a home veined with tiny passageways through stuff, brings comfort and keeps what would otherwise be a throat-gripping anxiety at bay. The most commonly hoarded items are bags, books, paperwork, newspapers, and old clothing.

Hoarding is also different from out-of-control clutter, which is a manifestation of chronic disorganization or simply not caring about keeping rooms neat. Someone in this predicament would welcome help digging out and getting rid of stuff. A compulsive hoarder, in contrast, would rather you amputate her body parts one by one than ask her, *recycling, trash, or Goodwill?*

There are enough compulsive hoarders like Bonnie—in danger of losing their homes or being beyond reach of rescuers in the event of a fire or other disaster—that communities throughout the country are establishing task forces to help hoarders declutter sufficiently to make their homes livable (in the eyes of the community). Either government-sponsored or purely volunteer, the groups typically consist of social workers, therapists, members of the fire department, and representatives of agencies that help the elderly (who are especially prone to hoarding). The first hoarding task force was created in Fairfax City, Virginia, in 1989; by 2007 five task forces were meeting and by 2016 there were twenty-seven in Massachusetts alone and more than one hundred elsewhere in the United States (as well as Canada, Britain, and Australia).

Exactly how many people are compulsive hoarders is open to question. A 2008 study called the National Comorbidity Survey

Replication, which asked some ten thousand adults about their mental health, found that 14 percent had hoarding symptoms at some point in their life. The European version found a lifetime prevalence of just 2.6 percent, however. The experts I spoke to cite the 2008 Hopkins Epidemiology of Personality Disorder Study as probably the closest to the mark. It pegged the percentage of people who are compulsive hoarders at any given time at 5.3 percent. The researchers had psychiatrists interview 735 people to determine whether they met the *DSM*'s criteria for compulsive hoarding by asking such questions as, "Do you find it almost impossible to throw out worn-out or worthless things? Give me some examples. Is this a problem for you or for others?"

The Hopkins study also yielded clues to the demographics of hoarding. Hoarding is more than twice as common in men (5.6 percent) as women (2.6 percent), though other research has found that those seeking help are predominantly female, suggesting men are more reluctant to recognize they're hoarding or to see it as a problem. Widowhood seemed to be a risk factor. And its prevalence increased with age, affecting 2.3 percent of those 34 to 44 but 6.2 percent of those over 55. That likely reflects at least three factors. As time goes on stuff begets stuff, requiring more effort to get rid of it. Also, as we grow older, memories often become more important, and aides-mémoire more critical. More problematic, the forms of cognitive decline that accompany aging also make hoarding more likely.

As many as 80 percent of people with hoarding disorder also acquire excessively, but the rest are like Bonnie. They don't buy any more stuff than the rest of us do. They just never throw out a single piece of mail, any magazine or newspaper, or even the boxes and bags and wrappers and containers that the requirements of daily living come in.

The media, starting with cable television's *Hoarders* on A&E and *Hoarding: Buried Alive* on TLC, feast on hoarders. When I began the research and reporting for this book, I set up a Google alert for "hoarding." This was not the wisest move. I learned of the unfortunate

Connecticut woman who died when the floor of her house collapsed in June 2014 under the weight of "mail, packages, bottles, lots of papers, newspapers, magazines, you name it," as a police sergeant told reporters. The hoard was "piled to the ceiling in most rooms." Authorities had to cut a hole into the one-story house and use a backhoe to remove enough clutter to allow them to get in.

The summer before, St. Paul, Minnesota, firefighters fought to get inside a burning home to save the owner, even enlarging some of the windows and doorways with power saws, only to find him dead inside, surrounded by stuff piled "floor to ceiling," as the fire marshal put it: books, cereal boxes, knickknacks. That April the body of Alice Klee, sixty-eight, who had been missing for two months, was found in her home in New Milford, New Jersey, under a pile of clothing, blankets, and trash in her bedroom. Her landlord had just received permission from a court to clear out Klee's apartment because she was months behind in her rent. "Her body was mummified, and the smell was masked by the stench of garbage and unattended cats," the town police chief told a local online news site.

These extremes threaten to hide a key aspect of hoarding. Just as one can have compulsions that fall well short of an OCD diagnosis, so the feelings that drive hoarding are present in most of us, particularly our penchant for imbuing certain objects with meaning beyond their objective, intrinsic worth. Dershowitz explained his compulsion to collect Judaica—a Seder plate that the Nazis had confiscated, a Torah frontispiece with Chinese lettering, and more from around the world—this way: "I bought as much as I could just to try to rescue them. Every piece is significant to me."* If you think you're immune to that, dig through your cardboard boxes or filing cabinets or other places where you keep "valuables," and make a pile of things to toss:

---

*The *New York Times* described the impending auction of Dershowitz's trove on Feb. 19, 2016.

your college diploma (the school has a record), one of your wedding invitations, your child's report cards, the book of matches from the restaurant where you had your first date with your spouse (guilty!), the photograph of your parents' wedding, your sports trophies or your child's, the Moses basket that your firstborn slept in (also guilty). If we stopped feeling these attachments, surely a facet of our humanity would be missing. Understanding the extreme form of that—hoarding—can shed light on the version that marks us all.

Hoardings Past

For a fairly prevalent behavior, and one that had drawn the attention of writers from Dante to Gogol, hoarding essentially flew under the radar of psychology and psychiatry until the 1990s. There was the occasional case report, though far fewer than make the news today. "Psychiatry had little interest in hoarding until about a generation ago," psychologist Randy Frost told me when we met at the International OCD Foundation annual meeting in 2013. "It may have to do with the fact that if something falls outside the *DSM* categories, lots of mental health professionals, even if they see the behavior, don't conceptualize it as a problem. Instead, they conceptualize it as laziness or sloppiness, and say 'just stop.'" The term "compulsive hoarding" was first used in a 1966 paper that described a single odd case report, with the adjective serving to differentiate normal saving and collecting from the pathological kind.

Psychiatry's, and society's, blind spot to compulsive hoarding as a mental disorder was pretty much the state of play in 1990 when Frost was teaching a twelve-student seminar at Smith College on OCD. One day a student asked about hoarding. "Her mother used to tell her, 'clean up your room or you'll wind up like the Collyer brothers,'" Frost said.

Among New Yorkers who grew up in the mid-twentieth century,

the Collyer brothers were as well-known as any mayor or president, thanks to a call that New York City police officers responded to on the morning of March 21, 1947. There was "a dead body in the Collyer mansion," said the caller. Several officers were dispatched to the home at the northwest corner of Fifth Avenue and 128th Street, where Homer Collyer, a lawyer, and his younger brother Langley, an engineer, lived. When the police arrived at the twelve-room, three-story brownstone, piles of newspaper nearly as dense as bricks prevented them from opening the basement door and mountains of junk blocked the front door and even upper-floor windows. A patrolman finally squeezed through a second-floor window, and he found . . . goat paths. They wound through piles of old stoves, books, boxes, bicycles, magazines, papers, potato peelers, the top of a horse-drawn carriage, countless umbrellas, car parts, an early X-ray machine, fourteen pianos, antique buggies, the chassis of a Model T and other detritus that eventually came to more than a hundred tons of possessions, piled from wall to wall and nearly floor to ceiling in every room, basement, and attic.

Wary of intruders, the brothers had rigged booby traps of debris, one of which had apparently triggered accidentally some days before the policemen's arrival. After two hours of burrowing through stuff, an officer found the body of the blind, bedridden Homer, sixty-five, first; he had apparently starved to death. Workmen spent eighteen days throwing junk out of windows. On April 8 they found Langley's body entombed in a junk avalanche. Hoarding had engulfed the brothers and seemed to swallow them whole, taking them from privileged childhoods in a distinguished New York family (their father was a doctor) and successful professional lives to an existence marked by unpaid taxes, mortgage foreclosures, utility shut-offs, and other signs of dysfunctional lives. The house was razed later that year.

When his student first brought up this story, Frost knew nothing about hoarding as a mental disorder. "It's a fringe symptom, and there are only a couple of case reports about a paragraph long in the literature," he told her. "But," he recalled when we spoke, "I suggested she put a notice in the local newspaper asking for people who had a clutter problem. She did, and we got about a hundred responses." These volunteers formed the core of his first study. "In interviewing these folks I found them so fascinating it just captivated me and it has ever since," he said.

A Classification Conundrum

That launched Frost on an odyssey that made him a rock star in the world of hoarding. He coauthored the first systematic study in 1993 (other scientific papers had been just case histories of individual hoarders). Titled *The Hoarding of Possessions*, it defined the behavior as "the acquisition of, and failure to discard, possessions which appear to be useless or of limited value."

Before 1996, fewer than ten scientific studies of hoarding had been published. The lack of interest was reflected in how psychiatry classified hoarding. "It was formally listed under obsessive-compulsive personality disorder, but clinicians were told that if it was a severe case you were supposed to consider a diagnosis of obsessive-compulsive disorder," said psychiatrist Sanjaya Saxena of the University of California, San Diego.

The scientific basis for that was tenuous, based largely on a partial overlap between hoarding and OCD. About 10 percent to 30 percent of people with OCD also hoard, studies found, while between 12 percent and 20 percent of people with hoarding disorder also have OCD. But people with OCD are less likely to hoard than they are to suffer from major depression, generalized anxiety, social phobia, or attention deficit hyperactivity disorder. Hoarding is only the fourth most frequent symptom of OCD (right before compulsive praying and other forms of scrupulosity), and is much less common than compulsions to wash or check. Psychiatrists knew that "neither obsessive-compulsive disorder nor obsessive-compulsive personality disorder dealt with hoarding very well," said UCSD's Saxena.

Most problematic, a hoarder's thoughts about discarding or keeping do not feel alien or intrusive, the way the thoughts of people with OCD do. (Remember how Shala Nicely knew with part of her brain that Fred was *not* in the refrigerator.) Instead, a hoarder's attachment to possessions, and the deep distress at the prospect of tossing it, feel indistinguishable from a normal stream of consciousness. To a hoarder, thoughts about stuff—keeping it, protecting it, deriving comfort from it—*are* her stream of consciousness. And, crucially, those thoughts are far from distressing, as the thoughts that drive OCD are (the stove is on, the toilet seat is contaminated). To the contrary. A hoarder like Bonnie derives comfort from seeing her possessions, from thinking about them, from knowing she has them. It is the prospect that she will be forced to throw out belongings, or the practical difficulties of living in such clutter, that causes distress.

Nevertheless, there was some logic to including hoarding as a form of OCD. The fear of parting with possessions that are personally meaningful (ancient newspaper clippings that remind you of the dreams you dreamed as a young newlywed) or possibly valuable (someone can use these boxes!) is similar to an OCD obsession, while the compulsive keeping seemed like an OCD compulsion. The *DSM-III-R*, published in 1987, therefore included hoarding in the symptom checklist for obsessive-compulsive personality disorder, and the *DSM-IV-TR* in 2000 advised that "a diagnosis of obsessive-compulsive disorder should be considered especially when hoarding is extreme."

Unfortunately for a profession that prides itself on its scientific underpinnings, when psychiatrists assembling the *DSM-5* wrestled with how to classify hoarding, they found "remarkably little empirical evidence to support the inclusion of hoarding as one of the OCPD criteria," they wrote in a paper describing their work. Listing hoarding with OCD also had problems: when people with OCD hoard, their piles are organized and their stacks are neat, aligned, and quite likely sorted by size, color, or other principle. They are more likely to hoard odd items, imbuing them with a magical quality much like avoiding sidewalk cracks. OCD hoarders may also feel compelled to carry out rituals related to their hoard, such as checking it or counting it. None of that describes true hoarders. The nail in the coffin of hoarding-as-OCD was neuroimaging. "Lo and behold, hoarders didn't have any overlap with other OCD patients in their brain imaging," Saxena said. "There are more differences than similarities."

The *DSM-5* booted hoarding out of OCD and OCPD. "Hoarding disorder" became its own stand-alone mental illness, not a symptom of either. Hoarding had arrived.

Personality

Two decades of research since Frost's seminal 1993 study confirmed the basic profile of hoarders that he introduced:

• They start to show a compulsion to hoard in childhood or adolescence. Hoarding allows them to feel prepared for every eventuality; maybe Bonnie would get a chance to redecorate her home (miracles do happen), in which case she would have her decorating magazines at hand. Hoarders tend to buy extras because they feel intense anxiety at the thought of being caught without something they need. That makes them carry more "just-in-case" items in their bags, pockets, and cars. Between 60 percent and 80 percent of hoarders also shop or otherwise acquire to excess. They keep nine broken old space heaters in case their tenth breaks and can be repaired with a working part from one through nine. They keep umpteen old pairs of unwearable jeans to have denim for patching their "good" pair. They experience a deep sense of comfort from knowing they will never, never be without something they need.

• They struggle to make decisions and are generally worse than nonhoarders at multiple-choice situations, such as ordering from a menu or picking which movie to see at the multiplex. "They have trouble picking from conflicting options," Saxena told me. That leaves them unable to choose between this watering can and those seventeen others, unable to decide which of forty-three toothbrushes they've hoarded from hotel giveaways they really need and which can be donated to the next charity drive, and unable to sort chin-high piles into "keep," "donate," and "toss." Decision-making is one of the brain's executive functions, which also include categorizing, sustaining attention on a task such as decluttering, or engaging in complex thinking such as sorting possessions into those that are truly valuable and those that fall short. "We think the difficulty making decisions is tied up with problems processing information," Frost told me. "It's way too inefficient: areas of the brain that are highly activated in hoarders are those where decision-making occurs," suggesting there is a bewildering cacophony of activity in the decision-making circuitry.

• The very act of deciding triggers in the hoarder an anxiety as psychologically painful as touching public toilets is to someone with the contamination form of OCD. The anxiety is compounded by the fear of throwing away something he should keep. Keeping everything that enters their lives allows hoarders to avoid deciding whether or not to toss something. The result is a landscape of piles that stretch throughout the home, grocery store receipts mixed with car registrations, empty soda bottles with a college diploma, yellowing newspapers with a wedding ring, spanking-new boots with crushed mud-encrusted flats from 1987.

• Hoarders tend to be perfectionists, which hobbles their decision-making even further: absent confidence that they can make perfect decisions about what to keep and what to toss, hoarders make no decisions. They procrastinate and have difficulty organizing or completing tasks because "they're worried about making mistakes," Frost said. "One woman couldn't bring herself to clean her home because she was afraid she couldn't get it perfect."

• Hoarders often display an intense emotional attachment to every object that comes into their lives. By avoiding discarding, the hoarder avoids the emotional pain of parting with something that has great sentimental value and the anxiety and grief that would return every time he thought of the now-absent object. Far from keeping worthless things, as the 1994 *DSM-IV* described, hoarders keep the same sort of things the rest of us do. Just more. Lots more.

• Hoarders see utility where the rest of us see trash, and a universe of possibilities in every object, which makes discarding anything feel like wasting. Hoarders have such a deep abhorrence of wasting, Frost and his Boston University colleague Gail Steketee found, that even the possibility of discarding something they might use one day feels as sickening as if they had violated a religious prohibition. Many people whose behavior falls short of a *DSM* diagnosis also abhor wasting, of course (doggie bag, anyone?), and many of us know people—or are people—who feel a tinge of angst when they see "perfectly good" furniture at the curb waiting for the garbage truck. And many people who don't meet *DSM* criteria nevertheless engage in a little just-in-case keeping: you never know when you'll want to watch that DVD or read that old magazine. The difference is that hoarders keep it all. Just in case.

Hoarders do not have to use something to value it. Merely knowing it exists suffices. A scrap of paper with a mysterious phone number might represent a wonderful opportunity, as one hoarder told Frost; of course she can't throw it out. But neither does she call the number, instead keeping it as pure potential, an eternal possibility unsullied by mundane reality, let alone disappointment. Bonnie, after all, never took the vacations advertised in the brochures she hoarded, nor did she plunge into even a tiny home improvement project to make her house look a little like the beautiful ones in the magazines she hoarded. Reality disappoints; unrealized dreams do not.

Bob Hartzell exemplifies hoarders' off-the-charts ability to see potential. Take the sleeves from Starbucks coffee cups . . . as Bob did, so many over the years that he could form holiday wreaths with them, fitting one inside the other and bending them into shape. Or take the cardboard boxes that printer paper comes in. At his last job, at a pharmaceutical distribution company, employees were allowed to take them home, and Bob did . . . a few at first, then a couple dozen, until he had at least two hundred in his apartment in Ohio. He planned to store screws, tools, and odds and ends in them, but over time the boxes accumulated in piles that rose from floor to ceiling. "I'm afraid to throw any away because I might need them," he told me. "There's this fear that it's a nice useful box and I would be stupid to get rid of it."

Bob has a particular affinity for containers. Pill bottles fill one large dresser drawer. The kitchen table is covered with plastic storage containers, plastic jars, bottles, pieces of tinfoil, pots, pans, and plastic bag after plastic bag after plastic bag. As the containers built up, he felt a stronger and stronger "anxiety of avoidance," as he called it, meaning that if he thought about culling his hoard, as his rational mind told him he should, anxiety seemed to flood his every pore. "My big breakthrough was having only one kind of thing, like bottles, in a box, instead of having it filled with unlike things," he said.

The medicine bottles in their very own boxes, however, soon posed a different problem. One day he vowed to throw them out, but then a suffocating anxiety gripped him: *I might need them one day,* he thought. *It's such a waste.* It took all the strength he could summon to throw the bottles into the garbage. Not setting them aside for recycling was a major victory, an admission that, *You know, some things really are trash.* It made him sick to his stomach, and a wave of anxiety that felt like his very veins were constricting spread over him, but he saw it through, and on garbage pickup day the bottles left forever. Unfortunately, Bob's eyes immediately landed on the now-empty box, labeled BOTTLES, at the top of a tall pile. It seemed so forlorn, so wasted, as bereft as a mother whose children had been wrested from her. He started saving bottles again. "It just sneaks up on you," he said wearily.

As we spoke, Bob walked through the home he shares with his wife, peering at labels, reaching up to peek inside boxes, bending down to read the labels on those at the bottom of a pile: "These are filled with papers and magazines and old newspapers . . . oh my god! These boxes here must be ten years old, and they're not labeled. I don't know what's in them." There were piles of old furniture, window shades, wooden shutters, cardboard boxes, broken chairs, computer boxes, a plastic hose, tennis racket, popcorn tin, throw rug, cat litter box, shelving, flowerpots. Bob is befuddled that things got to this point, and feels as if he is stuck in some bizarre chess nightmare: "It's like pieces are coming onto the board constantly, and I'm powerless to stop them or get rid of them."

A tendency to sentimentalize objects? Anxiety about discarding something that might be useful? Trouble making decisions? Yes, yes, and yes; Bob has the key psychological traits that compel hoarding. When I asked how he got this way, Bob fumbled a bit before zeroing in on his childhood in the 1950s and 1960s, when boys were discouraged from showing their feelings. Sadness, disappointment, frustration, and loneliness were to be kept under wraps. "If you said you felt bad, adults would say, don't feel that way," he recalled. "Or they'd ridicule you. I learned to keep my feelings to myself. It became a habit; just answer, 'I'm doing fine.' I think that's why I became attached to things instead of people: they don't judge you, and they don't ask anything of you."

Lest you think that hoarding has ruined Bob's life, think again. He has a well-paying job and his wife is a pianist and staff member at a prestigious university. Although he'd just as soon be able to let go of objects, retaining them is less painful, even therapeutic.

* * *

Whether the ultimate explanation for hoarding is difficulty in making decisions, imbuing countless objects with sentimental meaning, not wanting to be wasteful, or some combination, in each case the proximate motivation for hoarding is avoiding the anxiety the hoarder would suffer if he discarded things. It is hardly uncommon to act as one does because acting otherwise is too painful. For people with social anxiety disorder, interacting with other human beings is torture, so they keep to themselves. Hoarders cannot part with their stuff because the mere thought of doing so causes an anxiety as deep and sharp and excruciating as cutting off a limb.

Apart from this trio of traits, hoarders come in every human variety under the sun. Some are social, some are socially isolated. (If the latter, it is often a consequence and not a cause of hoarding.) Some can't hold a job, some are professionally successful. Some build walls of stuff between themselves and others in order to keep the world out, while for others hoarding becomes a way to fill the holes that life has left and to find a sense of permanence in the permanence of their never-to-depart possessions. It becomes a way to slay the existential angst that comes with the knowledge that nothing lasts, everything goes.

What hoarding seldom brings is joy or pride, two feelings that distinguish hoarding from collecting. Hoarders may see every item as a treasure but they do not display their haul. At most, all the hoarder feels is secure that her stuff is still there.

Michele felt that. One evening at the International OCD Foundation's meeting in Atlanta, she told me that her hoarding began after she joined a quilting club in the 1970s and started making fiber art. At first the supplies fit on a table, but eventually they sprawled onto the floor. Then it was rubber stamps, and fabric. "I'm an artistic person," she said. "So the biggest bedroom in the house"—an 1,100-square-foot, three-bedroom bungalow that she and her husband bought in 1970— "is filled with my stuff. I have so many projects," she said with a sigh. "I have a fabric room and a crafts room, and a room with rubber-stamp-art supplies. I do know that my 'creative interests' are at the bottom of my compulsion. I enjoy sewing, did some knitting, crocheting, fabric painting, dyeing, batik, photography, calligraphy, and more. I was an art major, and appreciate beautiful things."

Her projects rarely reach fruition, however. Michele often hits the Salvation Army store for blue jeans just for the pockets, for instance; "I think blue-jeans pockets are so cute," she told me. "I can make things out of them." She paused. "But then I didn't have room to put my sewing machine out, so I couldn't make anything." What was in the way? I asked her. "Books! I love books," she said, her face lighting up. "In the living room I have magazines in boxes, and books in boxes, and articles I cut out but didn't get to yet. But it's a neat clutter," she assured me. "There are big pathways going through it all. It isn't *narrow* goat paths at all." Although two living room chairs are covered with stuff, "there is a wide area to walk in," she said.

All three bedroom closets are filled with her clothes. "I collect T-shirts from places," she explained. She also rents three storage units, all filled. Although Michele does not have a strong sentimental attachment to her stuff, as many hoarders do, she is clearly hostage to the "I might need it one day" syndrome and paralyzed by what seems like a Sisyphean task. "I started going through some stuff once," she said. "I put labels on all the boxes. But it took so much time. It was just overwhelming to even start. And so many catalogues come in, you know? I have to go through them before throwing them out but I just don't have time. But maybe I could start with the kitchen, then the living room . . . then I could bring stuff in from the garage and sort it . . ." Her voice trailed off.

Out with It

She at least has the right idea. Hoarders understand what it would take to change their situation. The trouble is, they typically want absolutely no part of it. They know intuitively why they hoard and the purposes it serves; remember, the feelings that underlie a compulsion to hoard are not ego-dystonic, or alien to a person's true thoughts and core being, as is the case with OCD thoughts. They essentially define the person. As a result, "most hoarders don't even seek treatment unless a spouse threatens to leave, a family member issues an ultimatum, or a landlord threatens eviction," Terrence Shulman, a therapist who founded the Shulman Center for Compulsive Theft, Spending, and Hoarding in Michigan, said of the hoarders who find their way to him. "It's not about the stuff per se. It's about the emotions underneath. The struggle to get to whether you can address that is so overwhelming it can be paralyzing, but if there were a flood or a fire and they lost everything, they'd feel an enormous sense of relief."

Although there is no therapeutic recipe for overcoming hoarding, a form of cognitive-behavior therapy has been shown effective, at least partially and for some hoarders, in numerous studies. The cognitive part involves teaching a client or patient about hoarding, with lessons in setting goals—modest at first, like getting rid of a single item before the next session, or passing up a potential acquisition—as well as training in organizing and decision-making. The approach has been codified in a program called Buried in Treasures, named for the eponymous 2007 book by Randy Frost and Gail Steketee. Over thirteen weekly, two-hour sessions, participants led by a trained facilitator (not necessarily a professional; the manual is available free online) ponder why they keep a particular piece of clutter (which they bring in), and discuss what prevents them from tossing out clutter. The hoarder practices sorting, usually starting small, such as with a kitchen counter. (It helps to get a feeling of accomplishment, and nothing says progress like being able to use your kitchen again.)

This approach has been tested since about 2007, with results sufficiently encouraging that researchers have now run proper trials. In a 2013 study led by Frost and Steketee, for instance, forty-six people with hoarding disorder were randomly assigned to either this cognitive-behavioral therapy or wait-listed* for it. The intervention consisted of twenty-five or more one-hour sessions plus home visits, spread over nine to twelve months. Through a hybrid of cognitive and behavioral therapy, psychologists first help the hoarder understand her motivations; many have poor if any insight into why they hoard. The therapist also tries to teach the hoarder different, healthier ways of thinking about objects, about herself, and about her memories, questioning whether parting with useless items would really be an abomination, whether donating a deceased husband's clothes would really negate their love, and the like. After three months, 43 percent

---

*Researchers often use waiting lists for their control groups because people who try to enroll in a Buried in Treasures workshop are thought to be similar to those who actually participate in their motivation, severity of hoarding, and other traits.

of those receiving treatment were "much" or "very much" improved, according to evaluations of their homes by clinicians, whereas none in the wait-listed group were. (Hoarding rarely resolves on its own.) After another twenty-six weeks of treatment, 71 percent of the hoarders had improved, the researchers reported in the journal *Depression and Anxiety*, and most held onto their gains: a year later, 62 percent were much or very much improved.

Nathan Blech tried this sort of cognitive-behavior therapy, or at least an informal version of it, on his Meetup group as well as himself. When he invited me to see his Brooklyn apartment, the photographs he showed me beforehand made me wonder how I would even fit through the door. But that was "before." It was a time when Nathan kept hundreds of pounds of papers, including his grandfather's Holocaust memoir, written in pencil, for a family history project he felt compelled to take on (or else his family, many of whom had been killed by the Nazis, would be eliminated once again), and which spawned thousands of additional pages of notes, translations, and related family projects. It was a time when he kept six or twelve or sixty of nearly everything, from T-shirts to toothbrushes, so he would never run out. This was "after." Nathan had co-launched a Meetup group for hoarders, gathering twice a week in a Manhattan skyscraper, preaching what he practiced: over the course of several months he had weaned himself from accumulating (though it nearly killed him to say *no* to the deli worker's offer of six free hummus trays) and, item by item, culled his clutter.

Since much of it was paper, Nathan vowed to rid his apartment of more than a decade's worth of tax documents (not just the returns; the records, too) by buying a shredder. For days it sat in his apartment like a demon threatening to devour his identity. Everyone who has overcome hoarding has his own epiphanic insight, and Nathan's was this: if he could shred just one page of one return, the collection would be imperfect, like a "complete" Shakespeare without *Hamlet*. "Now the whole thing was incomplete," Nathan explained, "and that made it easier for me to shred the next page of the return, and then the supporting documents, and once I did 1997 it became easier to do 1993, and on and on." As he showed me around the kitchen, bedroom, and living room, Nathan was embarrassed that he still had multiple paper and plastic bags, dozens of folders of historical papers and research (neatly arranged on shelves in an enormous wall unit), and dozens of T-shirts (stored in built-in drawers). But when I pointed out that he had essentially eliminated the clutter shown in the photographs, and that the stuff he had left was nothing unusual, he beamed.

The Roots of Hoarding

The trigger for compulsive hoarding can be something chronic, such as Bonnie's deep melancholy over how her dreams had turned to yellowing newspaper articles. Or it can be an acute trauma, such as when losing a spouse or child causes survivors to keep everything that comes into their possession so that they, unlike the cruel universe, are not guilty of throwing away something precious. Indeed, one study done for the *DSM-5* found that many hoarders report their problem began when their spouse died or their children left home. People get snatched from us; damned if we let our stuff be taken, too.

Frost finds that about half of hoarders recall a stressful event around the time they began accumulating and keeping. These are people like Patty, who answered an ad I posted on Craigslist seeking hoarders. When she moved out of her parents' home after graduating from college, she told me, she piled her stuff into the old used car she had bought: the usual clothing, books, and electronics but also photocopies of virtually every letter she had written (many to her parents when she was away at college) in order to have a record of her life. One night the car was stolen; she never saw her stuff again. A few years later, she forgot to pay the monthly bill on a storage unit she had rented, and the contents—more clothes, records, furniture, tchotchkes, clocks, papers, lamps—were sold off. After that, Patty said, "I began to like to keep stuff, and to surround myself with stuff." It gave her a sense of security; if she could see it, she could be sure it wasn't going anywhere.

For people whose hoarding is sparked by a sudden loss of people or things, the behavior generally begins later than for people who do not recall such a trauma. In contrast, in people whose compulsion to hoard develops slowly over time, its origins often trace back to childhood. There's something in human nature—atavistic memories of scarcity? an innate drive to possess?—that leads most children to collect something, from dead beetles to expensive dolls or action figures. By age six, nearly 70 percent do so. Even if a child's urge to collect threatened to turn into full-blown hoarding, it would be tough to reach the extremes of goat paths: children are neither free agents nor armed with credit cards. Parents generally limit any tendency to collect, let alone hoard, through the age-old demand to *clean up your room*—and to get in there with garbage bags if necessary. Moms rifle through children's book bags in search of "forgotten" homework assignments and, while they're at it, toss old papers and junk, perhaps not suspecting their child regards them as treasures. (*Mom, where's my dead moth?!*)

Still, the first glimmerings of hoarding often emerge in childhood, around ages eight to ten. Just as adults who hoard often have difficulty with such higher-order cognitive processes as judgment and decision-making, so children who have poor executive function—a catch-all term that includes organizing, planning, and paying attention—are more likely to have hoarding tendencies. When you have trouble organizing you can't easily tell what you need, or what's extraneous or excessive. You can't find a book or a pen, so you acquire more.

Asked in one study when they began to hoard, elderly compulsive hoarders reported an average age of onset of 29.5. When the researchers asked more probing questions, taking the hoarders over the events of their childhood and adolescence, however, they recalled hoarding problems, or at least hoarding tendencies, at these younger ages. They had the same feelings of needing to acquire and keep, or being anxious or heartbroken about discarding, as they did in later life, but as kids they weren't able to act on them. That fits with other studies that ask hoarders to think back to when they first began to acquire excessive amounts of stuff: the average is about twelve, with 80 percent saying symptoms of hoarding had set in before age eighteen. (A 2010 study bracketed the age of onset as from eleven to fifteen.) The teen years, of course, are when people demand more autonomy over their actions as well as their own space. It is also when they develop financial autonomy through an allowance, after-school jobs, and other sources of spending money. Since hoarding can look a lot like the messiness and sloppiness that seems as inevitable a rite of passage as acne, families and even the teen seldom identify the behavior as hoarding, much less as a sign of a mental disorder.

Adult hoarders are more likely to have grown up in a hoarding family, researchers at Boston University told the OCD meeting, confirming other studies: 50 percent to 80 percent of hoarders have at least one close relative whom they considered a pack rat if not an outright hoarder. That sounds high, so it's important to know that, like any behavior with some degree of heritability, it is not inevitably passed down to the next generation. The Johns Hopkins OCD Family Study, which ran from 1996 to 2001 and evaluated just over eight hundred people with OCD, found that only 12 percent of the first-degree relatives of hoarders also hoarded: in a family with eight children of a hoarding father, that works out to just one of the siblings growing up to also be a hoarder.

Exactly how heritable hoarding is remains an open question. In 2013, British scientists reported that genetic differences play a role in hoarding by males but not females. They had 3,974 identical and fraternal twins, all fifteen years old, fill out a self-report on hoarding.

The basic rationale of twin studies is that because identical twins have identical genes, and fraternal twins share only half of their variable genes, comparing how alike the two kinds of twins are should offer clues about the size of the genetic contribution. If identical twins are more alike, that suggests a stronger role for inherited genes. The prevalence of hoarding symptoms in the twins was 2.6 percent of girls and 1.2 percent of boys, the scientists reported in PLOS One. But while more identical boy pairs than fraternal boy pairs were both hoarders (genes accounted for 32 percent of the variance in hoarding), there was no difference in the likelihood of hoarding between the two kinds of girl twins (the genetic input was a paltry 2 percent). In both sexes, the environment played a vastly greater role in the likelihood of hoarding.

Even if DNA does play a role, you can be sure there is no hoarding gene. The behavior is too complicated for that. More likely the genetic involvement works through numerous genes that shape brain circuitry involved in executive function, perhaps decision-making. The other way hoarding can run in families, of course, is if children model themselves after a hoarding parent or grandparent—not necessarily consciously, but by observing a way of life and concluding that it is perfectly acceptable. What is clear is that once hoarding sets in it is difficult to shake: the Boston University researchers reported that hoarding went away on its own in only one-seventh of teens.

For many people, being asked about their earliest memory of something brings a long pause, as they try to dredge up a remembrance of things past, but Grace didn't hesitate. "It's of playing on the floor with my sister, and these big, black plastic trash bags filled with things, and we'd lie on top of them," she told me. "I was four or five." Piled from the floor to about the height of an adult's hip, the bags held clothing and mail, broken electronics, newspapers and magazines—the stuff of her hoarding parents, whose idea of cleaning their three-bedroom home in Philadelphia was to cram things into those bags. "They were piled into walls so high we couldn't see over them," Grace said.

The front door opened into the living room, beyond which was the kitchen. Getting to any of them required walking carefully along the plastic runners that marked the paths between piles—bags and bags piled nearly to the ceiling, abandoned home improvement projects like shelving and cabinets shoved against walls, sofa and chairs swallowed by mounds of mail and papers and cardboard and plastic containers. "There was a path to everything," Grace said, "to the basement, which was also filled from floor to ceiling, to the washing machine in the room behind the kitchen, to the couch, to the kitchen," where the table had vanished years before under a mountain of plastic utensils and paper plates and unidentifiable containers. Gravity often had its way, and Grace and her sister became accustomed to hearing the "crunching and breaking of miscellaneous junk under our feet as we walked through the house." The family hid when the doorbell rang unexpectedly, and on the rare occasions when someone was expected her parents frantically stuffed mail and clothing into the ubiquitous black plastic bags and hurled them into the basement or the garage, desperately trying to make at least the living room seem merely messy.

The routines the family adopted to keep the world from knowing how they lived finally failed them one day, when a friend needed a place to wait for her parents to pick her up after a school trip. "My sister and I took the longest walk up the porch steps that day," Grace remembered. She tried to prevent the inevitable, cheerfully saying what a shame it would be to go inside on such a lovely day, but the friend was tired and wanted to sit down. "You could have picked her jaw up off the floor," Grace said. "We tried to distract her with a TV program but she could only focus on the mounds of trash around her."

Soon after, Grace's family moved to another house, a fixer-upper in a tough neighborhood (her parents had begun struggling financially). It seemed like a golden opportunity to cull the clutter and toss out much of the stuff. With her parents talking about a "clean slate," Grace envisioned mounds and mounds of black plastic garbage bags lined up at the curb the way other little girls imagine a trip to Disneyland. But it was not to be. The bags all came, collected in a mad rush on the day they needed to vacate the premises, without so much as being opened. So did drawers filled with trash; her father stuffed them into the moving truck as-is. So did years and years of mail. Grace's father insisted that everything was useful (or might be one day) and her mother was helpless in the face of decisions about what to keep and what to toss. "They just couldn't do it," Grace told me. Their stuff seemed as eternally bound to them as the ancient Mariner's accursed bird.

Grace, who graduated with a degree in psychology in 2012, was back home when I spoke to her. Like many millennials, her job (helping children with developmental disabilities) makes living on her own a nonstarter, financially. She and her sister have managed to carve out non-hoarding zones not only in their own bedrooms but also in the living room and kitchen. As soon as even two days of mail threatens to take up residency, they're brutal about sorting and tossing. They hope to move out eventually, though they have no doubt that once they do their parents will likely meet the same fate as the Collyer brothers.

Collectors

Scientists who study hoarders insist there is a vast gulf between people like Grace's parents, who meet the criteria for a mental disorder, and collectors. For one thing, collectors categorize their treasures, which belong to a specific, selective, well-defined category: matchbooks, yes; magazines, no; model trains, yes; clothing, no. Collecting is structured, planned, and selective. Hoarders acquire random stuff of all kinds. Collectors proudly display their trophies, be they baby spoons, orchids, unopened action figures, Morgan silver dollars, Broadway memorabilia, presidential campaign buttons, first editions, antique golf clubs, fifteenth-century maps, perfume bottles, Barbies, Hot Wheels cars, Madame Alexander dolls, vintage hats, telescopes, geodes, or fossil trilobites. Hoarders toss their possessions anywhere, often forgetting what's in the growing piles. Items in a collection are usually retired from normal use; a swizzle-stick collector would no more dunk one in an Old Fashioned than the Metropolitan Museum of Art would use its Chippendale chairs for a casual lunch. If hoarders don't use their stuff, it's because it's useless or unfindable. And collectors do not have the distress and impairment that many hoarders do.

Yet, like so many behaviors, collecting and hoarding have so much in common, especially the emotions motivating them, that drawing a sharp line between "charmingly eccentric" and "mental disorder" is a challenge. "Certain features are the same in hoarding and collecting," Randy Frost told me. "In both, there are attachments to possessions, which is something all of us have."

What drives collectors? For some, it's a desire to make sense of "the mess of the world," as well as to focus intensely on one small corner of that mess and know it in minute detail, wrote Michael Shanks, a professor of classical archaeology at Stanford University who explored collecting in his 2012 book *The Archaeological Imagination*. For others, it's a way of demarcating the self, of saying, *Here, this is part of who I am*. The person who has a collection of baseball cards or action figures, rocks or dolls or snow globes or (in two unusual cases Shanks discussed) items related to hands (gloves and glove-makers' forms, doll arms and ship prows and sculptures) or to the *Wizard of Oz* (books, costumes, and memorabilia)—such a person has imposed order on the world and planted a flag in a tiny part of it, defining himself in a unique way.

Collectors define themselves by their trove just as others use the iPhone they carry, the Galaxy tablet they use, the Restoration Hardware furniture they sit on to define themselves. Jon Cruz, who participated in the 2014 Collector's Night at the Brooklyn Historical Society, does that by amassing presidential campaign memorabilia, centered on the hundreds of pins from every candidate (primaries and general elections) since 1894 and including flourishes like an 1880 bandanna adorned with the likenesses of James Garfield and Chester Arthur. A teacher of government at a Bronx high school, Cruz told a reporter that he had been drawn to politics since he was eight, in 1984, and was "trying to talk to adults about NAFTA."

Collectors actively and even ostentatiously display the material objects that express their identity, values, taste, erudition, or other quality they take pride in. Kyle Supley, who also took his collection to the Brooklyn show, was so smitten with the clocks shown in the opening credits of the 1985 classic *Back to the Future* that at age eight he began methodically amassing every last one of them and is now up to two hundred—cuckoo clocks and Walt Disney clocks, cat clocks and Art Deco clocks and more. (Catch his YouTube video "Kyle at Age 12: Clock Collector.") "I think collectors are a little on the edge of being hoarders," he told the *New York Times*. "Given the chance, we would fill homes. So it has to be tastefully displayed." True hoarders, however, virtually never invite anyone to see their stuff, let alone display it, doing everything they can to keep the world out. How "everything"? When Will, a family friend, tried to enter the home where he grew up in suburban New York, where his sister still lived and hoarded, she wouldn't open the door; when he climbed in a ground-floor window she called the cops.

To help psychiatrists correctly classify hoarding for the *DSM-5,* scientists ran field tests to assess whether various diagnostic criteria accurately identified people with the disorder but did not mistakenly diagnose those without it. "You don't want to label as hoarding something that's a pleasurable activity like collecting," Columbia University psychiatrist Carolyn Rodriguez said when I visited her at the school's massive building atop Washington Heights in northern Manhattan one summer morning. "In England, something like 20 percent of people are collectors."

The participants in the field test included twenty-nine self-identified hoarders and twenty people who called themselves collectors (of, among other things, comics, coins, stamps, glass elephants, vintage wireless radios, toy soldiers, and model submarines). Questionnaires asked participants whether they had difficulty discarding things and how much clutter they lived with, including whether the clutter was sufficient to totally impede the use of key living spaces; whether the clutter or the idea of discarding caused "distress and impairment" (a near-universal criterion for diagnosing a mental illness, according to a key tenet of American and British psychiatry); whether these symptoms caused them "to avoid doing anything, going anyplace, or being with anyone."

None of the twenty collectors qualified as hoarders, researchers at the Institute of Psychiatry in London reported in 2012 in the journal *Comprehensive Psychiatry*, even though 90 percent admitted to difficulties discarding and 85 percent to distress at the idea of discarding. The only reasons they didn't qualify as hoarders is that their collections did not cause clutter or problems such as blocking access to some areas of the home, and certainly did not cause distress. A wonderful collection brings pride and joy. Hoarders, in contrast, say their stuff causes practical difficulties and, often, distress.

*   *   *

As with every compulsion, the line between pathology and eccentricity is far from clear. Hoarding experts insist that pathological hoarding is easily distinguished from collecting, primarily by the presence in the former of "distress and dysfunction," such as keeping hoarders from using the rooms and furniture in their homes normally. Without those, there is no mental illness. And Frost argues that "the nature of the attachment to their things is different in collectors and hoarders. People who hoard get extreme, rigid, inflexible attachments to things, and lots of them."

Frost, working with Steketee and clinical psychologist David

Tolin, systematized the distress and dysfunction criteria by developing a questionnaire to diagnose hoarding disorder. They were guided by the basic definition of hoarding as acquiring and failing to discard a large number of possessions that have little to no use or value (to an objective observer) with the result that living spaces are too cluttered to be used as intended and resulting in clinically significant *distress* or *impairment* (a.k.a. dysfunction) in social, academic, or occupational functioning. Each item is to be answered from zero (no difficulty or not at all) to eight (extremely difficult, or extreme difficulty), with numbers in between indicating mild, moderate, or severe:

1. Because of the clutter or number of possessions, how difficult is it for you to use the rooms in your home?
2. To what extent do you have difficulty discarding (or recycling, selling, giving away) ordinary things that other people would get rid of?
3. To what extent do you currently have a problem with collecting free things or buying more things than you need or can use or can afford?
4. To what extent do you experience emotional distress because of clutter, difficulty discarding, or problems with buying or acquiring things?
5. To what extent do you experience impairment in your life (daily routine, job/school, social activities, family activities, financial difficulties) because of clutter, difficulty discarding, or problems with buying or acquiring things?

The "distress and dysfunction" criteria in questions 4 and 5 present an obvious problem, one that has stirred controversy in other areas of psychiatry: namely, two people might have identical behaviors and symptoms of mental illness, but if those behaviors and feelings bother only one of them then he, and not the other (no distress or dysfunction), is mentally ill. For instance, someone could be just as depressed as another person, but if she finds this a perfectly acceptable way to feel and live ("if you're not depressed you don't understand what's going on in the world") then she isn't mentally ill. With hoarding, there's a risk of classifying one person as mentally ill but another, who accumulates just as much stuff and is just as attached to it, as not, because the second person has multiple houses to absorb her belongings and therefore suffers no dysfunction. Only in psychiatry do you find such situational definitions; high blood pressure is high blood pressure no matter whether it bothers you or not. Underlining the confusion within psychiatry, a leading expert on hoarding, writing in the *New England Journal of Medicine* in 2014, claimed that hoarders "may not necessarily report distress."

The "distress" criterion raises another problem. Is it possible that engaging in something that is both socially sanctioned and extremely common, such as collecting, does not cause distress precisely because of those attributes, whereas a behavior that psychiatrists deem a mental disorder and that society ridicules (see: *Hoarding: Buried Alive*) is practically bound to do so? Few hoarders who wind up seen by elder service caseworkers agree they're behaving irrationally, let alone that they have a mental disorder. "Most hoarders will tell you they never thought of it as a disease," Sanjaya Saxena told me—until family members or authorities told them it was and that they couldn't live that way. *That* caused distress, and presto: a behavior that had fallen short of a key criterion for mental illness now met enough criteria for an official diagnosis.

Mental illness falls along the great continuum of human variation; the question is where. Listen to hoarders like Bonnie and Bob and the others who let me into their lives, and you hear the reasons they give for keeping stuff, and the sorrow they feel when asked to discard it, that are strikingly similar to those of everyone else who feels attached to their college physics textbook (*that class changed my life*), their mother's wedding ring, their child's christening gown. The only difference is that the latter feel this attachment to only selected things. Hoarders' hearts embrace multitudes.

Bonnie Grabowski, with whose story I began this chapter, epitomizes the hoarder whose inability to part with stuff results from the deep sentimental attachment she feels to it, whether because it is all she has left of her husband and her dreams, or because it ties her to an earlier time in her life, when her children were young, when it felt like there was still a chance and time enough for the then-unhappiness to give way to something better. One of Frost's clients was unable to throw out anything that connected her to her past. As he was helping her declutter one day, she found an old ATM envelope in the pile of junk on her couch. With his encouragement, she managed the immense accomplishment (for a hoarder) of dropping it into the recycling box—and immediately began to cry. It felt like she was "losing that day of her life," Frost recalls her explaining. If she threw out too much, she said, there would be "nothing left of me."

Because many hoarders see sentimental value everywhere, the old *DSM*'s description of hoarding as "the inability to discard worn-out or worthless objects *even when they have no sentimental value*" (my italics) was off-base. To a hoarder, the most worthless-seeming junk can have immense sentimental value; every scrap and ort is a piece of their lives, and yanking one out threatens to make the rest fall apart. We all feel something like that, if not for an ATM receipt then for the Playbill from the show at which we shook hands with Adlai Stevenson (my parents) or the baseball scorecard from the last game a now-deceased parent took us to (my cousin) or the dress we wore on the first date we had with a now spouse (singer-turned-fashion-designer Victoria Beckham, who in 2014 told the British magazine *Stylist* that she has never parted with the suede minidress she wore in 1997 when she first went out with soccer great David Beckham, whom she married in 1999). The difference between that and hoarding is one of degree, not kind. Frost calls it a "special ability to see uniqueness and value where others don't." If you followed the old editions of the *DSM* to the letter, Bonnie and millions like her would not be classified as hoarders; the possessions in the floor-to-ceiling piles have deep sentimental value.

The tendency of many hoarders to imbue their acquisitions with deep emotional significance lies at the extreme of a continuum where we all find ourselves. In a bud vase on my étagère is a desiccated flower from my mother's funeral. Beside it are half a dozen pieces of confetti from the millennial New Year's Eve in Times Square: I had to work on January 1, 2000, and as I walked along the morning-empty streets from Grand Central Terminal to the *Newsweek* office at Columbus Circle, I picked them up, thinking, *In fifty years it will be so cool to touch these and know they fell from the most famous New Year's Eve site on the most notable New Year's Eve in modern history.* In my son Daniel's room are photographs of him with his soccer teams, the cheap trophies he got for Little League, the yellowing "Way to Go!" certificates from Miss Mango for "excellent behavior" in first grade. (I hasten to add that Daniel's room is neat as a pin now that he lives on the other side of the country, but these mementos are still there.) Are these signs of a mental disorder?

Although I mercilessly cull old clothing, papers, and even books (donating them to the local library), I keep these things, and a few others, because they connect me to people and times I will never see again. They are little tiles in the mosaic of personal identity. Our stuff expands that identity, deepens the meaning of our lives, provides security, and attaches us to our own past as well as to a world beyond ourselves.

CHAPTER NINE

Compulsive Acquiring, or I'll Take Two

> *The human animal is a beast that dies, and if he's got money he buys and buys and buys and I think the reason he buys everything he can buy is that in the back of his mind he has the crazy hope that one of his purchases will be life everlasting!*
>
> —Big Daddy, in *Cat on a Hot Tin Roof*

THERE IS no hoarding without acquiring, and in twenty-first-century America acquiring has become the national pastime. At a December 2006 news conference, President George W. Bush cast it as Americans' patriotic duty: "I encourage you all to go shopping more." For many of us, shopping, at least beyond what's needed to provide the necessities of life, can be an exciting, joyful, care-free indulgence, a splurge and a treat, a reward for a job well done or compensation meant to tip the balance of fair and unfair, just and un-just (*My boss lit into me at today's meeting; I deserve a new pair of sandals*). Like virtually every behavior people engage in to an extreme, excessive acquiring—shopping, shoplifting, or picking up free stuff—can spring from any of the three forces described in the Introduction: impulses in which we are seized by an irresistible urge, a pleasure-seeking drive akin to an addiction, or a need to dispel an unbearable anxiety that builds and builds until it feels like it will crush us. We're interested in the last version, of excessive acquiring as a compulsive behavior that people engage in to quiet anxiety.

* * *

On Jenny's way to meet me on a spring afternoon in Manhattan, the universe spoke to her: peeking out of a bag balanced atop a garbage can in front of an Upper West Side brownstone was a beautiful comforter. The week before, Jenny had vowed to other members of Nathan Blech's Meetup hoarding group that she would resist bringing into her apartment anything that she didn't absolutely, positively need.

Need, of course, is subjective.

The comforter seemed to be in pristine condition, and as Jenny remembered her vow she felt as if an angel and a temptress were lobbing mortars at one another from her two shoulders. The angel beseeched her not to take something that would only add to clutter so horrendous that the only places Jenny could move in her apartment were along its goat paths, around the computer desk, and on her bed, which she managed to keep clear. The temptress whispered that "this is a once in a lifetime deal." Her rational mind knew this wasn't so, of course; Manhattan is full of perfectly usable discards, so this was hardly a rarity. In any case, she didn't need another comforter. She briefly considered walking away empty-handed, but a toxic blend of insecurity and anxiety filled her chest. "If the universe put it there," she remembered thinking, "I should take it."

An actress who took mostly bit parts separated by weeks and sometimes months of no parts at all, Jenny never made much money. When she was growing up, her family struggled financially. She was taught to eat everything on her plate; "waste not, want not," was the household mantra, she said. Now, when something went on sale, she bought it. Actually, not exactly "it." She regularly bought eight or ten cans of her favorite tuna, she told me. But wait, I said; lots of people do things like that; maybe you're not really so unusual, let alone a compulsive acquirer. Jenny took a deep breath. And told me about the washing machines.

The one in her apartment broke a few years ago, and Jenny couldn't afford to fix or replace it. But as she was walking along the sidewalk one day, contemplating a future of Laundromats, she saw a washing machine at the curb. It was the same make and model as hers. She paid a neighborhood kid to haul it to her fifth-floor walk-up, then dismantled both it and her broken one (Jenny has been mechanically handy for years: as a hoarder, she can't have repairmen in her apartment). What was wrong with one was fine with the other, and vice versa, she discovered. It was as if one was yin to the other's yang. She cannibalized the found machine to repair the broken one.

No wonder she rejects the idea that it's a symptom of mental pathology to pick up "junk" on the street. Walking the sidewalks of New York, she said, "I just *see* things. Something will be behind a hydrant, or behind a pile of garbage, and I'll just know instinctively that it's . . . interesting. People like me, we see the potential in things that others don't. I know a hamper is not a living, breathing thing. But it *deserves a chance*, you know?" Even toilets do. She found a quite usable one on the sidewalk and disassembled it, making several trips to lug home the pieces. It was just what she needed to repair the cracked commode in her apartment. "That just doesn't wash with me, therapists saying it's crazy to think some piece of junk will be useful," she said.

There is a dollar store near Jenny's apartment, and one recent afternoon she passed it by. At first. But then she thought, *Oh, there's no harm in checking out the new arrivals*. Seeing canine diapers, she told herself she had enough for her seventeen-year-old dog, but then her brain demanded: *Do you know where they are?* The only way to quiet the anxiety was to toss a package into her shopping cart. Then she noticed vinyl tablecloths, which she regularly cut up to make doggie mats. The universe spoke to her again: the shelf was piled with plaids, whose Mondrian-like geometry make them ideal for cutting, with the straight lines and right angles for her scissors to follow. Again the angel and the temptress argued, but every time the "don't buy it" angel seemed to be winning Jenny felt an anxiety so gripping she compared it to when a severe allergic reaction constricts your throat. "I'm talking to myself, trying to rationalize why I don't need more diapers or tablecloths, and the next thing I know the world goes black and I feel powerless," she told me. Stacks of tablecloths went home with her.

During summer pilgrimages to her mother's rural home, she discovered an acquirers' mecca: outlet malls. "I would get thousands of dollars' worth of stuff for just a few hundred dollars, and UPS it back to New York," she told me. "It was unbelievable. I would spend entire days shopping until I was exhausted. Clothes, housewares, home furnishings, kitchen stuff, canned food, dry stuff like cereal and candy."

Even now she doesn't regret it, or at least not all of it. "One year I shipped home twenty-five tubes of anchovy paste: they were $2.99 in New York but only a quarter there!" She paused. "I still have some of that anchovy paste. And that was ten years ago." The frugality impulse was so strong that when she tried to resist, the throat-closing anxiety felt like a signal from her unconscious telling her to give in. Compulsively shopping "is just comforting," she said. "It's like building a wall or a fortress like the ones I made in kindergarten. I don't want to be this way but I can't overcome the compulsion." As we said good-bye and Jenny picked up the plastic bag with her found comforter, she wanted to tell me one more thing. Whoever put it out had also piled sheets, blankets, and the like outside the brownstone. "I left as much as I took," she told me—proudly or defensively. It was hard to tell.

Oniomania

In a 2006 study of 2,513 U.S. adults, psychiatrists at Stanford University found that 5.8 percent exhibited compulsive buying behavior, based on a screening questionnaire called the Compulsive Buying Scale. Compulsive buyers tended to be younger, Lorrin Koran and his colleagues reported in the *American Journal of Psychiatry*, and despite age-old stereotypes men were as likely to shop compulsively as women. More recent surveys have found a similar prevalence: a 2008 study in the *Journal of Consumer Research* estimated that 9 percent of Americans are compulsive buyers.

Excessive buying exemplifies the dilemma I described earlier: what looks like the same behavior can be a manifestation of impulsivity, an addiction, or a compulsion. "The behavior can be the same, but different people arrive at it by very different avenues," Susanne Ahmari, a clinical psychiatrist and neuroscientist, said when I visited her at Columbia University (she later moved to the University of Pittsburgh). "One behavior may stem from anxiety and another seemingly identical behavior will come from depression or mania or even just boredom." For other people, said April Benson, a psychotherapist who has made her name studying and treating overshopping, "it's closer to an impulse-control disorder: they get an urge to have something and they can't stop themselves from acting on it."

That was how psychiatrists in the early twentieth century viewed compulsive buying. The first scholarly reference to compulsive shopping came in a 1902 medical book, *Obsessions and Compulsions*, co-authored by a neurologist in Bordeaux, who treated a man who had *manie des achats*—mad shopping. It caught on: German psychiatrist Emil Kraepelin, considered the founder of modern scientific psychiatry, wrote about "compulsive buying disorder" and "buying mania" in his influential textbooks. Swiss psychiatrist Paul Eugen Bleuler (1857–1939), who is best known for coining the terms schizophrenia and autism, discussed it in his 1930 textbook, called compulsive buying *oniomania* (from the Greek *onios*, meaning "for sale") and described it as a "reactive impulse" or "impulsive insanity" much like kleptomania. He cited Kraepelin's discussion of "oniomaniacs in whom even buying is compulsive and leads to senseless contraction of debts with continuous delay of payment until a catastrophe clears the situation a little."

After the brief mentions by Kraepelin and Bleuler, for most of the twentieth century psychiatry showed little interest in compulsive buying. The phenomenon didn't even make it into the 1987 *DSM,* though it merited a few lines in the 2004 edition as an "impulse-control disorder not otherwise specified." The *DSM-5* of 2013 booted it out again. Researchers who studied consumer behavior paid some attention to compulsive buying, but for psychologists and psychiatrists "it basically just disappeared from the textbooks until the 1990s," said Donald Black, a psychiatrist at the University of Iowa and one of the country's leading experts on the behavior. "It was like no one thought about it."

Beginning in the 1990s, however, psychiatrists and others began reporting case histories of people who felt compelled to hit the mall—twenty cases in one study, twenty-four in another, and forty-six in a third. And that was when researchers began to realize they were dealing with a phenomenology of several distinct ontologies.

For some excessive shoppers, the behavior is a consequence not of a spur-of-the-moment impulse, as per Kraepelin and Bleuler, but of a buildup of emotions: depression, anxiety, boredom, and anger were the most common, Black concluded from the scientific literature as well as his own patients. "Euphoria or relief from negative emotions were the most common consequence," he found. If the payoff is relief, it's a compulsion, as I'll discuss below; if the payoff is euphoria, the behavior resembles an intensely pleasurable addiction. In that case, "there's an anticipatory element—they think about it, the excitement builds, and then they make the purchase," said Black. "People have described feelings similar to withdrawal if they can't shop. They experience mild dysphoria, irritability, even jitteriness." Between one-fifth and one-half of people (depending on the study) who buy to excess also have a substance abuse disorder, suggesting that these are the ones who are most likely to have the addictive version of excessive shopping, feeling a mood-boosting hedonic hit from whipping out the credit card again and again and draping those lovely shopping bags over their arms. Without that regular hedonic hit, the overshopper is as bereft and down as a gambling addict without her fix, and so has to shop and shop and shop again to maintain the thrill and the (temporary) high.

Closely related to shopping as a quest for a hedonic hit is shopping as a form of self-medication for boredom or depression, in which acquiring one more pretty thing assuages those and other painful emotions: *I don't have a date for Thursday night, but I have an amazing new pair of stilettos.* Loneliness, anger, and feeling inadequate, rejected, frustrated, and hurt can all trigger a shopping binge. "Most of the people I treat say it distracts them from whatever pain or distress they feel," said Terrence Shulman. Although the loneliness, anger, or hurt almost never have anything to do with shopping, shopping "acts like a soothing agent," he said, especially for people who feel "I'm not enough unless I have enough." A 2013 poll commissioned by "The Huffington Post" found that 40 percent of women and 19 percent of men said they shop as a way to cope with stress.

When overshopping is a true compulsion, in contrast, it brings little more than temporary relief from anxiety. Just as hoarders derive little joy from their stuff, instead offering it up like a sacrifice to placate the gods of anxiety, so compulsive shoppers experience anxiety and distress until they acquire and only relief when they do. "There is a rising anxiety that can be relieved only by going out and buying," April Benson said. "You feel driven to do something you don't necessarily want to do." Between 40 percent and 80 percent have an additional anxiety disorder. That's where we find the true compulsive shopper like Jenny. She did not *impulsively* scrounge the discarded comforter or get a lifetime supply of anchovy paste, and she derived no great pleasure from her acquisitions. Instead, she listened long and hard to what her feelings were telling her, and what they were telling her was *You feel that? You feel your throat closing up and your heart racing? That's your unconscious telling you that if you don't take this you will keep feeling as if you are waiting for word of whether the person you love most in the world survived the crash of the plane he was on.*

"The anxiety that drives the compulsive shopper could be anxiety about anything," Benson said. "It could be a fear of 'missing out' on something, like what everyone else is wearing, or missing out on the July sale at Nordstrom." The anxiety often involves self-esteem or feelings of worthlessness. *If I'm able to bring home another bag of outfits from H&M, I can't really be poor, can I?* Or it can arise from the thought of *not* buying. One woman whom psychologist Randy Frost tried to help was watching a shopping channel one day when a group of puppets was featured, he recalled. When no one bid on them, the woman began to fret that the puppets' feelings would be hurt if they "thought" no one wanted them. She bought half a dozen to make them feel wanted and relieve her own anxiety about their sadness.

Someone who buys compulsively does so because it quiets distress and anxiety but brings no pleasure, or at least no more than the *it feels good when I stop being in fear for my life* variety. A true compulsion as I'm using the term—following the lead of the emerging neuroscience— brings relief, not joy. Take the sixty-year-old woman who was being treated for hoarding disorder as part of a study at Boston University. When the clinical team first met her, they couldn't even get through the door of her apartment, and so met in the driveway. Sophie agreed that as a first step she would sort her stuff into categories—keep, donate, discard—marked with colored stickers. That was going well when, out of the blue, her abusive father called her for the first time in fifteen years. Sophie did the only thing that, she knew, could reliably hold back the suffocating anxiety that seized her when she heard his voice: she ran out and bought eight vacuum cleaners. Just as Jenny saw her acquisitions as "building a wall" to hold back the demands and cruelties of the outside world, so Sophie saw purchases as a bulwark against the return of a past she thought she had escaped.

Roots

Among people being treated for compulsive buying, the problem usually arose in the late teens or early twenties, an age that, not coincidentally, coincides with greater autonomy to go out on one's own, a bit of financial independence (all those babysitting gigs and lawn-mowing jobs add up), and—this being America—a driver's license. No particular pattern of early life experiences appears with any frequency in the personal histories of compulsive shoppers.

By the age of thirteen, Debbie Roes had already convinced herself that other girls in her school—in San Carlos, an affluent suburb of San Francisco, though Debbie's family was middle class—were prettier, cooler, smarter, and more popular than she would ever be. They were also the kind of girls who would show up in an amazing outfit every day and, Debbie swore, never wear it again. "I remember thinking I just didn't measure up," she told me one morning. "I so wanted to look like these girls, but I felt I never did."

That's when the shopping started. At first, it was something fun to do with friends, but soon it became more desperate. Whenever she had money—from babysitting, from her allowance, from the cash her father gave her after he and her mother divorced when Debbie was fourteen—she would hit the mall, often by herself; the social element had fallen by the wayside as the compulsion took over. "The money always felt like it was burning a hole in my pocket," she told me. A chubby tween, Debbie had also developed an eating disorder, and as she lost weight she felt the clothes looked fantastic on her. "As I got thinner I'd shop more and more," she recalled. "I'd think, 'Ooh, good, I can wear clothes I was too chubby to wear before'"—tight jeans and clingy sweaters and short skirts. "I never felt like I measured up," she said. "It was like, *yeah*, she's *prettier*, she's *more popular*, she's *richer, and* she's *smarter—but* I'm *better dressed.* I was always looking for validation, and the shopping helped with that. It was sort of a consolation prize that made me feel less bad and less unworthy. It was a way to deal with stress and disappointment. I'd white-knuckle it sometimes by not buying anything for a week or even a month. But I can only go for so long without shopping. When I give in, there's this incredible feeling of relief."

Debbie's compulsion to shop derives in large part from an anxious feeling that if she is not shopping she is missing something. "It feels like everyone is doing this and I'm not," she said. "I get anxious that there are these amazing sales, that if I don't go I'll miss a great bargain and will feel I messed up, or that I'll miss my one and only chance to get something that will make me look and feel really great, because it won't be there if I wait a day. I have to go *right now.* If I don't, the anxiety becomes unbearable." Needless to say, the relief lasts barely until she drives home. It comes flooding back as if she were a drunk whose euphoria-producing binge has turned into the ashes of regret by the morning after. Her resulting tension sets the stage for the next bout of compulsive shopping.

Several years ago, Debbie became a wardrobe consultant, something she recognizes was as risky as an alcoholic taking a job tending bar. "But I'm really good at shopping and thought I could help people," she said. Unfortunately, her shopping became even more compulsive with a new source of anxiety: if she did not look as fashion forward as next month's *Vogue*, her clients would lose faith in her. Not even getting bailed out of credit card debt by her father (twice) and by an ex-boyfriend stopped her compulsive shopping.

In early 2011 Debbie began to log every purchase, noting how often she wore it and if she returned it. The results were, she said, "abysmal." The next year was no better; her closet was even more full of things she had worn once or not at all. On the rare occasions when she pared her closet, she didn't break a sweat finding thirty-four items to give away: unlike hoarders, for whom parting with possessions is intolerable, acquirers generally have no such difficulty.* But then she took a cue from a program that April Benson developed, targeting the cognitive, emotional, and behavioral components of overshopping. Benson counsels her clients to train themselves to ask six questions when they find themselves on the threshold of a purchase:

Why am I here? (where "here" is a retail website or a bricks-and-mortar store)

How do I feel? If the answer is, "nervous about the fact that my only good suit is threadbare and I need to look presentable for tomorrow's job interview," or "stressed that I have literally nothing appropriate to wear to my friend's wedding this weekend," then a purchase is perfectly justified. If the answer is, "as if I'm about to explode like a shaken seltzer bottle if I don't buy this pair of shoes that I know I don't need," then you're likely being driven by a compulsion that's leading you into trouble. Continue to the next question:

Do I need this? See above. If the answer is anything short of job interview or wedding, continue to the next question.

What if I wait? If the answer is, "I'll look shabby for the job interview" (or wedding), then waiting doesn't make sense. If the answer is, "I'll explode with anxiety," then try extending

---

*In fact, getting rid of things can open up space for more acquiring.

yourself into the future: imagine a future you who is besieged with even greater anxiety than the current you, a strategy that can defuse the present anxiety without making the purchase. To wit:

How will I pay for it? In many cases the prospect of adding to your debt load provokes greater anxiety than foregoing the purchase. If so, focus on the emotions that come with that— how your heart will sink when you see your next credit card balance, how stressed you'll feel as you figure out which bills to postpone paying, how mortified you'll feel if you have to ask your spouse or family for financial help. Focusing on the negative emotions that will flood over you as a result of buying can swamp those you feel as a result of not buying. Analogously, people who have felt compelled to shoplift have been able to stop themselves by focusing on the terror they feel when they're arrested or jailed, and the humiliation they suffer when they have to tell their friends and family.

Where will I put it and what will I do with it? This can also help defuse present anxiety. Again, project yourself into the future; you're home with your purchase, looking for a place to put it. If your hoard of shoes or shirts or tchotchkes is already so immense—perhaps with many previous acquisitions still in their original wrapping or not used in some time—that the one you're contemplating will be as noticeable as a teaspoon of water added to the Mediterranean Sea, focusing on that can also bleed away the anxiety compelling you to acquire it. That helped Jenny reject many prospective prizes that she initially felt compelled to scoop up from the store or the street. Visualizing its future in her already-crowded apartment drained away the compulsion.

In addition to this practical checklist, however, Benson encourages her clients to think about and understand what drives them to overshop—"how it all began," she says—as well as to identify in-the-moment triggers that fill them with an anxiety that only shopping can dispel. "I had to learn what triggered it and what happened when I overshopped," Roes said. In January 2013 she started a blog, "Recovering Shopaholic," in the hope that going public about every purchase, every trigger, and every consequence would shame her into controlling her compulsive shopping. By mid-2013 she had hundreds of regular readers from around the world. She felt that, through the blog, she was giving voice to millions of people in the grip of the same compulsion that had made her do its bidding for thirty years. "I don't want my life to have been about being in malls. I want my legacy to be something helpful," she said. "Until this, I felt, well, there were a lot of things I didn't achieve—I never had children, and I never felt very accomplished in my career. But I was a heck of a good shopper."

With compulsive shopping, therapists often have success having patients first identify the emotional triggers that send them to the mall—sadness, feelings of inadequacy, anger, fear, frustration, shame, guilt, whatever. Then, the therapist asks the patient to think about what Benson, author of *To Buy or Not to Buy: Why We Overshop and How to Stop*, calls the "authentic and important underlying needs" related to the triggering emotions. For instance, guilt needs atonement or acceptance; inadequacy needs a kinder, more realistic assessment of one's relative worth. It doesn't work for everyone, but at least the approach takes into account the emotions that drive different people's overshopping, including the anxiety underlying the compulsive variety.

Shoplifting

While other compulsions can turn the mind into a prison, compulsive acquiring can make the metaphor real: alone among the true compulsions,* it can land you in jail. It's impossible to know how many people who steal compulsively get away with it, but by one estimate 87 percent of them are arrested at least once, though only about one in five go to prison.

Kleptomania is an impulse-control disorder and is quite rare, striking less than about 1 percent of the population. But there is also a compulsive form, resulting from a buildup of anxiety that can be dissipated only by the theft. That sounds like a convenient excuse, but the more people who described to me what drove them to shoplift, the more it seemed to carry a kernel of truth. They described feeling a chronic tension, one that rises to intolerable levels until they give in and pinch something, at which point the tension dissipates like a balloon with a slow leak. There is no sense of anger or vengeance in the kleptomaniac's theft; in the compulsive shoplifter, however . . . well, meet Kaitlyn.

When I spoke to her in 2014, it had been fifteen months since she had shoplifted, and when she had finished telling me her story I almost thought, *Wow, that's like Michael Jordan retiring at his peak*. For Kaitlyn, who was then fifty years old, was very, very good at shoplifting. She swiped her first trophy, a candy bar, when she was nine, but apart from a couple of times in her twenties she wasn't tempted to shoplift for years. A period of financial stress in her thirties gave her another case of sticky fingers, however: short of cash, she began lifting clothing, vitamin bottles, cosmetics, and food. Typically, she would be sitting at home fixating on her finances—the money she was making doing part-time marketing wasn't covering her bills, and she was running up credit card debt and borrowing from friends—when a palpable anxiety seemed to flood out from her core to her extremities. It felt as if her blood had somehow become hotter, thicker. When she

---

*That leaves out pathological gambling, drinking, and drug abuse, which are addictions with, in some cases, an overlay of impulse-control disorder.

argued with her boyfriend or had a lousy day, the anxiety made her ears throb, and she became as restless, itchy, and jumpy as a junkie. She would then remember something she saw at the mall and knew in her bones that that was the key to quelling the angst.

One of the first times she acted on that belief, she went into the local pharmacy to pick up a prescription and found that swiping things she needed—toothpaste, shampoo, soap, vitamins, cosmetics—was as easy as bending down to reach a bottom shelf, her purse conveniently yawning open. "I would go into a store, feeling this pent-up anxiety, and it would just happen," she said. "It was an amazing feeling of relief."

Kaitlyn had grown up with an alcoholic father who beat her brothers and terrified everybody else with his drunken, violent rages. Her mother took her stress out on Kaitlyn and frequently hit her. The family suffered from bouts of poverty and at times didn't have enough to eat. It was a difficult way to grow up, and when Kaitlyn hit those financial headwinds something just clicked in her mind: "Those things that were done to me, those years and years when I was violated . . ." Her voice trailed off. "I was trying to make it *even*," she finally said. She couldn't erase the abuse but, by shoplifting, she seemed to make "it"—the world; life; fate; the tally of good and bad, fair and unfair, joy and misery— "a little more even."

Terry Shulman, who treats many cases of compulsive shopping and shoplifting, says it's common among compulsive shoplifters to "feel compelled to make things right," often after being victimized or deprived. "It's as if they have this itch to even the score. They feel entitled to do what they're doing, as if they're avenging a past injustice."

In a typical episode, Kaitlyn was on her way back from vacation in Europe when a flight delay left her with time to kill at Amsterdam's Schiphol Airport, a mecca of high-end stores. She decided to fill her carry-on bag with as many "gifts" for her family and friends as she could fit. She took designer scarves, ties, Godiva chocolates, expensive perfumes and cosmetics. Instead of feeling alarmed at her behavior, she felt strangely soothed. Somehow the fact that she was stealing gifts for her family that she couldn't otherwise afford made it acceptable. After that, airport shops became favorite targets, and she regularly filled her bags with magazines, duty-free cosmetics, clothing, gifts—"and a *lot* of it," she said: she had gotten so cocky, she didn't break a sweat as she slipped things into her large carry-on bag, purse, or pockets. "As I got older I didn't *need* to do it anymore"—she had become a powerhouse Realtor who handles homes in an upscale area. "But I kept doing it. I knew where the store security guards were, I knew where the cameras were, and I felt like I was seeing and hearing more clearly than normal." She got away with it hundreds of times. She gave stuff to Goodwill and to family, she stuffed it in her closets and cabinets and drawers.

Through her thirties and into her forties, Kaitlyn's shoplifting intensified, and she "took anything and everything I could get my hands on," she said. Things eventually went south, however, and Kaitlyn was arrested for shoplifting three times in three and a half years. Her first arrest was for lifting $11.30 worth of vitamins and cold medicine for a sick friend. When she tried to stop after the first two arrests, she recalled, "It was like I was in hell. I was absolutely miserable. I said to my husband *I have to take something!*, and he would scream at me, *Why can't you just stop?!*

"I couldn't."

Her lawyer negotiated the charges down to misdemeanors, and after her guilty pleas she was fined and sentenced to two hundred hours of community service (with a Red Cross blood donation center). She was essentially scared straight—a success story that underlines why distinguishing between impulsivity, behavioral addiction, and behavioral compulsion isn't a theoretical exercise in psychological taxonomy but a crucial first step in crafting an effective treatment. "Fortunately" doesn't describe much about Kaitlyn's odyssey, but it does apply to the fact that her form of shoplifting was not an impulse-control disorder, as kleptomania is; for that, there are essentially no proven, effective therapies. But Kaitlyn's overshopping was a true compulsion, driven by anxiety. Shulman therefore started by asking her, as he does all compulsive shoplifters, why she thinks she did it. "I try to help enlighten my clients about what drives their compulsion," he told me. "Are they trying to make up for loss or abandonment? Are they trying to right a perceived wrong or injustice? I try to give them a sense of why the behavior is happening. Often they say they have no idea, but once they gain some insight they have a better chance of changing." He had Kaitlyn introspect about the anxiety that drove her to shoplift and ask if there was another way to dissipate it. "I always ask, why, why, why do you feel compelled to do this?" Shulman said. "I don't agree with Alcoholics Anonymous that the reason doesn't matter and all you have to do is 'just stop.' More often than not, the insight is helpful and necessary."

This is the cognitive part of the cognitive-behavior therapy he practices: getting a person to remember that her father never let her have new clothes. "That helps you know your triggers, your warning signals," Shulman said—in Kaitlyn's case, when someone told her she couldn't have or do something it triggered angry memories of the deprivation she experienced as a child and is still trying to make up for.

Although Kaitlyn had been clean for more than a year when we spoke, she still dreams of shoplifting and its unfailing power to drain her anxiety. "I fantasize about it like an ex-lover who got away," she told me. "It's kind of a wistful feeling. I felt my shoplifting was the best thing I ever had."

Bibliomania

A remarkable form of acquiring took hold in Europe beginning some 250 years ago, when a certain slice of society found itself in the grip of a mad compulsion to buy, own, keep, display, and boast about (but not necessarily read) books, a passion so widespread it acquired a name: bibliomania. Those in its grasp as well as those observing the afflicted saw in bibliomania undertones of madness, a foreshadowing of psychiatry's classification of many compulsive behaviors as mental disorders. In one of his thousands of letters to his son Philip, the English statesman and epistolist Lord Chesterfield (1694–1773), having heard that Philip was acquiring a taste for rare volumes, warned the young man to "beware the *Bibliomanie.*"

The lord looked prescient when, in an 1809 poem, Dr. John Ferriar of Manchester Lunatic Hospital asked, "What wild desires, / what torments seize / The hapless man who feels the book disease." It was a "tyrant passion," he warned, bringing an "anxious toil." The poem took the form of an epistle to Ferriar's friend Richard Heber (1773–1833), which was only appropriate. Heber was renowned for filling eight homes in four countries with what amounted to nearly 150,000 bound volumes plus thousands more pamphlets, the whole estimated (by one Paris bookseller at the time) to number as many as 300,000 individual works.

The year 1809 was a propitious one for bibliomania, for that was also when the English bibliographer and minister Thomas Frognall Dibdin (1776–1847) published *The Bibliomania.* Subtitled *Book-Madness; containing some account of the History, Symptoms, and Cure of This Fatal Disease,* it described "the madness of book-collecting" in unambiguously medical terms. The resulting collections, warned British writer (and father of a future prime minister) Isaac Disraeli (1766–1848), were "madhouses of the human mind." Bibliomania "has never raged more violently than in the present day," Disraeli observed in *Curiosities of Literature,* as some of the most respected men of the age were overtaken by a compulsion to acquire for display in their grand homes first editions; vellum editions; limited editions; large-page editions; and editions with uncut pages, silk linings, gold bands, tinted leather, "Etruscan bindings," and other symbols of erudition, taste, and wealth.

Few bibliomaniacs of the Victorian era left behind explanations for their mad passion, with the fortunate (for us) exception of Sir Thomas Phillipps (1792–1872). The illegitimate son of a textile magnate and a servant girl, Thomas was bitten by the bibliomania bug as a boy, acquiring just over one hundred books by age six. "All his pocket-money was spent in books," reported Britain's *Dictionary of National Biography* in 1896. "The main business of his life" (made possible by a hefty inheritance, though he was constantly in danger of blowing through it) was "the collection of rare manuscripts of all ages, countries, languages, and subjects." Phillipps termed his compulsion "the old Mania of Book-buying," and traveled the continent for collections to purchase: "chronicles, cartularies, household books of kings, queens, and nobles"; a collection of 1,300 Italian manuscripts here, 900 volumes of papers from the French Revolution there, as well as 500 or so "oriental manuscripts," and illuminated manuscripts originally created for kings, popes, and Medicis. At his death, scholars estimated, Phillipps had amassed some 60,000 manuscripts, as well as thousands of bound books, deeds, legal documents, Babylonian cylinder seals, maps, genealogical charts, letters, and drawings—twice the number of volumes as in the library of Cambridge University, and a fair start toward his goal of having, as he put it in a letter three years before his death, "ONE COPY OF EVERY BOOK IN THE WORLD!" It was sufficient, at any rate, that when he moved his collection from Middle Hill, his estate in Worcestershire, to Thirlestaine House in Cheltenham, it required a battalion of 230 horses, 160 movers, and 103 wagonloads to transport, psychoanalyst and art historian Werner Muensterberger (1913–2011) recounted in his 1994 book *Collecting: An Unruly Passion: Psychological Perspectives*.

When an official of the British Museum visited Phillipps in his later years, he saw a house where rooms were stuffed with large boxes of manuscripts, books, documents, and other treasures from years of accumulating. "Every room is filled with heaps of papers, MSS, books, charters, packages & other things," the Museum's Sir Frederic Madden wrote, lying "under your feet, piled upon tables, beds, chairs, ladder &c.&c. and in every room, piles of huge boxes, up to the ceiling." Writing to invite Jared Sparks, the president of Harvard University, to visit him at Thirlestaine House, Phillipps warned that "the Drawing Room is the only room we live in & three Bed Rooms for ourselves and our friends." He wrote to another friend, there "is no room to dine in except in the Housekeeper's Room!"

But why? He was "instigated," Phillipps wrote around 1837 in the preface to a catalogue of his collection, "by reading various accounts of the destruction of valuable manuscripts." His "chief desire" in accumulating what became England's, and probably the world's, most extensive collection of written works owned by a single individual came "from witnessing the unceasing destruction" of volumes by scavengers who cared nothing for the words themselves but only for the books' inlays of gold and other precious metals.

Phillipps's compulsion to collect other written works, such as deeds and charters, was also born of a fraught anxiety. It derived, he wrote, from his despair upon witnessing the destruction of such documents "in the shops of glue-makers and tailors" who extracted fiber from the paper. Were it not for his mad dash through Europe scooping up everything he could find, Phillipps seemed to believe, there would result a literary cataclysm akin to the fiery destruction of the library at Alexandria. He described his manuscripts as "a never failing solace in every trouble," as clear an admission as one can imagine that the books kept anxiety at bay.

A third goad to Phillipps's compulsive book collecting was that, as an illegitimate child, he felt deracinated in a way that only books could salve. In particular, his anxiety about his identity and roots, a curse of many illegitimate children, drove a preoccupation with origins and antecedents. As a result he gobbled up deeds, church records, and gravestone inscriptions. "His life work was effectively the outcome of his anxiety about his foggy past," Muensterberger argued.

Training his psychoanalyst's eye on Phillipps from the distance of a century, Muensterberger diagnosed "a kind of persistence behind which seems to lie a compulsive preoccupation, and like all compulsive action is molded by irrational impulses." ("Irrational" seems harsh; kinder to say Phillipps was smothering his many anxieties—that a book or document would be lost or destroyed were he not to acquire it.) Collections like Phillipps's "serve as a powerful help in keeping anxiety or uncertainty under control," Muensterberger argued. "Collecting is much more than the simple experience of pleasure . . . [serving instead as] a way of dealing with the dread of renewed anxiety."

Muensterberger was hardly alone in diagnosing anxiety at the root of at least some book collectors' behavior. The compulsive acquisition of books "relieves anxiety," Norman Weiner wrote in 1966 in the *Psychoanalytic Quarterly*. As with the relief most compulsions bring, however, it was only temporary: the bibliomaniac is compelled to "set out on another quest for a great book as soon as his anxiety returns," Weiner noted. Phillipps's anxiety that unique works would, without his intercession, be lost to the world certainly did not abate permanently after any acquisition . . . nor, it seemed, after 150,000.

While armchair psychoanalysis is always dicey, especially when the patient has been dead for a century, that's about as close as researchers have come to studying compulsive book buying. The phenomenon has "largely been ignored by psychoanalysts," Weiner wrote. Little has changed in the ensuing half century. The *DSM* has never recognized bibliomania as a formal disorder, and it is not a manifestation of, say, obsessive-compulsive disorder. One of OCD's defining features is that the compulsion feels ego-dystonic. Bibliomania, to the contrary, feels like a perfectly harmonious expression of one's deepest desires.

Harmony notwithstanding, as Phillipps got on in years, he grew almost frantic about the disposition of his collection, trying without success to interest Britain's national library in purchasing it. Bitter about the world's apparent indifference to his life's work, he stipulated in his will that his books remain forever at Thirlestaine House, not a single volume sold off or donated. After a chancery court ruled that impossible, largely because Phillipps's monetary estate was inadequate to provide for the maintenance of his collection, his trove was dispersed to national libraries, private archives, and the nascent collections of the likes of J. Paul Getty and Henry Huntington. It took nearly fifty years to sell the bulk of Phillipps's horde, Nicholas Basbanes recounted in his 1995 book *A Gentle Madness: Bibliophiles, Bibliomanes, and the Eternal Passion for Books,* and in 1929, thirty thousand manuscripts, documents, and books were still packed in crates and boxes at Thirlestaine House. They were still being sold, piecemeal and in vast lots, in the 1990s.

What was a burden for Phillipps and his heirs, as for the bibliomanes who preceded him, can arguably be seen as a boon for history. Much that would otherwise have been lost or destroyed was salvaged thanks to a compulsiveness and the anxiety that drove it. It would not be the last reminder of the good that compulsive behavior can do.

CHAPTER TEN

Compelled to Do Good

A FEW DAYS after comedian Joan Rivers died in the summer of 2014, the owner of a Manhattan cafe where she had performed the night before the diagnostic procedure that sent her into respiratory arrest spoke to a reporter about Rivers's astonishing drive. Steve Olsen, owner of the West Bank Cafe, told the New York *Daily News* that he had recently asked Rivers why, at age eighty-one, she still did so many stand-up gigs, not to mention reality shows, talk shows, online shows, and award show red-carpets. "She said because it kept her alive," Olsen recounted. And as the television networks combed through their archives for Rivers clips to show during their retrospectives on her life and career, at least two showed the same footage: an interview she did a few years before her death in which she was asked, for the umpteenth time, why she never stops working. Rivers took out one of those old-fashioned spiral-bound day planners and flipped the pages to a month far in the future, on which all thirty day boxes were empty. *That, right there*, she said, pointing emphatically, is her greatest fear: that no one will invite her to perform, that her fans will forget her, that she will be professionally dead while there is still a breath in her body and a crackle of electricity in her brain. And so she worked as compulsively as a kid trying to break into the business.

The compulsion to do good in the world, even if the good is merely bringing laughter to a few dozen well-lubricated customers in a dark Times Square club, emanates from as many sources as a river of snowmelt water: the joy of seeing one's work make an impact, as when a young teacher's students become the first in their African villages to learn to read; the pride a composer feels when the world premier of her opera lights up the audience's faces; the fist-pumping glow one competitor feels after vanquishing all others on the playing field of sport, business, or academia. If the do-gooding takes the form of volunteering, or choosing an occupation because it offers the opportunity to help others, it can be driven by the sense of connectedness that comes from being involved in a community of like-minded people, and the satisfaction of being perceived as a "good person." "Actually seeing that your efforts made a tangible difference seemed to predict volunteer longevity," Carol Sansone, chair of the Department of Psychology at the University of Utah, who has studied people who volunteer for local AIDS groups and struggling schools, told me. The extreme do-gooders profiled in Larissa MacFarquhar's 2016 book *Strangers Drowning* were driven by a sense of duty (often religiously inspired) so powerful they were willing to put themselves and their children at mortal risk in order to help people they had never met, such as by adopting a couple dozen children or founding a leper colony in a panther-filled forest.

But the pull of these positive emotions is mirrored, in some people, by the push of negative ones. A 1984 analysis of extreme do-gooders found they were driven by "compulsivity" often stemming from "identification with the victim," psychologist Nancy McWilliams wrote in the journal *Psychoanalytic Psychology*. Rather than being drawn to act by duty or the warm-glow effect, compulsive do-gooders are moved by the repulsive force of anxiety. Filled with a palpable sense of itchy, jumpy, brain-racing, muscle-clenching, throat-gripping, can't-sit-still angst at the very thought of *not* volunteering, creating, excelling, donating a kidney, or otherwise acting in a way that does the world good, they feel compelled to actions that, directly or indirectly, benefit the rest of us. It's just that those benefits are not the motivating force: quelling anxiety is. If in so doing they also bring smiles to an audience, well, then we who benefit from their compulsions can be thankful.

That's why Joan Rivers's compulsion to perform is part of this chapter rather than that on the workaholism of obsessive-compulsive personality disorder. The OCPD-fueled drive to work comes from the anxiety that no one will do a job as competently as you will, and of believing that any slacking off or lowering of standards will allow intolerable mistakes and sloppiness to seep into a world already awash in the imperfection and disorder you are desperately trying to keep at bay (cf. Liza Jane's refusal to wipe the hard drive of a busted computer). A compulsion like Rivers's is different. Its genesis lies in an anxiety more existential. This anxiety is the kind that comes from contemplating one's own mortality, or the existence of suffering in the world, or the presence of evil . . . and saying, *not on my watch*.

For behaviors that even cynics acknowledge are not uncommon, generosity, altruism, volunteering, and other forms of doing good have gotten remarkably little attention from scientists. Studies of what compels some people to be unusually giving or selfless, or to act in other ways that benefit humankind, are rare. A notable exception is research into one of the most extraordinary forms of altruism: donating a kidney to a stranger.

Giving Away Part of Yourself

It is one thing to register to donate your organs upon death, which about 45 percent of Americans do, or to donate blood, which about

5 percent of those eligible do. It is quite another to donate a kidney, especially to a stranger, a process called nondirected donation. Barely two thousand such "altruistic" kidney donations have ever been made in the United States. Even though every healthy person has a spare kidney, donation is an extraordinarily selfless act: donors receive no payment (just their medical bills are covered), they undergo extensive pre-op medical and psychological testing, they often have to travel out of state for the procedure, they can suffer postsurgical pain during a weeks-long recovery period, and for their trouble they often meet skepticism and even hostility from family and friends (ranging from *How could you jeopardize yourself, and thus our family, for a stranger?* to *So you think you're better than everyone else because you gave away a kidney?*).

The phenomenon puzzled scientists, too. According to core tenets of evolutionary biology, humans undertake altruistic acts for, para-doxically, selfish reasons: to earn a chit that can be exchanged for a reciprocal favor later, to help a relative who shares some of your DNA, or to enhance your reputation in a way that will be adaptive in the eyes of natural selection. In this case, altruism is pseudoaltruism, a view that prevailed from Freud until the late twentieth century. Donating a kidney to a stranger was regarded as so psychologically unbalanced that it was illegal in Great Britain until 2006, and regarded as a sign of psychopathology in the United States until late in the twentieth century.

More recent research has been kinder. In a 2014 study, psycholo-gists invited nineteen people who had donated a kidney to a stranger to have their brains imaged. Along with twenty nondonors, serving as controls, they underwent both structural magnetic resonance imaging (MRI), which measures brain structures, and functional MRI (fMRI), which assesses brain activity during specific tasks—in this case, look-ing at eighty images, one at a time for a couple of seconds, of faces with fearful, angry, or neutral expressions. Structural MRI showed that the donors' right amygdala, which processes the sense of fear, was about 8 percent larger than the controls', Abigail Marsh of Georgetown University and her colleagues reported in *Proceedings of the National Academy of Sciences*. Functional MRI found that the same structure showed significantly greater activation when the volunteers looked at faces with fearful expressions, evidence of heightened sensitivity to that expression. These findings jibed with previous research suggesting that the biological basis for altruistic behavior lies in the brain's sensitivity to others' distress, and that facial expressions of fear are powerful elicitors of compassion. People who are extremely sensitive to these cues "may be unusually motivated to respond altruistically to others," Marsh concluded. "My guess is, you need the amygdala to understand someone else's fearfulness or distress, and to represent it in the brain. People who are very altruistic are very sensitive to others' fear or distress. Seeing it in others makes them feel it themselves." They understand at a visceral, emotional level what being afraid feels like.

That made my ears prick up. Extraordinary altruists epitomize the cliché "I feel your pain." They pick up on others' fearfulness and distress to the point of feeling it themselves, thanks to the amygdala's double role of perceiving those feelings in other people and generating the felt sense of them in oneself. Marsh learned one more thing: "I always ask donors why they did what they did," she told me. "Many people said it was a quick decision, that they hadn't known you can donate a kidney while you're alive, and when they found out, their reaction was, *Oh wow, I can actually do this.* It's almost instantaneous: *I have to help.* That suggests it's an emotional more than a rational decision," as the fMRI results suggest: people do not methodically calculate the risks and benefits of donating a kidney and then reach a dispassionate conclusion. Instead, they feel distress akin to anxiety, one they can alleviate only through an extraordinary act.

Marsh's study spurred me to contact several kidney donors, in hopes of understanding what drove them. Harvey Mysel, who founded the Living Kidney Donor Network in 2006 after he received a kidney from his wife, said that in his experience people donate because their faith compels them to ("Do not neglect to do good and to share what you have, for such sacrifices are pleasing to God," Hebrews 13:16). But are some donors driven to do what they do because they can't stand the idea that another individual will suffer and possibly die for want of what they can provide? That would be the anxiety-based motivation that would qualify the act as a compulsion, one undertaken because doing otherwise allows a crushing near-panic to grip your throat and never let go.

Amy Donohue, a stand-up comic in Phoenix, was in her early forties when a woman she followed on Twitter sent out a plea: her mother was on the transplant list for a kidney; would anyone be willing to be a living donor? It was only after Amy tweeted back, *Sure, why not?*, that she did a little online research to see what the heck she had gotten into.

That spur-of-the-moment decision, driven by the gut and the heart rather than the head, exemplified the pattern seen in the fMRIs of kidney donors—that an acute sensitivity to other people's distress underlies their decision. "Where does that come from?" I asked Amy. She fumbled a bit, as if trying to figure it out herself, mentioning that, yeah, her friends and family often say she's unusually compassionate, and that after her mother threw her alcoholic father out of the house when Amy was eight she had to step up and help take care of her younger sister. She had clear memories of preparing way too many Crock-Pot dinners. And then it came pouring out. "What the fuck happened to humanity?" Amy cried. "When did we forget to help other people? People don't even donate *blood*. There is such hypocrisy! When I see how many people need a kidney I am so outraged!" Although Amy's decision to donate a kidney based on a tweet may have been driven by gut-level compassion, the drive to follow through (even at the cost of her job) was compelled by something angrier: a fed-up, *I'm going to take a stand* determination not to be like the selfish, self-centered millions that infuriated her. Then, more quietly, she said there was something else I should understand about her decision. "I got more out of it than she did," Amy said, referring to the woman now living with her kidney. "I don't have children," she went on. That compelled her to find another way to leave a legacy, to plant one little flag in the earth saying *I was here.*

I don't want to be like Mark Twain's hammer-wielder to whom everything looks like a nail, seeing everything through the prism of anxiety. But as Amy spoke it was clear there was an undercurrent of anxiety in her drive to leave something behind, to make a difference. Most people want to do that, but it triggers deep anxiety only in some. Amy's was not a pathological anxiety, but it was powerful enough to drive her to a magnanimous act.

Cara Yesawich, an award-winning advertising executive who lives in suburban Chicago, was fifty-four in 2010 when she donated a kidney. Although she was stone-cold fluent in the data on living donors' survival and health—excellent—she waited until her two sons were grown, just in case. She will tell anyone who'll listen that "living donors are the only way to reduce the waiting list and save lives." (She was part of a complicated chain of pairs that resulted in eight patients receiving a donated kidney.)

When we began chatting, Cara was all business, reeling off the statistics (tens of thousands of people on what is likely a five-year waiting list for a kidney, with five thousand dying each year), lamenting that more dialysis centers and transplant programs do not educate their patients about living kidney donation, and giving the expected answer about why she chose to donate: "To help someone. I wanted to make a difference and I knew I could change someone's life," she said. "I wanted someone to be able to live, to be with their family, to get a chance at life." But lots of people have that desire without acting on it. What is it that pushes donors over the hump that blocks everyone else? Cara, who was a volunteer in Marsh's MRI study, remembered something her father used to ask her: *Why do you have to get so involved with people, Cara?* "I guess it's true," she said slowly, thinking aloud. "I do pick up on people's emotions. I don't like seeing people in pain or suffering. I guess I'm like the cliché: I do feel their pain."

Anxious Altruists

For Cara and Amy, anxiety of the Joan Rivers variety was part of what compelled them to heights of altruism. As it happens, scientists had recently begun studying how, in people with a specific psychological makeup, anxiety underlies the drive to do good. This work grew out of studies on attachment theory, which was created by British psychiatrist John Bowlby in the mid-twentieth century to explore the roots of unhappiness, anxiety, anger, and delinquency. The idea is that children develop a sense of emotional security in the first years of life, absorbing the idea that the people who take care of them are reliable sources of safety and comfort. Or at least some children do. The unfortunate others learn that those who are supposed to protect and take care of them—for simplicity, let's say their parents—can't be relied on: they are sometimes there to offer comfort and sometimes not. Attachment security is the sense that one is worthy of being loved and that people will be there for you, particularly in times of stress or distress.

Bowlby was trying to explain the behavior of very young children, in particular how babies become dependent on their mothers for protection and comfort. But as attachment theory was extended, he and his acolytes found that a child's sense of attachment reverberated into adulthood. Children who were "securely attached"—confident that someone will always be there for them—grow up to be well adjusted, comfortable with closeness and interdependence, trusting they will find solace in those they are closest to, and able to form close relationships. They tend to view problems as manageable and believe that obstacles can be overcome. But insecurely attached children never developed that sense of trust. They feel uneasy and alone rather than safe and secure and conclude that they cannot count on those closest to them. One result can be what psychologists call an anxious attachment style. A child like this typically tries desperately to become close to people, anxiously trying to gain their protection and coerce love and support. As an adult she becomes desperate for closeness and is plagued with anxiety at the thought that her partner will not be available in times of need, that he will let her down, or leave her. She typically has little confidence in her own abilities and skills to overcome problems or pain.

The relevance of attachment theory to do-gooder behavior such as kidney donation is this: people who feel insecure are, in general, less generous or altruistic, said psychologist Omri Gillath of the University of Kansas, who studies the relationship between attachment and altruism; those who feel emotionally secure are more so. "Your sense of security is like a finite mental resource," he explained. "If you have very little, you have to focus it on yourself in order to deal with threats. But if you feel a greater sense of security, it's as if you have some to spare. Your own emotional needs are largely taken care of, so you can turn your attention and emotional resources toward others." That echoes what Marsh found about the correlation between well-being and the rate of kidney donation: when people's own psychological needs are pretty much satisfied, they have emotional and mental wherewithal left over for others. If their existence is an inescapable morass of emotional discontent, they don't.

But there is an interesting exception to this. An anxious attachment style is associated with intense personal distress at the sight or knowledge of others' suffering. Such people may feel compelled to help others, through altruistic actions or other forms of generosity, "because they are overwhelmed with emotions over other people's suffering," Gillath said. "They think, 'This can happen to me,'" and the anxiety that provokes can be relieved only by jumping in to do everything they can to mitigate that suffering. "When insecure people who are high on the anxiety dimension volunteer, their level of anxiety decreases," he said. "They actually gain emotional security."

Years ago, when I attended a week-long retreat in Dharamsala at which the Dalai Lama heard from neuroscientists about research on the brain's power to change its structure and function as a result of both experiences and mental training, one Buddhist scholar put it this way: "There is helping because you really want to help, and there is helping because you feel so distressed by the sight of suffering that you act to alleviate your own suffering," said Matthieu Ricard, a French-born monk. Some people, that is, feel compelled to help others because the distress they feel from the existence of suffering, great and small, is overpowering. When anxious people volunteer, therefore, it is often for that reason.

That jibes with what studies have found about kidney donors, whose empathy seems to derive from an acute sensitivity to the suffering of others. But such anxiety can also drive less extreme giving.

* * *

Kenn Dudek took a minimum-wage job at a nursing home just as deinstitutionalization was sweeping the country. "It was a time when the thinking about these illnesses was simply wrong, as we now know," he told me. "I met a guy who was there because he had been diagnosed with what we'd now call bipolar illness. He told me he had played trumpet in one of the Big Bands, and all I could think of was, how the heck did he wind up here? He was a good man and an interesting man, but he had an illness that made it hard for him to function. I just felt there was a whole group of people who were treated very badly, including by the mental health profession. It was the time of thorazine and other highly sedating antipsychotics, which were given out to people with schizophrenia and bipolar like Tic-Tacs. It left them drooling and lethargic and unable to do much more than shuffle."

It seemed like a tragic waste, with blame aplenty to go around. "Psychiatry, psychology, social work—those fields deserve some of the responsibility for why this went south for decades," Dudek said, referring to the poor care people with mental illness received in what was supposed to be a time of scientific enlightenment. New graduates would start with the most serious mentally ill patients, and then with experience would move on to the less severe, easier cases. The reward for experience, in other words, was not working with patients who most needed help. "I couldn't believe how badly the mentally ill were treated, starting with how mental health professionals treated them," said Dudek.

In 1944, six former psychiatric patients and two volunteers formed "We Are Not Alone," a group whose hope was to alleviate the social isolation that severe mental illness—schizophrenia, bipolar disorder, depression—brings. In 1948, they purchased a townhouse in Manhattan's Hell's Kitchen neighborhood, then a place of murderous rival gangs, and created Fountain House. It offers education, especially for young adults who have a psychotic break at college, and training programs to prepare people for jobs. Dudek became the president of Fountain House in 1992. "These are the weirdest illnesses: they become you," Dudek told me. "Suddenly you *are* a schizophrenic, not a person with schizophrenia. Your personhood is subsumed in your diagnosis, your humanity is stripped away. From the beginning of my career I felt I could see the person inside the diagnosis. I could never *not* reach out and try to find the person instead of the illness." The injustice he witnessed early in his career compelled him to make this his life's work.

Something else drives him through the not-uncommon seventy-hour workweeks and midnight calls. Dudek was brought up in a tight-knit Catholic community outside Boston, his father a World War II veteran who suffered from post-traumatic stress disorder and who, despite an IQ of 160, could find employment only as a milkman and custodian. Dudek sees, in the mentally ill people at Fountain House, the shadow of his father, and of lives that could be so much more than they are. There is at least one more source of his drive. Dudek's little brother, two years his junior, died at the age of four. "It drives me in some fashion I don't fully understand," Dudek said. "I believe I am living two lives. I think that's probably one source of the compulsion to do this work."

Compelled to Create

A strand of thought in psychology holds that the purpose of every deliberate action humans undertake is to cheat death. The actions range from having children who also have children who also have . . . , thus propagating our genes into perpetuity, to leaving a creative legacy that will outlive our mortal body. You can hear some of the latter in the reasons artists through the centuries have given for why they create. For Jeff Koons (b. 1955) "there is a responsibility that art should somehow be able to have an effect on mankind and make the world a better place," he said in a 1986 interview. Willem de Kooning (1904–1997) cut through the verbiage and came up with the central truth: "I don't paint to live, I live to paint."

In most works of art, that compulsion is not apparent to the untrained eye, but in some it is as obvious as paint on canvas. In his *Obsession: A History,* Lennard Davis recounts the tragic tale of the neo-conceptual artist Mark Lombardi, whose signature works were drawings—diagrams, really—depicting networks of relationships. He "compulsively laid out series of circles and connecting arcing lines" depicting the flow of money around the world, Davis wrote, between and among politicians, companies and individuals, such as "Bill Clinton, the Lippo Group, and Jackson Stephens of Little Rock, Arkansas," as one drawing is titled.* Lombardi did not wing it, however. He carefully researched every connection and transaction he could find. According to the catalogue for *Mark Lombardi: Global Networks*, he amassed more than fourteen thousand three-by-five index cards on which he scribbled notes about the flow of money underlying the Iran-Contra conspiracy during Ronald Reagan's presidency, "The Tower Commission Report," and other conspiracist hits of the 1980s. His friends described Lombardi as "consumed" and "frenetic" during his work. Lombardi would "work, without sleep, for days at a time," said one, suggesting "a form of mania." He clipped articles from newspapers and newsweeklies and tracked down government reports on scandals, often by badgering secondhand booksellers for copies. Lombardi committed suicide by hanging in 2000.

"There is a restlessness that characterizes some artists and other creative people," Marcy Segal told me. She began studying creativity in 1977, at the International Center for Studies in Creativity (at Buffalo State College), and went on to a career advising corporations and other groups on how to bring out their employees' inherent creative abilities. She has been the driving force behind World Creativity and Innovation Week, which was launched in Canada in 2001 and spread globally. Like many people in the growing field of "creativity studies," Segal believes everyone has the capacity to be creative—or, more precisely, to be "little 'c' creative": maybe not discovering the uncertainty principle or painting *Guernica*, but inventing a device to lock a public restroom stall when its door is broken or devising substitutes for chocolate chips when you find the cupboard bare of Toll House.

Segal's work has focused on the temperaments that underlie creativity—she has identified four—and the specific kind of "restlessness" that, in each case, drives people to create. For people with an artisan/

---

*The names refer to players in the Whitewater scandal that engulfed the Clintons during Bill Clinton's first term in office.

improviser temperament, she said, the restlessness comes from feeling, "I've had enough" of this way of doing things or of this imperfect device. "They start thinking about other ways," she said. "There's a restless energy there. It's about feeling edgy in their current circumstances, and they put that uncomfortable feeling to use. It pushes them to create." Or, as physicist Arthur Schawlow (1921–1999), who shared the 1981 Nobel Prize in physics for helping invent lasers, said, "The most successful scientists often are not the most talented, but the ones who are just impelled by curiosity. They've got to know what the answer is." (We'll substitute "compelled" for "impelled," since Schawlow's field was physics and not psychology.)

Segal's "catalysts/idealists" experience restlessness over the state of the world. "They think, 'Things don't have to be this way,'" she said, "and they're restless as long as things don't change." For the third group, whose creative drive comes from an enjoyment of mastery and accomplishment, "incompetence and stupidity makes them restless," Segal said. "They feel compelled to do something" about the sorry situation around them or their perception of themselves as not accomplishing enough. Finally, people with the creative temperament Segal calls guardians/stabilizers feel restless when things are not going smoothly. When their organization, family, or society as a whole seems to be headed for a train wreck, they feel driven to intervene before the derailment. "The output of the restlessness in all four temperaments can be creativity in any domain," Segal said, from art to science to business.

Teresa Amabile, a professor at the Harvard Business School who has studied creativity since the 1980s, made her mark in the field with what's called the componential theory of creativity. That model holds that creativity requires an individual to have specific skills relevant to the domain where she aims to be creative as well as what she calls "intrinsic task motivation"—what we're calling anxiety-fueled compulsion. Amabile calls it "passion: the motivation to undertake a task or solve a problem because it is interesting, involving, personally challenging, or satisfying," as she put it in a 2012 working paper. Substitute "compulsion" for "motivation" and you have creative drive. Not every creative person feels this strongly compelled, but you need at least some of that feeling to persevere against the forces of convention and skepticism that seek to thwart creative ideas. In 1995, for instance, physicist Joe Jacobson of the MIT Media Lab was at a beach and ran out of reading matter. That tickle of annoyance—in Segal's words, a feeling of "I've had enough" and "things don't have to be this way"—drove him to spend the rest of the afternoon brainstorming what became electronic ink, the technology behind the Sony eReader and the Amazon Kindle.

The Rose

In 1958 painter Jay DeFeo (1929–1989), then twenty-nine, began what would become *The Rose*. At roughly eleven feet by eight feet, eleven inches thick, and more than two thousand pounds, the work consumed DeFeo for eight years. She labored endlessly and repetitively, a Beat-era Penelope scraping away layers of paint only to add more (an astounding eight inches thick in places). Although DeFeo created thousands of other works, it was *The Rose* "that came to dominate her oeuvre and reputation," wrote museum curator Marla Prather of the Whitney Museum (the painting's home since 1995) in a foreword to the 2003 book *Jay DeFeo and The Rose*, "never seeming to leave her in psychic peace."

She was powerless to resist its call, as novelist and former journalist Martha Sherrill described in her essay in the 2003 volume: "The process of its magnificent accretion seemed to consume her. It was as though the work exerted a strange magnetism, pulling everything toward it—people, paint, needles from the Christmas tree in DeFeo's studio, and the artist herself—refusing to let go. . . . People joked that the work would be finished only when the artist herself died, and a myth grew up around them, DeFeo and *The Rose*: a religion, a relation-ship, a compulsion. . . ." In one 1959 letter, DeFeo said of the torment that came from her compulsion to work on the painting, "I want the struggle, as painful as it can sometimes become," for its absence would be infinitely worse. The painting became the white whale to her Ahab, the monster to her Dr. Frankenstein.

The Rose was eventually transported to the Pasadena Art Museum in 1965 (after a slab of plaster and molding were gouged out of DeFeo's building on Fillmore Street near San Francisco's Haight-Ashbury district so it could be removed from her upper-floor apartment). Even then DeFeo was compelled to make changes. She felt "a sense of obsession," then-curator James Demetrion said, and spent three more months on the painting before she would allow it to be shown to the public.

And the work itself? At once classical, rococo, and baroque, it is a sea of "hacked and carved" layers of paint nearly sculptural in their depth, depicting a sort of starburst (volcano? womb? philosopher's stone? the eponymous flower?) from which a myriad of lines radiate—or, perhaps, to which they are drawn from the farthest reaches of the universe, as if DeFeo were depicting the mesmerizing, omnipotent, appalling, magical pull that compelled her indentured servitude, "a victim in the hurricane pulled toward the eye," as Davis put it. Thomas Hoving included it in his 1997 book *Greatest Works of Art of Western Civilization*. When the Whitney hauls it out of storage to put it on view in temporary exhibits, the task requires eight handlers the better part of a day to remove it from its protective steel cage and transport it with an immense gantry, a truck, a forklift, and numerous dollies.

DeFeo and Lombardi were in illustrious company. Over the course of 444 days in Arles, France, spanning 1888 and 1889, Vincent van Gogh created some two hundred oil paintings, including such famous canvases as those depicting sunflowers and fishing boats, as well as more than one hundred drawings and watercolors—which works out to a new work every thirty-six hours. As Harvard neurologist Shahram Khoshbin told the *Los Angeles Times* in 1985, "When you look at those paintings and realize that each one was done in a day, you realize that it takes tremendous compulsion for someone to do that."

No less than visual art, the written word has spurred compulsions to create and to have. Four of the greatest novelists of nineteenth-century Europe—Dickens and Balzac, Trollope and Zola—were also the most prolific, though that word doesn't do justice to their output. The quantity of journalism and literature, criticism and letters they produced was staggering, their work habits compulsive to the point of monomania, their writing sessions interrupted by almost nothing but the need to eat and sleep. Line up the *Complete Dickens* or the *Complete Balzac* beside the *Complete Shakespeare* and you will see that the nineteenth-century writers make their sixteenth-century predecessor look like a weekend scribbler. Rejecting the habit of earlier writers of taking quill to paper when the muse (or creditors) called them, these novelists engaged in marathons of writing. Trollope wrote forty-seven novels plus sixteen other books.* Balzac invented more than three thousand fictional characters and produced more than a hundred plays, stories, and novels, writing at his desk for fifteen to eighteen hours a day.

On Zola's mantel was the inscription *nulla dies sine linea*—no day without a sentence. Indeed. He wrote thirty-seven novels, ten other books, and piles upon piles of criticism, letters, and journalism. But it was because he sat for interviews with a committee of some fifteen doctors that we have evidence that the marathon writing was driven by anxiety and thus qualifies as compulsive. After questioning Zola about his writing habits and state of mind, the medics concluded that

---

*His mother, Frances Trollope, wrote 114 novels from age fifty to seventy-six, so perhaps the compulsion to write ran in the family.

he had such a passion for "order" that "it sometimes reaches a morbid stage, for it provokes a certain suffering in cases of disorder," as Arthur MacDonald recounted in his 1898 book, *Émile Zola: A Study of His Personality, with Illustrations*. The term obsessive-compulsive disorder did not exist in Zola's time. But Zola's "suffering in cases of disorder" seemed to drive him to battle the forces of disorder by imposing structure on an unruly world through fiction—where the creator is free to corral his characters and their world however he likes—as well as through criticism and journalism, where the power of analysis and reporting can impose order on chaos. Zola's driving emotion was fear, MacDonald asserted, and he "accomplishes certain things from fear" of what would happen "if he should not. . . . The intellectual sentiment that causes Zola to work is not a pleasure, but the necessity of accomplishing the task he has imposed upon himself."

Zola's passion for order, and the anxiety that engulfed him when he contemplated the consequences of not writing, were only the beginning of the sources of distress, the committee of physicians found. He was also a victim of "the doubting mania." A form of OCD, doubting mania manifested itself as anxiety that he would not be capable of writing—something he reacted to by, essentially, never ceasing to write, almost like a tightrope walker who knows that if he stops he will plunge to his death. Zola's medical team identified other manifestations of OCD, including a compulsion to count. "When in the street, he counts the gas-jets, the number of doors, and especially the number of hacks," MacDonald reported. "In his home, he counts the steps on the staircases, the different things on his bureau." MacDonald wondered whether the writer's compulsion to write and other mental quirks "has given rise to the intellectual ability" and accomplishments that Zola achieved. "Pathological facts have been such constant concomitants of great talent and genius," he concluded, "that the relation . . . suggests the idea of cause and effect."

Of all the nineteenth-century novelists, however, it was Dosto-yevsky who saw most clearly into the tortured wellspring of his output. Asking rhetorically what the purpose of his writing was, he answered himself (in *Notes from the Underground*): "I shall perhaps obtain actual relief from writing," he speculated. For instance, a distant memory "came vividly to my mind a few days ago, and has remained haunting me," he recalled, adding that "I must get rid of it somehow." The only avenue of relief he could imagine was "to write it down."

Today, Dostoyevsky, like Zola, would be a candidate for hyper-graphia, the compulsive or overwhelming urge to write. The usual evidence for it is the quantity of the writing, but the more interesting aspect is the overpowering need to write, a need as compelling and as anxiety-provoking as any OCD patient's compulsion to wash or check or count or straighten.

The "Incurable Writing Disease"

When Alice Flaherty's twin boys died soon after they were born pre-maturely in 1998, the Harvard Medical School neurologist felt as if the abyss of grief that sucked her in would never let her out. But after a bit more than a week, she felt something else entirely: an overwhelm-ing need to write, and write, and write, to put every idea she had on paper, to channel the flood of ideas crashing like waves against her brain into the printed word. Before then, she had been a prolific writer, taking such copious notes when she was doing her medical residency that she was able to turn them into a neurology textbook. After her sons died, however, "It was as if someone had thrown a switch. Ev-erything seemed so full of importance, I had to write it all down and preserve it," she told *Psychology Today* in 2007.

Feeling powerless against the drive to write, she scribbled notes on her forearm while stuck in traffic. She scrawled random thoughts on

Post-its when she woke up in the middle of the night. She could do nothing else for four months. Even odder, when her twin girls were born a year later and lived (despite also being premature), Flaherty was again consumed with an overpowering compulsion to write down all that she felt and thought. One result was her 2004 book, *The Midnight Disease*, about both writing (the neurobiology of creativity) and not writing (causes of writer's block), with a brief tour of hypergraphia like her own: an unstoppable compulsion to write, and to write in vast, copious, Dostoyevskian quantity. "Something in me was pressing to get out, if only myself escaping myself," Flaherty wrote. "Words fled from my head like rats from a sinking ship," and "the rats could not get out fast enough."

Poet Tina Kelley describes a palpable sensation of discomfort and fidgety restlessness that besieges her if too many days pass without writing. "When I'm working through any sort of drama in my life, my first impulse is to write about it in my journal, just to get it out, and then to write a poem about it again, to get it out of my system," she told me. "I've always felt writing is curative." At the start of each day, she "has to" write down what happened yesterday, a compulsion which, if resisted or ignored or even set aside due to the press of other things "or just because life is crazy," grows into a physical unease, she said. Kelley has written two books of poetry—*Precise* and *The Gospel of Galore*—and, since it's hard to keep the wolf from the door on a poet's income, spent many years as a reporter for the *New York Times*. Her time there coincided with the terrorist attacks of September 11, 2001. From September 15, 2001, to September 10, 2002, the paper ran more than 2,500 "portraits of grief," impressionistic mini-profiles of those who lost their lives that day. Kelly wrote 121 of them. In that case, too, she was driven by the unbearable weight of imagining not memorializing the victims with a deft detail or two—the fireman who wore the only size 15 boots in the department, the financial worker who as a child cut the grass by attaching a self-propelling mower to a cinder block and watching with satisfaction as it went round and round. "It would have been such a disservice not to do them," Kelley said. Her compulsion can be quieted only by giving in to it, so she writes, and writes, and writes.

The compulsion to write has probably existed since the Babylonians first took a stylus to clay. In the fifth century B.C., Hippocrates knew it as "the sacred disease," while Juvenal, the Roman poet of the early second century A.D., described what he called "the incurable writing disease." Although Zola's version of it drew the attention of his era's men of science, the compulsion to write has been largely overlooked by more recent researchers.

That began to change in the 1970s. In a seminal paper, Boston neurologists Stephen Waxman and Norman Geschwind linked hypergraphia in seven epilepsy patients to a veritable lighting storm in their temporal lobes. That electrical activity triggered the patients' seizures, but it also seemed to compel them to write. One woman who was twenty-four at the time of the study had, since age fifteen, "spent at least several hours per day writing things down," carrying "several tablets of writing paper with her at all times," the physicians reported in the journal *Neurology* in 1974. Her stated reason was "to be sure of what I do," and to that end she compulsively recorded "what she had done in the preceding few hours," including seizures and hallucinations. But she also made voluminous lists, including of the records in her collection, songs her father played on the harmonica, items of furniture in her apartment, and likes and dislikes. She recounted "having written at least several hundred times the words of a song she had learned at seventeen," the researchers reported, "using whatever was available (scraps of paper, napkins). . . . She also reported sometimes feeling compelled to write a word over and over or to copy, once or several times, the printed labels on items she purchased."

Another patient with epilepsy compulsively typed out day-by-day accounts of his experiences, though like most products of hypergraphia the entries fell somewhat short of literary merit. "It was cool last night so I opened the windows and left the air conditioner off. I had a very bad night. I was awake about every two hours. I hung three pictures today on screws I put in the wall. It made me so weak I had to lay down. I slept for two hours." The need to capture every moment, lest it flee into the black hole of memory, and to be understood by whoever his readers might be—including his later self—is almost palpable on the page, as with the frequent use of parenthetical expressions to ensure his meaning is not lost: "On weekends (Sat. and Sun.) I don't go walking." "There is a compulsive quality to much of the written material we have examined," Waxman and Geschwind wrote with the understatement typical of scientific papers.

Neurologists traced the hypergraphia to the source of the patients' epileptic seizures: the brain's temporal lobes. Their location just behind the ears makes sense for structures that process auditory input, including in the language-comprehending structure called Wernicke's area. But they also have extensive connections with the limbic region, which processes and generates emotions. That, Geschwind argued, was likely one source of his patients' hypergraphia: a deepening of the emotional responses so that they feel more, and more profoundly, than people in whom the limbic system is not being regularly hypercharged by the electrical storms of the temporal lobes. "It is speculated," Geschwind wrote, "that these behavioral alterations [including compulsive writing] are the result of an intermittent spike focus in the temporal lobe that leads to an alteration in the responsiveness of the limbic system." Or, stripped of medical jargon, in the throes of emotions as sharp as a bayonet—the result of intense limbic-system activity triggered by a temporal lobe seizure—you feel compelled to put words on paper (or screen), an outpouring that feels as if it is the only release from the suffering of unrequited love or tragic loss, of exile, war, or injustice. "Since all events become charged with importance," Geschwind concluded, "the patients frequently resort to recording them in written form at great length and in highly charged language." And sometimes in both language and image: in addition to producing three hundred works of art in 444 days, Van Gogh also feverishly penned more than two hundred letters of at least six pages each over the same period, describing the events of each day. He, too, had epilepsy.

When compulsive writing is not paired with a Dostoyevskian talent, you get the Boston recluse Arthur Crew Inman (1895–1963). The son of a wealthy Atlanta family whose fortune was made in cotton trading and manufacturing, Inman suffered a nervous breakdown after two years at Haverford College and dropped out. Living on family money, he eventually moved to Boston, where he wrote what became a 155-volume, handwritten diary of more than 17 million words. (A two-volume, 1,661-page version, *The Inman Diary: A Public and Private Confession,* was published by Harvard University Press in 1985, which called it with admirable understatement "one of the great literary curiosities of our age.") It included not only his own history and that of his country and adopted city, and seemingly every thought he ever had about politics, revolution, nightmares, and compulsions, but also the histories of the young women he hired as "talkers" to sit for hours in his darkened apartment and tell him the stories of their lives.

Libby Smith, an editor of *The Inman Diary* who spent seven years reading the original, helped Inman fill out a questionnaire designed to identify personality and behavioral quirks. He scored high in "compulsive attention to detail," manifested in his drive to make lists and adhere to a strict schedule; "deepening of all emotions," "grandiosity," and "sense of personal destiny." Together, they reflect (or produce) an emotionally toxic stew of anxiety that could be dissipated only by pouring every thought, observation, feeling, and sensation onto the page. Inman diagnosed himself this way: "I live in a box where the camera shutter is out of order and the filter doesn't work and the film is oversensitive, and whatever that is beautiful or lovely by rights registers painfully or askew. . . . The simplest factors of existence, sunlight and sound, uneven surfaces, moderate distances, transgress my ineffective barriers and raid the very inner keep of my broken fortifications, so that there exists no sanctuary or fastness to which I can withdraw my sensitivity, neither awake nor asleep."

CHAPTER ELEVEN

The Compulsive Brain

THE FORTY-SIX-YEAR-OLD South Korean man had been in fine health all his life, when one day he suffered a medical catastrophe: an aneurysm had formed in a blood vessel connecting two critical brain arteries, and it ruptured. In most such cases the victim becomes partially blind, stripped of peripheral vision. For this gentleman, the consequences were somewhat odder.

The burst aneurysm caused extensive damage to the left side of his orbitofrontal cortex, the structure just behind the eyebrows (hence "orbito") which is responsible for higher-order cognitive functions such as planning and judgment, and to the caudate nucleus, which sits just beneath the cortex. Although long thought only to control voluntary movement, the caudate, which from the side looks like a squat question mark, turns out to have cognitive functions, too: it plots actions that will lead to goals, and tells the orbitofrontal cortex how much attention to pay to incoming sensory information. Because of the latter role, caudate malfunctions can tag a piece of information as being a cause for greater worry than it really is, resulting in obsessive-compulsive disorder, as I'll discuss below.

In early 1997 the man underwent neurosurgery to repair the aneurysm and remove the buildup of cerebrospinal fluid in his brain. Within a couple of months he seemed to have mostly recovered, except for one striking change in behavior. One July day, he ventured out to a park for his first walk since his aneurysm burst, when a tiny object on the ground caught his eye: it was a bullet from a toy gun. He picked it up. Then he picked up another toy bullet. Whenever he returned to the park—indeed, whenever he went outside—he felt an overwhelming compulsion to search for toy bullets. Nothing else particularly interested him—not coins, not papers, not anything that might have value, only the tiny round pellets, the size of a pencil eraser, which he searched for by walking with his eyes cast downward, combing streets and park paths for hours in even the rainiest, most dismal weather. In the two years before he came to the attention of neurologists and psychiatrists at Samsung Medical Center in Seoul, he had collected more than five thousand bullets. He kept them in bottles, neurologist Duk Na and colleagues reported in 2001 in the journal *Neurology*, and never felt any desire to take them out or handle them, or to collect anything else.

Damage to the orbitofrontal cortex in other patients triggered different forms of compulsive collecting. A forty-nine-year-old Frenchman treated at the Salpêtrière Hospital in Paris for a brain tumor in 1995 was found, in a CT scan, to have two large cavities in his frontal cortex, and within two years he felt driven to search out discarded household appliances. He wandered his hometown, Salpêtrière neurologist Emmanuelle Volle and her colleagues reported in *Neurology* in 2002, compelled to search out telephones, washing machines, television sets, vacuum cleaners, refrigerators, and videocassette recorders (this was, after all, the 1990s). He went about this methodically and efficiently, setting out twice a month as if for an appointment with destiny. The man stored the first thirty-five television sets in his living room and, when it could not hold any more, filled his daughter's room, then hallways, a bathroom, three cellars, and, finally, ventilation shafts with his scavenged treasures. Apart from a compulsion to collect appliances, the man showed no cognitive deficits, though he did have trouble mustering enthusiasm for anything else.

* * *

These Korean and French patients were on the losing side of experiments of nature that left big holes in their brain, triggering bizarre compulsions. From this, we might be tempted to conclude that damage to the frontal regions and/or caudate is the cause of compulsions. Were it only so simple.

Neuroscientists are far from nailing down the brain basis for compulsive behaviors. What they have is a hodgepodge of ways compulsions can seize the brain. More than anything, the research is showing that there are many, many ways for a brain to feel irresistibly, compulsively, driven to a behavior. Remember, for instance, the multiple psychological reasons why people hoard, including deep emotional attachment to objectively worthless items and impaired decision-making that leaves the hoarder unable to identify what can go and what should stay. Since all mental activities, including feelings and thoughts, reflect brain activity, each psychological trait must have a neurobiological basis.

Yet that basis has been maddeningly elusive. For years, psychiatry has been pummeled for failing to find objective diagnostic criteria for the hundreds of ills it identified. There is nothing like a blood pressure cuff or, more realistically, a neuroimaging test. Psychiatrists and neurobiologists have made a valiant effort to remedy that, putting seemingly every mentally tortured soul into an MRI tube to measure brain activity and identify what went wrong, but the effort has largely failed. That state of affairs so troubled psychiatrist Thomas Insel, then director of the National Institute of Mental Health, that in 2013 he slammed psychiatry's diagnostic manual for "its lack of validity" and for failing to base diagnoses on objective laboratory tests. "Patients with mental disorders," he wrote on his NIMH blog, "deserve better."

The OCD Circuit

Psychiatrists tried, god knows. The greatest progress has been made in identifying the brain basis for obsessive-compulsive disorder, so much so that OCD has become an exemplar for turning a psychiatric disorder into a neurological one. The first steps came in the late 1980s, when psychiatrists and neuroscientists at the University of California, Los Angeles, ran a newspaper ad inviting people with compulsions to volunteer for a brain imaging study. Hundreds responded, and after a standard psychological evaluation two dozen were given brain scans using the technology of the time, positron emission tomography, or PET. What leaped out was a consistent pattern of elevated activity in three regions: the orbitofrontal cortex, the nearby anterior cingulate, and the striatum deep in the brain's interior just forward of the ears.

The orbitofrontal cortex has a plethora of functions. It weighs complex decisions, especially those involving risk, and is also responsible for ruminations and worries. For purposes of OCD, its key job is that of error detector: it compares actual events to expected events, noting, for instance, when a reward that the brain has learned to anticipate does not arrive. Neurons in the orbitofrontal cortex fire when something goes wrong, when experience clashes with expectation, or when something seems amiss, such as a slightly askew picture on a wall, uneven piles of books, cans not sorted by label, or any of the myriad of other niggling imperfections that send someone with OCD into a panic. The result is an intrusive, insistent, gut-level feeling that something is wrong. The elevated orbitofrontal activity in people with

OCD seems to be the reason they perceive errors the rest of us are blind to.

The anterior cingulate houses a slightly different kind of error-detection machinery. It fires when you make a mistake or when you make a choice that you know, subconsciously or intuitively, is wrong in some way. A common example is when, in the popular psychology test called the Stroop task, you name the color ink that a color word is written in when the two are discordant (such as *green* written in red ink). The anterior cingulate typically detects errors that you make, not things that are off in the world outside the brain.

The striatum receives signals from and sends signals to so many other regions that it's the neural equivalent of one of those 1940s telephone switchboards, blooming with wires, but raised to the nth power. It has been implicated in voluntary movement, learning, memory, and goal-directed behavior, but the key for OCD is that one of its components, called the caudate nucleus, sends inhibitory axons to many other brain structures. It is one of the brain's "quiet down" centers. (The caudate was damaged in the unfortunate gentleman who developed the bullet-collecting compulsion.) The more active the caudate, the more traffic flows along these axons, and the stronger the *shhhhh*. When the caudate is abnormally active, then, the inhibitory message goes from a sedate *hush* to a powerful *shut up*. One of the structures that gets nearly silenced has the job of itself inhibiting activity in yet a third structure down the line. (If you're a toe-bone-connected-to-the-foot-bone fan, we're up to the ankle bone.) When the silencer is silenced, the gunshot sounds at full volume—and when the inhibiting structure is blocked due to overactivity in the caudate, activity in the next structure, a switching station called the thalamus, has no brakes on it. Result: heightened thalamic activity. The thalamus acts as kindling to the cingulate and its neighbor, the orbitofrontal cortex, with the result that both of those structures are also overactive. Which is precisely what neuroimaging of people with OCD shows. Remember that overactivity in the orbitofrontal and anterior cingulate means hyped-up error detection.

Together, the orbitofrontal cortex/anterior cingulate/caudate circuit—or, in the common shorthand, a cortical-striatal circuit—is known as the "worry circuit" or "OCD circuit." "It's basically the circuit that tells you something bad is about to happen—like you'll get contaminated, covered with germs—and you have to do something about it," said UCSD's Sanjaya Saxena. "The pattern of activity in OCD is very consistent from patient to patient. There is elevated activity in the orbitofrontal cortex, the caudate nucleus, thalamus, and anterior cingulate. And when you get better, activity decreases in all these areas."

The brain glitch responsible for OCD stands out for several reasons, including that it was the first to be deciphered. But another reason is that it involves patterns of activity, not the "chemical imbalances" that the public—thank you, direct-to-consumer pharmaceutical ads—has been brainwashed into believing are the cause of mental disorders. This isn't a book about what a train wreck that idea has been, leading to the proliferation of prescriptions for drugs that supposedly correct those imbalances but whose benefits are very, very slight or nonexistent, and turning most psychiatrists into just diagnosticians and drug dispensers more than therapists who seek to work through a patient's problems via psychotherapy. For our purposes, what matters is that it is empirically wrong: abnormalities in the brain's wiring, not neurochemical imbalances, underlie most mental illness. And OCD was the first to show that.

The worry circuit exists in healthy brains as well. "You know that feeling you get when you step off a sidewalk to cross the street and suddenly a car that you didn't see is bearing down on you?" the IOCD Foundation's Jeff Szymanski asked me. "It's *the same circuit* that's telling people with OCD that something is dangerously wrong." Some brains are born with a low threshold for feeling that (their OCD circuit fires at the least provocation), while others develop that low threshold. "So you protect yourself, or get out of there, or do anything you can to defuse the danger—or the sense of danger," Szymanski said. That reinforces the sense that you were in danger, validating the anxiety, and telling the brain that the threat was probably real. The OCD circuit becomes even more active, sending "Danger! Danger!" at the slightest provocation. The brain also learns that giving in to the warning by executing a compulsive behavior relieves anxiety. Score one for Pavlov (more on whom below).

Identifying the OCD circuit represented a significant step toward understanding the brain basis for the disorder. Overactivity there is not so unambiguous as to be diagnostic, however: neuroimaging cannot reliably detect OCD. The characteristic worry-circuit activity jumps out when scientists look at hundreds of brain scans; if you average the activity in one hundred normal brains and then in one hundred OCD brains, you'll find this telltale difference. But a particular OCD brain might or might not show this pattern, Yale psychiatrist Marc Potenza told me: "We're not at the point where we can make a psychiatric diagnosis with brain imaging." Height offers an analogy. If you average the heights of one hundred men, and compare that to the average heights of one hundred women, the former will be greater. But any particular woman might be taller than the average man, and any particular man might be shorter than the average woman.

Whenever a brain exhibits some abnormality or quirk, the question arises: Where did *that* come from? There are only two possibilities: it was present at birth, and is thus the result of brain-development genes inherited from mom and dad or of some event in the womb; or it emerged after birth, and is the result of something the person experienced. Compulsions can be caused by both nature and nurture.

Family studies have shown that OCD is five to seven times more frequent in first-degree relatives of patients than in unrelated people, suggesting a genetic component: if a close relative has the disorder you are more likely to as well, but "more likely" does not mean "definitely." That reflects the fact that there is no such thing as an "OCD gene" that, like those for Tay-Sachs and sickle-cell disease, produces the disorder in everyone who inherits it from both parents. Instead, in complicated psychiatric conditions, multiple genes play a role. In 2012, for instance, scientists at Massachusetts General Hospital ran the first genome-wide association study of OCD. Enlisting 1,465 people with OCD, more than 5,500 unaffected controls, and 400 trios consisting of an OCD patient and both parents, they analyzed some 480,000 gene variants and got hits in two places. One, the MGH team reported in *Molecular Psychiatry,* was near a gene called BTBD3, which seems to be involved in brain wiring (it directs the output fibers of one neuron to the input fiber of another). The other hit was to a gene called DLGAP1, which is involved in choreographing the formation of synapses. In mice, which have a version of this human gene, deleting it produces OCD-ish symptoms. That suggests a healthy working version of DLGAP1 is necessary for normal brain development, while an absent or aberrant version of the gene somehow leads to the circuitry underlying OCD.

A third OCD-related gene entered the picture in 2014, when researchers at Johns Hopkins University scanned the genomes of more than 1,400 people with OCD and more than 1,000 close relatives. They found that DNA variants near a gene called protein tyrosine phosphokinase (PTPRD) were more likely to be found in people with OCD and their relatives than in people without the disorder, they reported in *Molecular Psychiatry.* In lab animals, the PTRPD gene has been shown to regulate a number of cellular activities, including growth and differentiation. In particular, it promotes the growth of axons and dendrites, which carry signals into and out of neurons; anything going awry with those processes could lay the foundation for aberrant wiring that becomes an OCD circuit. But while these genetic studies are steps forward, they fall far short of convincing explanations:

many OCD patients do not have the aberrant genes, and many people with the aberrant genes do not have OCD. All the genes do is increase one's risk of developing OCD.

Environmental factors that make children more likely to develop a compulsion are even murkier. One idea is that people become compulsive when they feel the world is an unpredictable and threatening place and their compulsive behavior is the one thing they have control over (even though they don't). Some psychologists have speculated that parental obsession with germs can be imparted to kids, but it's equally likely that children will react to that message by a perversely opposite behavior, reveling in all the dirt and grime they can find. Beyond that, the causes are anyone's guess.

A Hoarder's Cortex

One reason hoarding was classified as a standalone diagnosis in the *DSM-5,* rather than remaining a form of OCD, is that the patterns of brain activity in the two disorders are distinct. That is, the brains of people with pure hoarding disorder show none of the telltale over-activity in the cortical-striatal "worry circuit" found in the brains of people with OCD. The neurology fits with the psychology: hoarders don't ruminate excessively, they don't suffer from perpetual feelings that something is amiss. They're basically fine until and unless someone disturbs their packed-to-the-rafters world.

An early clue to the brain basis of pure hoarding came from Phineas Gage, whose brain became world famous. Even if you have heard his story, stick with me; this is the seldom-told part.

A railroad foreman, Gage was overseeing a crew clearing a track bed in order to lay rail near Cavendish, Vermont, in 1848, when an explosion shot a forty-four-inch tamping iron straight into his skull under the left cheekbone and clear through his brain. Spearing his frontal lobes, it exited the top of his head and landed thirty yards away.

Miraculously, although Gage seemed shaken, he was able to walk to an oxcart that took him back to his boardinghouse, where a local physician tended to his wounds, replacing dislodged skull fragments. After recovering from his acute injuries, the formerly even-tempered and soft-spoken Gage became prone to unprovoked and profanity-filled rages, and turned "pertinaciously obstinate" and "capricious," Dr. J. M. Harlow wrote in 1868, "impatient of restraint of advice when it conflicts with his desires."

Generations of neuroscientists tell the story of Phineas Gage because his was the most dramatic experiment of nature (or railroad crew) to link damage to a region of the brain with a precise emotional and psychological outcome: the prefrontal region impaled by the tamping iron is the locus of emotional control, reason, planning, and similar high-order cognitive function. But scientists who study hoarding dug up a less-known consequence of his accident: Phineas developed a "great fondness" for souvenirs, according to Harlow.

That would hardly be enough to link frontal lobe damage to hoarding, but a 2005 study of eighty-six brain-damaged patients suggested that Phineas was no anomaly. Before they sustained brain damage, the patients had no history of psychiatric disease or unusual collecting behavior, let alone hoarding. But when neuroscientists probed more deeply, it turned out that thirteen of the eighty-six "exhibited abnormal collecting, characterized by massive and disruptive accumulation of useless objects," Antonio Damasio, then at the University of Iowa, and his colleagues wrote in the journal *Brain*. In particular, the patients accumulated newspapers, magazines, junk mail, catalogues, appliances and appliance parts, food, clothing, broken furniture and furniture parts, televisions, scrap metal, car parts, grocery bags, food containers, empty bottles, and cardboard boxes. "In all cases, the abnormality of collecting behaviour was severe and persisted despite attempted interventions," the scientists wrote.

All the hoarders had damage to the frontal cortex reminiscent of the Korean toy-bullet hoarder and the French appliance hoarder. It was not surprising, then, that most also had deficits in functions controlled by the frontal cortex: their memory and organizing skills were below normal, supporting Randy Frost's observation that executive function deficits such as not being able to figure out how to even start making a dent in the mountains of stuff underlie many cases of hoarding.

Damasio's hoarders also had damage in the anterior cingulate, the structure that in OCD patients screams *something is wrong*. But the hoarders' anterior cingulates were remarkably quiet. It apparently detected nothing amiss whatsoever, despite goat paths and ceiling-high piles of stuff. In contrast, subcortical structures that, in lab rats, drive the animals to acquire and retain objects were unimpaired. That led the Iowa team to posit that hoarding arose in their brain-damaged patients because the prefrontal regions that usually ride herd on acquisition were sidelined by injury. Result: "the drive to collect food and other objects operates without its usual acquired cognitive constraints," the scientists wrote, resulting in a "disinhibited hoarding drive running relatively free."

Free indeed. One of the volunteers, a sixty-nine-year-old housewife with a damaged frontal cortex, filled a two-car garage with mostly broken furniture, appliances, lawn ornaments, pet supplies, and clothing scrounged from neighbors' trash piles. She never tried to use or repair the items. "Her closets and drawers were overflowing," the Iowa team wrote, "and more clothing . . . was stacked throughout the house." When a twenty-seven-year-old was left with damage to the frontal cortex, after neurosurgery to repair a brain aneurysm, he began collecting tools, wire, and scrap metal, also from neighbors' trash, filling his basement and garage. A welder who also sustained frontal damage developed a behavior akin to the bullet collector's: he felt compelled to collect grains of corn scattered in fields near his home after the harvest (this was Iowa, remember). "He collected corn almost daily," the scientists wrote, "accumulating large piles and continuing to collect as it rotted and attracted rodents. . . . He also began to bring home found scrap metal and discarded automobile and appliance parts."

The Iowa study identified structural anomalies in the brains of people who suddenly became hoarders. To glimpse the mental activity hoarders engage in when faced with the decision at the core of their disorder—keep or toss?—required looking for functional anomalies.

A study a few years later did just that. In research presented to the 2007 meeting of the American College of Neuropsychopharmacology, UCSD's Saxena also found that the anterior cingulate seems to be functionally AWOL in hoarders. He performed neuroimaging on twenty compulsive hoarders and eighteen healthy controls. Compulsive hoarders had significantly lower activity in the anterior cingulate than controls. The worse the hoarding, the lower the anterior cingulate activity, Saxena found: "It's as if in ordinary circumstances, like looking at the condition of their home, they *can't* tell something is wrong."

But was that lower activity causally related to hoarding? To find out, psychologist David Tolin of the Institute for Living in Hartford, Connecticut, and his colleagues performed an ingenious experiment. They had forty-three compulsive hoarders, thirty-one people with OCD, and thirty-three healthy people come to their lab with a few of their belongings, such as junk mail or an old newspaper. While lying in an MRI tube, the volunteers watched a video screen display one piece of junk mail or newspaper at a time, interspersed with papers belonging to the researchers, in each case preceded by a screen with the word *yours* or *ours* so the volunteers did not waste time discerning who that old receipt belonged to. (Tolin has also done the experiment with other possessions, such as empty food containers and toys.) In each case, he asked: Should the assistant shred this one? How about this one? Or this? These were actual, real-time decisions, not a lab game: if the volunteer gave the okay the item would be shredded in front of their eyes. They had six seconds to decide.

Not surprisingly, the hoarders chose to discard significantly fewer of their own possessions than the OCD patients or healthy volunteers did, Tolin's team reported in 2012 in *JAMA Psychiatry*. The amount of anxiety, indecisiveness, and sadness the hoarders said they felt while making their decisions was much greater than the OCD and healthy participants felt. And the more anxiety, indecisiveness, sadness, and "not just right" feelings they experienced, the fewer of their possessions they agreed to have shredded.

For the most part, the pattern of activity in the hoarders' brains resembled that of nonhoarders. There were two screaming exceptions, however: the functional MRI picked up distinctive patterns of activity that seemed to underlie the distress the hoarders reported from deciding whether or not to allow their papers to be shredded. When hoarders had to pick "save or toss" for the *researchers'* papers, there was relatively low activity in the anterior cingulate cortex, the region Damasio and Saxena had identified as being damaged or indolent in many hoarders.

When the hoarders in Tolin's fMRI looked at their own stuff and had to decide to keep it or toss it, activity in the anterior cingulate and insula soared, both compared to baseline and to healthy brains. The more severe the hoarding, the greater the activity spike. In addition, the higher hoarders rated their sense of indecisiveness (*What should I do? I know I should say it's okay to shred that ancient envelope, but . . .*) and the severity of their "not just right" feeling, the higher the insula and anterior cingulate activity.

The finding of increased activity in the anterior cingulate may seem to contradict the Saxena and Damasio finding that hoarders have abnormally low activity there. But remember that those observations were made when the hoarders' brains were essentially in neutral, not being asked to think about anything. In the Tolin study, hoarders' brains were forced to judge whether something was or soon would be amiss, namely, whether giving the okay to shred a dearly beloved supermarket circular was a mistake of cataclysmic proportions. Under these circumstances, the anterior cingulate behaved like a teenager who'd slept all day and awoke half an hour before a big test, exploding with frantic activity as if to make up for lost time. The anterior cingulate seemed to say, *My job is to assess whether something is wrong in a situation, and the situation is that you're asking whether it's okay to toss that old paper? Hell yes, there's something wrong!* The hoarders felt anxious and afraid they'd make a misery-inducing decision. The anterior cingulate screamed, "Mistake! Mistake!" at full volume.

As for the insula, this structure deep in the folds of the cortex had long been a mystery, with conflicting findings about its function. Damasio finally cracked the secret: the insula processes and interprets bodily sensations, such as a fast heart rate and sweating, and links it to an emotion—in this example, anxiety. The insula also seems to assess the emotional salience of stimuli, monitor errors, and evaluate risks. To anthropomorphize, the insula takes input about bodily states linked to emotional experiences, figures out what emotions triggered the bodily state (fear, euphoria, anxiety . . .), and then sends its conclusions to higher-order cognitive regions so you consciously think, *Hmmm, my heart is racing, I must be nervous.* This likely comes into play when hoarders are forced to decide whether to condemn long-held papers to capital punishment in a shredder. Their first reaction is anxiety, which leaves a somatic imprint, perhaps a racing pulse. The insula receives that input and translates it into "the emotion in play here is anxiety."

Together, the anterior cingulate and insula are "at the core of a 'salience network,'" Tolin and his colleagues wrote. Low activity in this network contributes "to the diminished motivation and poor insight frequently observed in patients with hoarding disorder." Unable to distinguish the significant and worthwhile from the trivial and worthless, they keep and value all of it. But when hoarders are confronted with possessions they have already accumulated, these regions become hyperactive, producing a feeling that something is not right, a sense that you are in danger of making the wrong decision. Hence the decision to keep, save, hoard.

At least one more brain region underlies hoarding. For a 2008 study in *Molecular Psychiatry*, researchers at King's College London had twenty-nine OCD patients (thirteen with and sixteen without hoarding symptoms) and twenty-one healthy controls lie in an MRI tube. The volunteers viewed three types of pictures: of objects commonly hoarded by patients (old magazines and newspapers, empty food containers, clothes, and toys), of scenes that healthy volunteers had rated highly disgusting and anxiety-provoking (mutilated bodies, spiders, cockroaches, human waste), and of neutral or mildly positive scenes (furniture, nature, pets).

When viewing photos of hoarded stuff, which they were instructed to imagine belonged to them, hoarders showed greater activation (compared to nonhoarders) just behind the forehead, in a structure called the ventromedial prefrontal cortex. That was intriguing, for this region has two key functions: it is decision-making central, and it suppresses emotional reactions to negative images, thoughts, and experiences. In the latter role, you can think of the ventromedial prefrontal as the comforting mother who tells an upset child, *There, there, it's not so bad*—or, in the case of hoarders seeing junk, *Don't worry about the grease on that old pizza box; we can clean it up and use it to store newspapers!* As a decision-maker, the ventromedial prefrontal is especially important in making choices in situations where the outcomes are uncertain, ambiguous, or possibly risky. In the hoarders, it was as if this structure were frantically trying to figure out whether to be upset about the theoretical annihilation of hoarded stuff even though it belonged to a stranger, and simultaneously trying to quiet the anxiety provoked by the instruction to imagine it as their own and being ordered to toss it.

I wish I could describe comparable neuroimaging research on compulsive shoppers, exercisers, gamers, and Internet surfers. Unfortunately, the few studies that have been done have used so few volunteers, have not been replicated, or have used such questionable designs that they tell us almost nothing. For instance, a 2011 study in the *Journal of Consumer Policy* imaged the brains of twenty-three compulsive shoppers when they were shown things for sale, when they were shown the price, and then when they decided whether or not to buy. Seeing the item, the shoppers had higher activity (relative to controls) in the nucleus accumbens, a key part of the dopamine circuit, Gerhard Raab of Germany's Ludwigshafen University of Applied Sciences and colleagues reported. Seeing the price, the shoppers showed relatively lower activation of the insula (which interprets the emotional reasons behind bodily states such as a racing heart) and the anterior cingulate, the error-detection structure that is hyperactive in OCD. That might lead you to craft a story of compulsive shoppers getting deliriously excited when anticipating acquiring a shiny new bauble, and not caring about price, perhaps lacking the neural machinery to judge an item's value. Except for one thing: when the volunteers decided whether or not to buy, the anterior cingulate became *more* active. Again, it's all too easy to glibly explain that compulsive shoppers' error detectors finally kick into gear . . . but a finding of lower anterior cingulate activity at the point of making a purchase decision would inspire an equally reasonable-sounding explanation ("they can't tell when they're about to make a mistake"). Without an a priori hypothesis about the brain activity behind a behavior, neuroimaging becomes a fishing expedition where you can't tell if the catch is a prized marlin or an old boot.

When Yale's Marc Potenza and Robert Leeman reviewed the neurobiology of behavioral addictions and compulsive behaviors in the *Canadian Journal of Psychiatry* in 2013, their account was shot through with warnings like "there have been seemingly opposing results" and diplomatic caveats like "methodological details may contribute to these differing results." The only safe thing to say about compulsive behaviors is that they probably involve dysfunction of the brain's dopamine-fueled reward circuits. Fortunately, that's something where the science has a decades-long foundation to stand on.

The Strange Case of the Parkinson's Patients

At one level, the neurobiology of compulsions runs on conditioned learning, the kind discovered by Ivan Petrovich Pavlov (1849–1936). The Russian physiologist was studying the digestive system, using dogs as his laboratory model, when he noticed that food caused the canines to salivate. But so, too, did the mere arrival of a lab worker. Since every time food appeared an assistant in standard scientific attire also arrived, Pavlov hypothesized, perhaps the dogs were reacting to the lab coats. In a series of experiments, he identified the conditioned stimulus and response. Most famously, Pavlov rang a bell when the dogs were fed. The dogs learned to associate the ringing, another conditioned stimulus, with food. After a few rounds of this the mere sound of the bell, with nary a scrap of meat in sight, triggered drooling.

People in the grip of a compulsion are like Pavlov's drooling dogs. A compulsion pairs an urge to get rid of a painful emotion—anxiety—with a behavior that succeeds in doing that. Anxiety about missing an important text is vanquished by constantly checking your smartphone. The receding of that anxiety becomes paired with the behavior: voilà, conditioned learning. That's the argument Szymanski was making when he explained that giving in to an OCD compulsion relieves anxiety, teaching the brain to do so.

But the desperation and anxiety that drive compulsive behavior can't be explained by Pavlovian conditioning alone. Patients with Parkinson's disease, of all things, revealed that something else is going on.

For reasons known only to the gods of evolution, the neurochemical dopamine has jobs in the brain as different as driving a bus and cooking meth. In the substantia nigra, a structure near the base of the brain, dopamine carries signals that allow smooth, controlled movement. When dopamine-producing neurons die, the result is tremors in the hands, arms, legs, jaw, and face; and impaired balance and coordination—Parkinson's disease. Dopamine is also responsible for sending you to the moon and back during the most mind-blowing orgasmic experiences. That's because it operates not only in the substantia nigra but also within the reward circuits, which are centered on the nucleus accumbens (of OCD infamy). These circuits calculate how rewarding an experience feels compared to how rewarding you expected it to be. Experiences that meet or exceed expectations feel great, bringing the brain a sense of reward.

You can imagine the possibilities for crossed wires in these quite separate movement and reward systems. Pharmacologists didn't.

For decades physicians had treated Parkinson's disease with the drug levodopa, which is a precursor to dopamine. The idea is that if you feed the brain lots of dopamine precursor, it will churn out more dopamine, sort of like turbo-charging deliveries of flour and sugar to a bakery might yield more cupcakes. In the 1990s, however, a new class of drugs was introduced. Called dopamine agonists, they are, like levodopa, also essentially replacement therapy. But they act further downstream, fitting into dopamine receptors. At the risk of belaboring the analogy, it would be like getting customers to eat the sugar and flour directly, without waiting for the ingredients to be baked into cupcakes.

Once a dopamine agonist docks with a dopamine receptor, it triggers an over-the-top reaction. Think of it as plugging a little 1970s-era clock radio into an outlet, getting tinny sound, then one day plugging in a 400-watt guitar amplifier instead, and the first chords of "Smoke on the Water" blow out your eardrums. That's what taking a dopamine agonist is like: same receptor, different molecular entity plugged in, super-charged result. "Dopamine agonists act on receptors like a superdopamine," said psychiatrist Michael Bostwick of the Mayo Clinic in Rochester, Minnesota. "They glom on."

Easy to say now. But in September 2000, a team of neurologists and psychiatrists at Hospital Universitario Doce de Octubre in Madrid, Spain, reported that ten of their levodopa-treated Parkinson's patients had suddenly become pathological gamblers. Slot machines were the preferred vice. That suggested "it could be related to the do-paminergic" treatment, Dr. José Antonio Molina and his colleagues wrote in the journal *Movement Disorders*. This hint of a link between sudden compulsive gambling and dopamine drugs had "apparently never been reported" before.

But something close had been. In 1989 neurologist Ryan Uitti and colleagues found that thirteen of their Parkinson's patients developed hypersexuality soon after beginning levodopa therapy. His discovery, however, appeared in a low-profile journal, *Clinical Neuropharmacology*, and attracted little notice. And over the course of just two weeks in 1999, neurologist Mark Stacy, then director of the Muhammad Ali Parkinson Research Center in Phoenix, learned that two of his Par-kinson's patients, whose medication he had just increased, immediately went on a gambling spree and lost $60,000 each. But he presented the observation in a poster at the Movement Disorders Meeting, not publishing a paper until 2003.

By then, the new generation of dopamine agonists had been in use for nearly a decade, which might make it seem odd that compulsive behaviors were not linked to the drugs until 2000. "But it just wasn't something you asked," said neurologist Erika Driver-Dunckley. "Pa-tients would come in and you'd ask about their movement disorder. Why would it occur to anyone to ask if a Parkinson's patient had sud-denly developed compulsive urges to gamble or look at porn?"

After the Spanish report, however, neurologists started both ask-ing and scrutinizing their old notes. At the Muhammad Ali Center, Driver-Dunckley and Stacy began combing through the database of Parkinson's patients seen from May 1, 1999, to April 30, 2000. Presto: of 1,281 taking dopamine agonists, nine had also mentioned a sudden onset of compulsive gambling, they and their colleagues reported in the journal *Neurology* in 2003.

That small incidence didn't exactly constitute an epidemic, but remember that this was a look-through-the-files, retrospective analysis limited by the "don't ask, don't tell" quandary that Driver-Dunckley alluded to: neurologists had no more reason to ask a Parkinson's patient if he had started feeling inexorably drawn to casinos than an ophthalmologist had reasons to ask about bunions. Once she did start asking, Driver-Dunckley told me, "Patients would bring up that they'd gone through a divorce because they'd cheated with a prostitute, or that they'd lost all of their money gambling. That was unusual enough by itself, but even more so because Parkinson's patients have been described as goody-two-shoes"—straitlaced, risk-averse people whose dwindling supply of dopamine leaves them bereft of the brain signals that deliver hedonic hits. "After just a couple of cases I thought, huh, this might be significant," she continued. "They weren't telling me they had spent a *little* more money gambling than they usually did. It would be, 'I just spent all of my retirement savings gambling.' Some blew it all in a week, and some did it by going to casinos every week for a month. But it wasn't just gambling and hypersexuality. We also had people who developed compulsive hair combing or house cleaning."

To overcome the limitations of retrospective analysis, from 2002 to 2004 Mayo's James Bower and J. Eric Ahlskog asked their Parkinson's patients if they had begun showing any unusual behavior after being prescribed dopamine agonists. Eleven said they had developed a compulsive drive to gamble, in most cases within three months of beginning the dopamine regimen or increasing dosage, the Mayo team reported in 2005 in *Archives of Neurology*. Most were taking pramipexole (trade name Mirapex), which locks onto the dopamine receptors that are especially abundant in the nucleus accumbens—reward-circuit central. "This was the paper that showed this is consequential and something we should pay attention to," said Mayo's Bostwick.

One of the eleven patients was a fifty-four-year-old married pastor who had been in the habit of dropping twenty dollars or so during his once-every-four-or-five-year visits to a local casino. But on the dopamine agonist "he began to gamble almost daily and over several months lost about $2,500, which he kept secret from his wife. He reluctantly brought this up to his neurologist," the researchers wrote. The sixty-three-year-old who began gambling at casinos two or three times a week on the Parkinson's meds, compared to once every three months before, told his neurologist that he felt an "incredible compulsion" to gamble even when he "logically knew it was time to quit." A forty-one-year-old computer programmer, who had never gambled in his life, said that after he started taking the Parkinson's meds he felt "consumed" with the need to gamble online, losing $5,000 within a few months. "In addition to gambling," the Mayo researchers wrote about this poor soul, "he compulsively purchased items that he did not need or want."

Neurologist Joseph Friedman of the Alpert Medical School at Brown University reported a more unusual compulsion in a Parkinson's patient on a dopamine drug, an accountant who "tallied figures over and over again," Friedman told the in-house magazine of Massachusetts General Hospital in 2006. "Another patient couldn't stop trimming her hedges in winter, another obsessively pulled weeds and one couldn't go grocery shopping because she couldn't stop reading labels on cans." In every case, as soon as doctors took them off the dopamine-boosting meds, the compulsions melted away.

Only a minority of Parkinson's patients develop a compulsive behavior on a dopamine agonist. When Mayo neurology fellow Anhar Hassan and her colleagues reviewed the records of 321 Parkinson's disease patients from 2007 to 2009, by which time movement-disorder physicians were keenly aware that the drugs were linked to compulsive behaviors and made sure to ask about them, sixty-nine patients, or 22 percent, had developed a sudden-onset compulsion while on the drugs. The prevalence reached one in three among patients on the higher doses, the Mayo team reported in *Parkinsonism and Related Disorders* in 2011. Hassan counted twenty-five newly compulsive gamblers, twenty-four patients with compulsive sexual behavior, eighteen newly compulsive shoppers, six suddenly compulsive computer users, and eight "compulsive hobbyists."

Among them was the sixty-three-year-old woman who began spending three hundred to four hundred dollars per week buying flowers and twelve hours a day arranging them, an activity she had never before shown much interest in. One fifty-seven-year-old man began staying up late and compulsively building furniture and making pottery. A fifty-one-year-old burned the midnight oil rewiring or painting his house, while a fifty-five-year-old man began compulsively cleaning bathtubs. The men seemed to gravitate toward male clichés, such as the fifty-six-year-old who started purchasing new watches daily at Walmart and the sixty-three-year-old who loaded up on Lamborghinis and Bentleys (yes, plural). "Also compulsive ice-cream eating," the researchers added. The women's new compulsions also seemed almost absurdly stereotypical, such as the fifty-three-year-old who began compulsively buying costume jewelry and the seventy-two-year-old who began buying kitchen items so compulsively as to leave Martha Stewart in the dust.

Scientists are mystified about why one Parkinson's patient taking a dopamine agonist starts gambling compulsively while another starts compulsively gardening. They have made a little more progress understanding which Parkinson's patients are most at risk of succumbing to a dopamine-fueled compulsion. Men seem especially susceptible, as do younger patients, those in whom the disease struck relatively early in life, those with impulsive personalities, and people who have had Parkinson's for two decades or more. But the link is now indisputable: a 2014 analysis in *JAMA Internal Medicine*, using a Food and Drug Administration database of adverse drug reactions reported by physicians, found that the proportion of reports involving compulsive behaviors was 278 times higher for dopamine agonists than for other drugs. "The likelihood of a causal connection," wrote Joshua Gagne of Harvard Medical School, "is high."

The *What* Circuit?

If the dopamine-fueled pleasure-and-reward circuit were as simple as originally thought, the Parkinson's patients would not be in this book. Their behavior would be described as an addiction, motivated by a drive for the hedonic hits that gambling can bring, not a compulsion motivated by a desperate need to avoid or quiet anxiety. But *pleasure circuit*, it turns out, is a misnomer.

In 1954 at McGill University in Montreal, Peter Milner and James Olds were conducting an experiment that involved inserting an electrode into a rat's brain. Their target was the reticular formation, which regulates sleep-wake cycles. The electrode curved off its intended path, however, and landed just above the hypothalamus, which is part of the limbic system's Emotions Central. The landing site thus received the stimulation intended for the reticular formation. In the experiment, whenever rats pressed a lever their limbic system received an electrical stimulus from the implanted electrode. How much did rats like this? If a rat had an opportunity to press the lever while en route to chow, it lost all interest in dinner and instead hit the lever, stimulating its brain "frequently and regularly for long periods of time if permitted to do so," the researchers reported in 1954 in the (now defunct) *Journal of Comparative and Physiological Psychology*. "The control exercised over the animal's behavior by means of this reward is extreme," they continued, "possibly exceeding that exercised by any other reward previously used in animal experimentation."

The McGill team found the same effect when the electrodes were implanted in the nearby nucleus accumbens, Olds wrote in a 1956 article for *Scientific American* called "Pleasure Centers in the Brain." Even if rats had been deprived of food all day and were lured down a ramp by an enticing amuse-bouche, given the opportunity for electrical stimulation of the limbic system they never made it to dinner. Instead, they happied themselves nearly to death rather than taking a moment from their lever-pressing (up to two thousand times per hour) to scamper over to the food dish. Later, given a choice between pressing a lever to stimulate their brain's "pleasure center"—let's defer to Olds's 1956 nomenclature for now—or one that would warm up a cage cold enough to hang meat in, the rats opted for the former. When research in the 1970s established that the neurons in the regions Olds called the pleasure center run largely on dopamine, dopamine was crowned the brain's "pleasure chemical." And lo, the idea of a "pleasure circuit" became dogma.

Then things grew more complicated. Think back to the McGill rats, whose behavior was interpreted as pleasure-seeking. But rats, like people, engage in repetitive behaviors for lots of reasons. What if the rats, which were a few ganglia short of being able to articulate their feelings, were not sensing pleasure every time they pressed the lever but experiencing anxiety if they didn't?

Looking back on decades of such experiments in 2010, psychiatrist Morten Kringelbach of Oxford University and psychologist Kent Berridge of the University of Michigan wrote in the journal *Discovery Medicine* that "[t]he pleasure electrodes may never have lived up to their name." Although studies "also found compulsive lever pressing in some patients, it was never clear from these patients' subjective reports that the electrodes did indeed cause real pleasure." Instead, electrical stimulation of the nucleus accumbens produced a mildly pleasurable feeling, but rarely with an intensity that the rats apparently experienced. That has led researchers to suggest that stimulating the dopamine circuit never caused intense pleasure at all, but rather a compulsive drive to obtain the stimulation. And thus was brought to the fore the distinction between liking and wanting: one can want, even need, to do something but derive no enjoyment from it. Just ask someone with OCD.

The dopamine circuitry, rather than living up to its original moniker as a pleasure center, is more like a prediction machine. It forecasts how rewarding something will be and then compares reality, once it arrives, to that prediction. If reality falls short, you feel a sense of incompleteness, dissatisfaction, of being left anxiously hanging by the behavioral equivalent of waiting for the E flat after the G-G-G in the opening chords of Beethoven's Fifth Symphony (as I described in Chapter 4). In that situation the nucleus accumbens generates a feeling of wanting to try again to make reality live up to its dopamine-created hype—by playing another hand of poker, trying another bite of cheesecake, hitting the mall again. The compulsion arises from the need to make reality accord with prediction, to complete the quest for reward, to satisfy the expectation. But if and when that happens, the result is not happiness as we usually conceive it but, at best, relief, a sense of alright-ness. It's the E flat.

A study with monkeys showed what was happening in the brain. To establish that the animals' ventral tegmental area functioned like that of humans, the scientists gave them a drop of sweet syrup, which they love, while recording their brain activity with electrodes. As expected, the reward/pleasure circuit became active and there was a burst of dopamine; the ventral tegmental area indeed seemed to register rewarding, pleasurable experiences, and to run on dopamine, as the human version does. The monkeys were then trained to watch a video screen, learning that when a green light appeared a drop of sweet syrup would descend from a tube within reach of their mouths a couple of seconds later. A red light, however, was the prelude to nothing. Green light = reward, red light = disappointment.

As the monkeys made the Pavlovian connection of color to reward, their ventral tegmental area became active and awash in dopamine when they merely saw the green light. It didn't wait for the syrup: knowing the treat was coming was apparently as enjoyable and rewarding as the treat itself. Starbucks addicts likely have a similar experience: if you see that green-and-white mermaid, a feeling of pleasure washes over you even before you take that first sip of iced vanilla macchiato. In the monkeys, there was no second spike when the monkeys actually licked up the syrup. This was evidence that activity in the "reward" circuit, fueled by dopamine, was producing the *expectation* of reward, not the satisfaction of the reward itself. If it marked pleasure, dopamine-circuit activity would have risen when the monkeys actually received the syrup. But it didn't.

The arrival of the dopamine spike *before* the arrival of the reward is analogous to the seconds between when you set the slot machine's lemons, cherries, and JACKPOTS! spinning and when they stop. Achieving a reward and merely anticipating it—whether winning new powers in a video game, winning at the slots, or anything else—each produce activity in the ventral tegmental area, the mother lode of dopamine. Once you get a taste of the pleasure that awaits you, your reward-expectation circuitry lights up like a winning slot machine. You feel compelled to continue. Oh, and near-misses make the ventral tegmental area as active as outright wins: missing the green pig with our angry bird or reading a total dud of a text rather than the invitation we were hoping for stokes the dopamine circuit almost as powerfully as true wins. Disappointments cause dopamine levels to crash, making us feel disappointed, anxious, unfulfilled, driven to get the promised pig or text we expected. Activity in the dopamine circuit is not so much about pleasure as about expecting pleasure, and when we don't get it we feel driven to seek it out, desperately and compulsively.

* * *

Dopamine neurons respond to the difference between the prediction or expectation of rewards and the occurrence of those rewards, neurobiologist Wolfram Schultz, then at the University of Fribourg in Switzerland, argued in the *Journal of Neurophysiology* in 1998. There are, he posited, three possibilities:

1. If rewards arrive without having been predicted, the dopamine circuit becomes activated, with neurons firing away. Reality surpassed expectations and the dopamine neurons go wild. (*There are margaritas at this church picnic? Yes!*) You feel euphoric, which is why Jamie Madigan described the effect of winning unexpected loot in *Diablo 3* as a dopamine freak-out. Getting a Porsche for your birthday when you expected another tie is way more thrilling than knowing the Carrera was in the cards.

2. If rewards occur as predicted, the dopamine circuit fires, but less intensely.

3. If predicted rewards do not come, dopamine neurons' activity drops off a cliff. This is the situation in the brains of the Parkinson's patients: the meds stimulated the firing of their dopamine neurons, but nothing in reality met the heightened expectation of reward. So they went thrill seeking at casinos or (thrills being in the eye of the beholder) pottery-making. What starts as increased activity in the dopamine circuit from artificially activating it with drugs becomes a compulsive drive toward more and greater rewards that, in what feels like a comment on the human condition, can never match the expectations generated by the brain.

Since we are not dopamine slaves, that's not the end of the story. The orbitofrontal cortex and other prefrontal regions can inhibit the neurological activity driving us to execute that behavior. The greater the activity in the striatal regions that house the dopamine machinery, the more likely activity in the prefrontal regions will fall short. Or, conversely, the weaker the activity in the prefrontal regions, the less activity is needed from the dopamine circuitry to drive a compulsive behavior. Which one wins determines whether we can squelch the compulsion or are forced to give in to it.

Conclusion

If this book has left you with anything, I hope it is the realization that there is no bright line between mental illness and mental normality. Many psychiatrists use that fact to argue that the bar for diagnosing mental disorders is too low, and that too many people who should be diagnosed as mentally ill are slipping through the net. Studies that raise the estimated prevalence of depression or PTSD or ADHD not only ratchet up the pressure to increase funding for research on that particular illness; they also implicitly plant in society's collective brain the suspicion that experts are underdiagnosing other mental disorders, too. That notion gets picked up by the media and turned into listicles of "warning signs" for this or that psychiatric ill, and presto—more and more of us have a mental disorder, and soon the exploding numbers call into question the very notion of mental normality.

That point has been made countless times by experts who have pushed back against ever-expanding psychiatric diagnoses. This is not the book to re-litigate that case.* But the fact that anxiety has become the most prevalent psychiatric disorder holds lessons for those of us who do not believe that everyone is, even a little, mentally ill. Most important, it sheds light on the seeming ubiquity of compulsive behaviors. Not the extreme compulsions of OCD and hoarding, to be sure. Instead, by recognizing that anxiety is (to paraphrase the insight of medical historian Roy Porter quoted in the Introduction)

---

*For the best presentation of the case against the creeping expansion of mental diagnoses, read psychiatrist Allen Frances's 2013 book *Saving Normal: An Insider's Revolt Against Out-of-Control Psychiatric Diagnosis, DSM-5, Big Pharma, and the Medicalization of Ordinary Life*. The subtitle says it all, so I'll add only that Frances oversaw the *DSM-IV*, and feels morally obligated to make amends.

the lunacy that our age deserves, the puzzling and the disconcerting become understandable. The compulsive behaviors that anxiety drives us to range from organizing kitchen cabinets to our most idiosyncratic specifications to acquiring things we don't need, from saving a single fading dried flower from a funeral to desperately swiping through our phones for fear of missing out, all in an effort to keep the angst at bay. The saddest thing I came to understand in researching and reporting this book is that so many of our behaviors draw us into them not because they bring joy but because they promise to quiet anxiety. But the most heartening thing was the realization that the ability of compulsive behaviors to quiet anxieties great and small is one of the greatest gifts our brains can give us.

ACKNOWLEDGMENTS

I AM ENORMOUSLY GRATEFUL to the people, named and unnamed, who agreed to tell me about their compulsions. They did so in the hope that others would understand why they do what they do, and why saying "just stop" is not only pointless but heartless. If I have not furthered that understanding, it is entirely my fault. My enormous thanks, too, to the psychologists, psychiatrists, neurologists, and neuroscientists who patiently explained their research to me and did not throw me out of their offices when I asked, for the umpteenth time, what qualifies a behavior as compulsive rather than addictive or impulsive. Finally, let me acknowledge those who helped me at the very beginning and at the very end of the work on this book. Thanks to Douglas Main, who helped me find enough scientific research to feel confident that there was a book to be written about compulsions, I was able to put together the proposal that became the basis for this book. And, thanks to my editor, Karyn Marcus, the book you read is much better than the manuscript I originally submitted.

INDEX

ABOUT THE AUTHOR

Sharon Begley is the senior science writer at ST*A*T, the life sciences publication of the *Boston Globe*. Previously she was the senior health and science correspondent at Reuters, the science editor and the science columnist at *Newsweek*, and the science columnist at the *Wall Street Journal*. She is the coauthor (with Richard J. Davidson) of the 2012 book *The Emotional Life of Your Brain*, the author of the 2007 book *Train Your Mind, Change Your Brain*, and the coauthor (with Jeffrey Schwartz) of the 2002 book *The Mind and the Brain*. She is the recipient of numerous awards for her writing, including an honorary degree from the University of North Carolina at Asheville for communicating science to the public, and the Public Understanding of Science Award from the San Francisco Exploratorium.